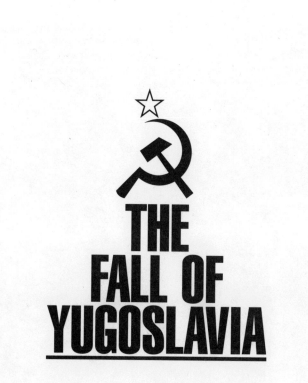

THE
FALL OF
YUGOSLAVIA

THE FALL OF YUGOSLAVIA

WHY COMMUNISM FAILED

SVETOZAR STOJANOVIĆ

 Prometheus Books

59 John Glenn Drive
Amherst, NewYork 14228-2197

Published 1997 by Prometheus Books.

01 00 99 98 97   5 4 3 2 1

Library of Congress Cataloging-in-Publication Data

Stojanović, Svetozar.
    [Propast komunizma i razbijanja Jugoslavije. English]
    The fall of Yugoslavia : why communism failed / Svetozar Stojanović.
        p.   cm.
    This book is a revised translation of: Propast komunizma i razbijanja
Jugoslavije.
    Includes bibliographical references and index.
    ISBN 1-57392-146-7 (cloth : alk. paper)
    1. Yugoslavia—Politics and government—1945–1980. 2. Yugoslavia—Politics
and government—1980–1992. 3. Communism—Yugoslavia. I. Title.
DR1302.S7713   1997
949.702'3—dc21   97-7426
                                                                                       CIP

Table of Contents

Part Three

WHAT HAS HAPPENED TO COMMUNISM AND MARXISM?

I remember my astonishment when he expressed his congratulations to the victors, as well as his deep pity for them, because the vanquished know where they stand and what they have to do, whereas the victors still cannot imagine what awaits them.

Ivo Andrić, "A Letter from 1920"

Man, a Sisyphus, only occasionally succeeds in convincing himself that the rock he is rolling to the top of a mountain has fallen back, when, in fact, he has only been rocking it back and forth at the foot of the mountain.

Dobrica Ćosić, "The Believer"

Foreword

With the exception of the postscript to the fourth chapter and also the new sixth chapter ("The Pseudomorphosis of Communism in Serbia"), this book presents the English translation of the Serbo-Croatian version completed in November 1994, and published under the title *The Collapse of Communism and the Destruction of Yugoslavia* (Belgrade: Filip Visnjić and the Institute for Philosophy and Social Theory, April 1995).

I would like to quote from my short foreword to the Serbo-Croatian edition:

> The book I hereby present to the reader represents the fruit of six years of work with the research project "Social Change in Yugoslavia at the Crossroads of the Two Centuries" at the Institute for Philosophy and Social Theory of the University of Belgrade. The greatest social change of all, however, came unexpectedly in the course of this work in the form of the tragic destruction of the Yugoslav state.
>
> Since 1989, up until today as I write these words, I have spent each fall semester as a professor at the Center for Russian and East European Studies, the Department of Philosophy and the Department of Sociology at the University of Kansas (Lawrence, Kansas) in the United States. This experience, in addition to the work and discussions with colleagues at the Institute for Philosophy and Social Theory in Belgrade, has been of immeasurable benefit toward the writing of this book.
>
> The text of the fifth chapter was published in the fall of 1993, by the same publisher as that of the present book, as a separate brochure entitled *Authority without*

Power: Dobrica Ćosić as Head of State (this was recently published in Italy as well). Since this chapter is obviously about a constantly changing situation, I have decided to add postscripts (I–IV) under the title of "The Serbs under the Blockade of Serbia." The first three postscripts were completed and distributed to friends on 15 January, 15 March, and 15 June 1994, respectively. The fourth postscript has just now been completed and handed out to the same friends. No changes have been made in the postscripts nor in any other parts of the original book manuscript to adjust them to the subsequent developments. It will be left to the reader to gage to what extent I was right and wrong in my assessments.

15 November 1994

I would like to add a few more words now. Most importantly, I wish to point out that I have deliberately written a book that crosses the realms of several social science and humanities disciplines, as well as genres of writing. It also incorporates several different approaches: historical narration and analysis, systemic analysis and social theory, the autobiographical, portrait sketches of politicians and statesmen, and even philosophical examination of the condition of humanity at the crossroads of the two centuries and millennia. In other words, this book is written in a "postmodernist" form and style.

I initially intended to place the third, most theoretical part, at the beginning, considering the lack of similar attempts at building a theory of the collapse of communism, a theory of postcommunist developments as well as a theory of the transformation from Marxism into post-Marxism. The reader will note that in the explanation of the implosion of communism I place the emphasis on a particular type of constellation of structural-systemic causes and historical contingencies such as Gorbachëv and Yeltsin. However, in order to broaden my audience, and not to restrict it to social scientists, philosophers, university students, and the like, I did not want to discourage potential readers with such a structural-systemic and theoretical approach from the beginning. I therefore have opted to introduce these ideas through a study of the Yugoslav case. Naturally, the general assertions I make later about the disintegration of communism and communist federations referring primarily to the case of the USSR are also applicable in large part to Yugoslavia.

A special place in the history of communism is held not only by the Soviet Union but also by Yugoslavia, which is why I have afforded them by far the bulk of attention. If we want to arrange all of the former communist countries in Europe onto a spectrum beginning with the USSR as a general communist matrix and model, as the superpower leader of the Warsaw block, and finally as a pseudo-federation—Yugoslavia has to be placed at the opposite end of this spectrum as the most reformed and independent communist country, and as even a contradictory mix of federation and confederation.

With the exception of my first book, *Contemporary Metaethics* (1964), my previous books have mostly dealt with Marxism, communism, and socialism. With this new, fourth book I wrap up a tetralogy devoted to those issues. To avoid repeating the titles of the previous books in the tetralogy I shall refer only to the number of their order (and the corresponding chapters and pages):

I   *Between Ideals and Reality* (New York, London and Toronto: Oxford University Press, 1973).

II   *In Search of Democracy in Socialism* (Buffalo, N.Y.: Prometheus Books, 1981).

III *From Marxism and Bolshevism to Gorbachëv* (Buffalo, N.Y.: Prometheus Books, 1988).

I am greatly indebted to my colleagues Daniel Chirot, David A. Crocker, and William L. McBride who read the *initial* versions of the book manuscript and made invaluable suggestions.

Translation of this book into English was done in sections by Julie Clark, Elissa Helms, Vida Janković, and Linda Krstajić. To all of them I owe my thanks. General editing of the translation was carried out by Gordon Bardos and Diana Fabiano, to whom I am very grateful. I also owe my gratitude to Christopher Citro, my research assistant in the fall of 1996 at the University of Kansas, Lawrence, Kansas. Of course, when so many people are involved in one way or another in the translation of a book, the publisher must take on a lot of work but is also entitled to the last word. I therefore owe special thanks to Paul Kurtz, Steven Mitchell, and Ranjit Sandhu. This is my third book to be published by Prometheus Books (actually the fourth if *Tolerance and Revolution*, which I co-edited with Paul Kurtz, is taken into account).

Svetozar Stojanović
30 November 1996

Part One

From Stalinism to Titoism

AUSTRIA

Budapest

HUNGARY

ROMANIA

SLOVENIA
Ljubljana

Zagreb

CROATIA

VOJVODINA

BULGARIA

BOSNIA AND
HERZEGOVINA

Beograd

YUGOSLAVIA

SERBIA

Sarajevo

MONTENEGRO

KOSOVO

Sofiya

Adriatic
Sea

Skopje

MACEDONIA

ITALY

Tirana

ALBANIA

GREECE

0   100 km

0   100 mi.

EUROPE

SICILY

AFRICA

Mediterranean
Sea

Bill Pitzer- PITZO*Graphics*

One

Varieties of Stalinism

What Is the Time Now in Moscow? And in Belgrade?

"What's the time now in Moscow" (D. Ćosić in the novel *The Sinner*) is one of the nicest metaphors about international Stalinism. The time in Moscow did, indeed, change continually and unforeseeably in rhythm with the super-despot's twists and turns, while all the other communist parties set their own clocks in time with the Kremlin's.

And yet, the real Stalinism was a diffuse phenomenon, although incomparably less so than Bolshevism (its genus or family). Long ago I proposed some corresponding conceptual and other distinctions for Stalinism by particularly using the example of the Yugoslav Communist Party (YCP).

From the time of their formation after World War I, the communist parties in Eastern Europe were *in opposition, in the underground, or under occupation* . . . and not *in power* as was the Soviet Communist Party (SCP/b). Similarly, one should not underestimate the differences between the Stalinism of the YCP during the *antifascist and civil war and revolution,* on the one hand, and the ruling Stalinism in the USSR or in Yugoslavia, once that Party assumed power, on the other hand. Let me say in passing, that the political

15

regimes in the first Yugoslavia actually abetted the hardcore Stalinists (a special type being the convict-Stalinists) by their harsh persecution of communists. Furthermore, Stalinism in power was one thing and the Stalinism of the communist parties in the Western parliamentary democracies was another. That *"parliamentarism"* lies at one end of the Stalinist spectrum, and *totalitarianism* lies at the opposite end.

The *original* Stalinism, which set its seal on all the later ones, came out on top in the inner-Party struggle among the ruling Bolsheviks. Other communist parties as well were fully able to realize and manifest Stalinist potentials only after assuming power. As Stalinism in the USSR was the result of the *Stalinizing process*, its *phases and degrees* have to be differentiated. Not only did the anti-Stalinists and the non-Stalinists fall away from the stalinization path in all the communist parties, but so did the *incomplete Stalinists* as well.

For this reason, the key question is to what degree had the YCP become Stalinized prior to Stalin's onslaught in 1948. Three years apparently had not been sufficient for that ruling party to *complete* the stalinization process. It is also important to note that the YCP's ideology in 1948 was in full conformity with regard to Moscow, whereas in practice certain differences had already accumulated.

The *"highly developed"* Soviet Stalinism was marked by terrorist industrialization, terrorist statization of agriculture, and terrorist purges in the Soviet Communist Party(b) itself. The conflict between the YCP and Stalin, however, occurred at a time of the fairly enthusiastic (not mass terrorist) industrialization of Yugoslavia. More importantly, it occurred at a time when the YCP had not yet irreversibly plunged into the mass terrorist collectivization of the village. How significant this was is evident from the fact that such terrorization of the peasantry in the USSR, starting from 1928 and onwards, marks the watershed between Leninism and Stalinism. Prior to the Stalin's offensive 1948, the YCP likewise had not engaged in mass terrorist purges in its own ranks.

By a curious play of chance, every 10 years—1928, 1938 (the completed stalinization in the USSR), and 1948—crucial events took place in the history of Stalinism. Just as had the SCP(b) 20 years earlier, the YCP in 1948 reached a cross-roads but—in contrast to the SCP(b)—it turned to its own type of NEP,[1] after a *period* of forcing the peasants into the so-called work cooperatives.

The biggest irony in the YCP's history, however, was that its most Stalinist potential was manifested only at the time it openly resisted Stalin. This is why some 30 years ago I described Tito's "No" as a "Stalinist anti-Stalinism." In doing so I primarily had in mind the forced establishment of the so-called peasant work cooperatives that were dissolved only after Stalin's death! I also had in mind the imprisonment of "bourgeois elements" in the Popular Front, the annihilation of the last remnants of small private businesses and trades, the brutal terrorization of real or imputed cominformists, the convictions (based on earlier Soviet denunciations) and even the execution in Slovenia of a group of former Dachau and Buchenwald concentration camp inmates during World War II. My own father, a prewar merchant, a "bourgeois fellow-traveler" of the communists (though never a member of the YCP) from the very outset of the uprising against the occupiers in 1941, was a candidate on the Democratic Party's list for deputy within the framework of the Popular Front, in the first postwar elections. He was arrested soon after Stalin's first letter to Tito in the spring of 1948 and sentenced to 14 years at hard labor of which he spent more than three years in prison. This was one in a series of actions which in practice meant implicit acceptance of Stalin's "criticism" but which was verbally rejected. Conclusion: it was a typical feature of our Stalinist anti-Stalinism to intensify repression, especially that of the secret political police, a phenomenon that was to remain the lasting hallmark of Titoism.

Stalinism moved in a vicious circle of *self-enlarging and self justifying* mass terror. Even the most active manifestation of loyalty to Stalin was not enough to save anyone from wholly arbitrary terrorization. Under such circumstances, a mood of *panic* spread rapidly and even penetrated intimate human relations. In a certain sense,

---

1 . New Economic Policy.

the family was the basic foundation of the expanded reproduction of Stalinist totalitarianism. In those days school children brought home a godlike image of Stalin. Distraught parents most certainly dared not call this image into question in front of their children, but sometimes even bent over backwards to uphold and strengthen it. And in order not to collapse under the burden of self-debasement, many parents swiftly convinced themselves that the super-cult of Stalin was justified. A similar totalitarian mechanism was operative in Yugoslavia with regard to Tito and his leadership, both before the break with Stalin and, even more so, with the heightened terrorization after the break.

Stalinist terror constantly produced its own justification as well. The harsher the consequences of Stalinism, the more it considered itself indispensable. For instance, when the private peasants did not possess sufficient farm produce for the requisitioning demanded, the repressive measures "had" to be more intensive because the towns were threatened with increasing hunger; and since even intensive terrorization did not augment agricultural yields, the "only solution" was the forced collectivization of their farms. This resulted in even greater shortages of agricultural products, and so forth and so on. This is also an approximate picture of Titoist policy before the peasants were allowed (on very small holdings) to produce for the market. All this happened several years after the break with Stalin. But it was already a Bukharinist turn in Titoism.

In Yugoslavia as well, there was a pronounced difference between the Stalinists as initiators, orderers and executors of *mass terrorism* and the Stalinists who were *naive believers*. It would be unjustified to equate the *uninformed* Stalinists with those who became Stalinists even though they were *well informed*. Up until the end of World War II, there was only a small number of Yugoslav communists who really knew what the situation was like in the USSR. The rest, living at a great distance and possessing scant knowledge of Soviet affairs, were Stalinists in the sense that they blindly supported Stalin, the SCP(b) and the Soviet Union, in the belief that communist ideals were genuinely being materialized there. This latter group eagerly longed to see the Soviet utopia and its quasi-divine charismarch. Some did succeed in this but were repaid by bitter disappointment, some even losing their lives. They had made a journey into a positive utopia that ended in a negative one. Even some of the YCP chiefs showed symptoms of uninformed Stalinism for a certain time. Even Djilas, who had not up to that time been in the USSR, was shocked when confronted with the behavior of some Soviet soldiers on Yugoslav soil at the end of World War II.

Neither should we pass generalized judgments on the Stalinists because of the *generational* differences. An important component of *idealistic* as against *realistic* Stalinism, was the utopian nature of the *young* generation. These youths, virtually still teenagers, who joined the Communist Youth League and the YCP only in 1941, unlike some of their *older* comrades, were not genuinely tormented by the former Moscow trials or the Hitler-Stalin Pact. After all, such problems were being rapidly pushed into the background, even by the experienced communists, when the German occupation and the liberation struggle began. No wonder, since even a section of the Russian anticommunist émigrés in the West altered their stance vis-à-vis the USSR, when Hitler attacked that country. It would also be unjust to lay special blame on the young and inexperienced Yugoslav communists for their loyal devotion to Stalin and the USSR, when we know that some of the most prominent intellectuals in the West nurtured similar illusions. Tito himself believed that the USSR would defeat Germany within six months. The Yugoslav Partisans hoped they would receive military assistance from the USSR, even when that country was on the brink of defeat. After the war, Yugoslav communists also expected economic aid from the USSR although that land was even more devastated than Yugoslavia.

Unless one perceives the differences among the Stalinists, it is also impossible to understand what was to happen subsequently during the destalinization process, or the liberal communist reforms, or finally the recent implosion of communism. Some quondam insufficiently informed, idealistic, and naïvely loyal Stalinists, such for example as Gorbachëv and his associates, became transformed into the principal initiators and leaders of communist reformism and even into decisive actors in the process of the self-negation of communism.

When we try to explain the Titoists' treatment of the cominform-ists in their own ranks, from 1948 onwards, we must also bear in mind the distinctions among the Stalinists. A good many communists were imprisoned as being cominformists only because they insisted that their leaders should have attended a Cominform meeting in Bucharest in order to defend themselves from the accusations leveled against them. They had no inkling of the possibility that such a delegation would not have returned to Yugoslavia alive. The leadership, headed by Tito (who, in his own words, experienced Stalin's attack with great astonishment) was thoroughly acquainted with the situation in the USSR. Yet that leadership required the communists who were quite ignorant about all this to take up a proper attitude straightaway. Such communists were not even aware of the real nature of their own leadership and naïvely responded to the call freely to voice their opinions of the Cominform Resolution against the YCP, at their Party meetings. The narrowest top leadership of the YCP was quite patient with some of the leaders who were hesitant. But, at the same time, the leadership hurriedly arrested the young and ill-informed cominformists. Incidentally, Stalin committed a serious blunder in 1948 by disparaging the YCP and its wartime and revolutionary contribution, thereby alienating numerous idealistic Stalinists in the Communist Youth League and in the YCP. The Titoist leadership that had taught the communists to worship Stalin now required them, virtually overnight, to turn against him. The realistic Stalinists, Tito and Kardelj, before all others, who had sojourned in Moscow before the war and were best acquainted with Stalinism, began dealing brutally with even the youngest Stalinist idealists.

In the Bare Island (Goli otok) concentration camp (our own anti-Gulag), as in other such camps, real and imputed cominformists were subjected to appalling terrorism—and this at the time that Tito and his closest associates enjoyed the pleasurable amenities of the Brioni Islands and even sailed past the torture sites in his floating palace, the cruise ship "Galeb," as he voyaged on his "missions of peace" around the world.

Aleksandar Ranković, Tito's right-hand man, was later to admit that almost half of the imprisoned cominformists were innocent. He did not, however, feel the need to draw any political conclusions from this fact as to the possible consequences for the YCP leadership. This leadership continued claiming successes while distancing itself from all responsibility for its misdeeds, as though they had been caused by natural disasters. The fact that at least one-fifth of the YCP membership declared itself in favor of the Cominform Resolution seemed not to have had any connection with the previous policy of that leadership of unquestioning loyalty to Stalin. And not to mention the treatment in the concentration camps for the cominformists which in some sense was even more inhumane than that in Soviet camps: some cominformists were cynically given the freedom to exercise "self-management and self-re-education" in the camps, which led to brutal physical and psychological torture amongst the inmates who in this way competed to deserve being paroled. One must also not forget that in Yugoslavia some communists, even some noncommunists and anticommunists, who criticized the Yugoslav leadership from liberal and democratic positions, were deliberately incarcerated in perfect Stalinist style, as being *cominformists*.

Not only were the cominformists subjected to torture but their families, friends, and even chance acquaintances were also persecuted. If we agree that the physical isolation of genuine cominformists was necessary, this certainly could not justify the brutality toward them. Here, now, is a political fairy tale of mine: Tito decides to confine the cominformists on a wooded Adriatic island (that is, again, far from the eastern and northern borders of Yugoslavia, so as to prevent their liberation in the event of a Soviet military intervention) and to send selected communists, who rejected Stalin's accusations with the right arguments, to work among the inmates for the purpose of patient persuasion without torture.

And as we are speaking of the suffering cominformists, it should be emphasized that very few of them recognized the organic link between their own fate and the mass terrorism perpetrated on the anticommunists and noncommunists in which they themselves had earlier participated. By becoming an institution and a habit, terrorism possesses a powerful tendency sooner or later to turn upon its own protagonists and adherents. It is enough for erstwhile "comrades" to be renamed "enemies" to have even more horrifying terrorist methods used against them, because they betrayed the "common revolutionary cause." The "class enemies" were "only" executed or incarcerated, whereas former "comrades" were also subjected to moral annihilation.

What course would our history have taken had Stalin not demanded the overthrow of Tito and his trio (Kardelj, Ranković, and Djilas) but had continued setting them up as models to other communist leaders and had then craftily induced them to forge ahead into the mass terrorist collectivization of agriculture, into a more rapid and more radical nationalization of private property, into still more brutal persecution of "bourgeois elements," into the organization of countless trials similar to the so-called Dachau and Buchenwald trials? In a word, if he had urged them to turn the whole of Yugoslavia into a specific "Gulag Archipelago"? After all, Stalin's emissaries at the first Cominform Meeting in 1947 had already induced the Yugoslav delegation arrogantly to criticize the French and Italian Communist Parties and thus unwittingly to contribute to its own isolation when its turn came the following year.

And what would have ensued if Stalin had attempted to persuade Tito to create a Balkan federation with Bulgaria and Albania, and to integrate it straightaway into a kind of Warsaw alliance (which was established only in 1949 after Tito had already successfully defected) and then had militarily intervened against Yugoslavia by invoking these "international" institutions?

However, nothing of all this would have been indispensable to Stalin in his younger days. He would have known how to invite Tito and his trio to some celebration, give them a handful of medals and decorations and then arrange for them to perish in an airplane accident on their way home. He would then have had the occasion to "mourn" them at their funeral just as he did at Kirov's. True, Stalin, "missed" doing this as early as mid-1946 when Tito was last in the USSR, before the rift. Subsequently, using various pretexts, Tito sent others from among the leadership to the Soviet Union.[2] This is one of the reasons for the "paradoxical" conclusion that the YCP could not have successfully resisted Stalin had it not been led by a Tito with his highly developed Stalinist characteristics and experience.

After the break with Stalin, Tito and his ideologists re-styled earlier differences, even lifting them to mythic proportions by means of hindsight projections. We were to believe that when Tito assumed the leadership of the YCP on the eve of World War II, the YCP was a non-Stalinist, almost anti-Stalinist, Party. This was a case of retroactive metaphysics: the "essence" of the YCP was the same both when it obsequiously followed Stalin and when it wrenched itself free from his coattails!

During the war, the Soviet leadership did indeed secretly rebuke Tito for calling his military detachments "proletarian" and for setting up a temporary government at the second session of the Antifascist Council of National Liberation of Yugoslavia (AVNOJ) in November 1943. Furthermore, in a speech of 27th May 1945 in connection with the forced withdrawal of his troops from Trieste, Tito criticized the policy of spheres of influence, which the USSR considered an insult and therefore protested. In addition, the Titoist leadership ob-

---

2 . Djilas was in Moscow at the last meeting before the conflict broke out. On that occasion something occurred that he has never made public but which I learned from him personally. Namely, in January 1990 the Moscow journal *Literary Gazette* and the Belgrade weekly *NIN* arranged in Moscow a Soviet-Yugoslav discussion on the "Stalin-Tito Conflict." Of the Yugoslavs, among others, Djilas and I participated. After Djilas spoke I asked him whether Stalin had ever suggested in one way or another that he (Djilas) should assume Tito's position. Djilas responded by describing the following scene. In Stalin's dacha, during a working dinner, attended by the highest Soviet leaders, and of the Yugoslavs only by Djilas, at a certain moment the conversation lapsed and was followed by a long silence. All those present fixed their eyes on Djilas, who intuitively felt that Stalin was about to suggest a change in the Yugoslav leadership. So he (Djilas) broke the silence by an abrupt warm praise of Tito. After a while, Stalin cut Djilas short with an energetic, dismissive wave of his hand and a sharp look, returning to topics of the previous conversation.

structed Soviet intelligence services in their efforts to recruit agents within the YCP, even after the war. Finally, while the war was still in progress and especially after it, the Soviet side looked askance at the equal glorification of Stalin and Tito by the Yugoslav communists.

Nevertheless, the fateful discord between the Soviet and Yugoslav leaderships cropped up only after Tito attempted to create a Balkan federation *under his leadership* while the immediate cause for Stalin's assault was his belief that Tito's army was making ready to invade Albania.

Yugoslav Stalinism and Antifascist Patriotism

On the eve of Hitler's attack on Yugoslavia, the YCP was a fully disciplined section of the Communist Internationale. The leading Yugoslav Stalinists endeavored primarily to assist the Soviet Union, overthrow the government in their country, and integrate it into the USSR as one of its republics. They supported Stalin's pact with Hitler. We need only look at Resolution of the Fifth National Conference of the YCP, dated 1940, which defined World War II as an "imperialist" war and stated that the "English and French imperialists sparked a new conflict."

When he saw how enthusiastically the Ustashi government was welcomed in Zagreb in April 1941, Tito moved the central headquarters of the YCP to Belgrade. His first thought undoubtedly was to survive, but his decision was also motivated by the prospects for eventual resistance to the occupational forces. The bulk of the partisan units that launched the uprising in July 1941 were made up of young persons who had just joined the Communist Youth League and the YCP. True, they did aspire to come to power, not less than did the older communists, but they were at least equally motivated by patriotic antifascism. *The culture of resistance and revolt against foreign invaders*, so pronounced in the Serbian regions of Yugoslavia, exerted great influence on them.

During the German occupation in Serbia, I was 10 to 14 years old. My postwar decision to join the Communist Youth League was decisively influenced by the fact that several young communists passed through our home on their way to join the Partisans. I was also influenced by the fact that my father, as a patriot, cooperated with the Partisans—for which his life had hung on a thread on several occasions. Likewise, another circumstance that left an impression on me was that a Jewish woman, who managed to survive the war, was hidden in our home for a period of time.

Unless one clearly differentiates the motivation of the leading communists from that of the younger ones, one cannot understand the relationship between Stalinism and patriotic antifascism. These two components of Yugocommunism were in a state of tension, but Stalinism became dominant as soon as the question of priority was raised, because for the communist leaders patriotic antifascism possessed an instrumental and not intrinsic value. After all, the essential feature of Stalinist totalitarianism was to treat *everyone and everything* as a sheer means to its end.

Thus, for example, by subsequent ideologization, it was "established' that the communists played the decisive role in the 27th March 1941 overthrow of the Yugoslav government's pact with Hitler, signed two days earlier. However, the communist contribution to this event was negligible. During the whole time they ruled, the communists concealed from the people the fact that Tito had immediately rebuked the then communist leadership in Serbia for surrendering to the mass antifascist enthusiasm.

The YCP sent out a call for an uprising against the occupiers on the 4th of July 1941 only after Hitler's attack on the USSR, which was launched on the 22nd of June of that year. This was in line with Stalin's appraisal that the attack radically changed the nature of World War II from being an imperialist war to a liberation war.

One of the first moves of the *Yugoslav war Stalinism* was to liquidate those communists who had earlier opposed the "Bolshevization" of the YCP. Thus, Živojin Pavlović, author of a book entitled *The Soviet Thermidor*, in which he criticized Tito for Stalinizing the YCP, was killed on liberated territory (the Užice Republic) in the fall of 1941.

As the liberation war in Yugoslavia grew in momentum, so did the aspirations of the communists to monopolize antifascism. For this reason, the 4th July 1941 date was finally selected to mark the beginning of the uprising, as it was on that day that the YCP called for the struggle to begin. As long as it could, the leadership glossed over the fact that the armed struggle had been launched before that date by the noncommunist Serbs in Croatia and in Bosnia-Herze-govina, in their efforts to save themselves from the Ustashi genocidal assault.

My thesis on the instrumentalization of antifascism is also con-firmed by the negotiations conducted in March 1943 in Zagreb, by a partisan delegation led by Milovan Djilas. This delegation proposed to the German Command that their mutual hostilities should cease for the purpose of concentrating their forces on their conflict with the Chetniks, before the expected landing of the Western Allies on the Adriatic coast. To the very end of his life, Tito denied that these negotiations were conducted on his orders because he knew that the truth would cast doubt on the proclaimed antifascist purity of the Partisans, a matter of key significance for the assertion of their patriotic moral superiority above that of Draža Mihajlović's Chetniks.

The official history of the National Liberation War did not ascribe any significant differences to what the Chetniks represented, on the one side, and the Nedić, Ljotić, and even the Ustashi formations, on the other. In order to understand what I mean by this, I must first remind the reader of the existence of two crucially different dimen-sions in Serbian traditions. One such tradition is the *rebel-deon-tological* one and the second is the *opportunist-utilitarian* tradition. The first was manifested, for example, in the desire to reject in entirety the Austro-Hungarian ultimatum in 1914, in the refusal to accept the Yugoslav government's pact with Hitler in 1941, as well as in the outbreak of the Partisan and Chetnik uprisings against the occupiers in that same year. The second tradition was manifested in the partial acceptance of the Austro-Hungarian ultimatum by the Serbian government, in the signing of the accord with Hitler, in the goodwill shown to him by the Simović government as soon as it assumed power after the 27 March 1941 coup d'etat, in the Chetnik decision to refrain from continuing the uprising and, most of all, in the Nedić quisling government and its armed struggle against the Partisans up to the end of the war.

In Serbian history these two dominant tendencies constantly conflict and interplay and occasionally mitigate each other's effects. When a fatal danger appears to threaten their national dignity or independence, the rebel-deontological elite often prevails by bestowing its voice to the masses and their actions but also by conveying the impression that the majority of the Serbs are ready to sacrifice their lives for higher values. In fact, the Serbs are generally educated to feel shame if they evince fear or the readiness to be "flexible." But, when due to the activities of a relatively small uncompromising avant-garde, huge sacrifices ensue, a decisive role is then taken up by the opportunist-utilitarians and even, in some instances, by those who pursue a *collaborationist* orientation.

It is in this light that I see what was happening in Serbia during the 1941–1944 occupation. As is known, the Partisans and the Chetniks rose against the German occupying forces and succeeded in freeing a considerable area of the land in the second half of 1941. However, the two groups of freedom-fighters became soon separated not only as to their ultimate wartime aims, but also by dint of the defeat of the uprising and especially by their attitudes to the mass reprisals against the civilian population. The German troops executed 100 Serb civilians for each of their solders killed and 50 for each who was wounded.

The bulk of the Partisans fled beyond Serbia while the few remaining ones did not cease harassing the enemy, despite the civilian casualties. These sacrifices however, shocked the Chetniks of Draža Mihajlović and marked them psychologically and politically until their final collapse. "It is not yet time to fight," became the Chetnik watchword. They waited, more or less, for the Allied victory over Hitler and then to participate in the war in the concluding military operations and impose a solution of the question as to who the postwar rulers in Yugoslavia would be. Meanwhile, the Chetniks went on fighting the Partisans with the latter paying them in the same coin.

In this ostensibly winning combination, there was "only" one oversight: Churchill was no less an opportunist and utilitarian than Draža Mihajlović. He therefore withdrew his support from the Chetniks and extended it to the Partisans. Mihajlović's position was quite fragile from the moral standpoint as well; he ultimately wanted to save his people at the cost of the wartime losses of the leading antifascist powers. If we compare the two antifascist formations in Yugoslavia, we can note that the source of the Mihajlović movement's collapse was his unwillingness to continue fighting the occupying forces. The moral decadence of Titoism manifested itself in the continuation of the civil war even after its victory had been attained.

More light is thrown on the relationship between communism and antifascism in our country by the main patterns that were taken over from the Stalinized history of the Bolshevik revolution and the USSR. That is why antifascism was no obstacle to the Yugoslav communists in their "sharpening of the class struggle" as well as in their rapid shift from a "bourgeois phase" of the revolution to the "proletarian" one. In doing this, they annihilated actual and potential enemies and rivals, even those who were also antifascists. And when the communist terrorization led to grave defeats, the leadership of the YCP and the National Liberation War distanced themselves in true Stalinist fashion from the acts of terror as from "leftist deviations," although the terror was inspired by that leadership.

Another evidence of the official ideologization regarding the intrinsic antifascism of communism was the declaration that every anticommunism in Yugoslavia was profascist and even fascist, at least "objectively" so, if not by deliberate choice. All potential rivals of the communists, not to mention the real enemies, were proclaimed "fascists," or "the servants and helpers" of fascism, or "enemy collaborators" and the like. These terms were used as justification for mass arrests and executions when the communists assumed power. They also made use of the confiscation of the property of "enemy collaborators" (often falsely accused as such), which was their most favorite form of statization.

There was also a close link between the instrumentalization of antifascism and the absence of *enlightened* denazification in Yugoslavia, after the end of World War II, even in Bosnia-Herzegovina and in Croatia where numerous Ustashi and their accomplices were to be found. I shall have more to say on this topic in Chapter 3. At this point, let me only add:

Relatively more Nazi-fascists were imprisoned and executed in Yugoslavia than in Germany, Austria, or Italy, but unfortunately much less effort was exerted to explain why there was such a large number of them in our country. The communist leaders and ideologists were guided by the tacit premise that Nazi-fascism in some of our national communities was just a kind of "accident" in comparison with their "essence" as personified in the communists and the National Liberation War.

This was one of the reasons for imposing the specific "equalization" (*uravnilovka*) in the evaluation of the contribution and sacrifices made by the members of the various nationalities in the National Liberation War. This false symmetry was also evidence of the arrogant assumption of the victors that the nations in the new Yugoslavia could not be *unconditionally* considered equal but that they should be treated according to their contribution to the National Liberation War.

This attitude also held true for the national minorities. Because of the large number of occupational soldiers and collaborators from amongst their number, the German minority was virtually entirely banished from Yugoslavia, while some had left of their own accord. But this was not the case with the national minorities in Yugoslavia of those occupational countries in which communists came to power. In keeping with this policy, Yugoslavia waived the payment of war reparations of certain countries while insisting on such reparations from other countries.

Tito never ceased exploiting antifascism in order to uphold his Stalinism, even in the field of culture. To portray this I shall cite one of his prewar attacks on some left-wing intellectuals:

29

But the Trotskyists are also active in the literary field. With their alleged "scientific" viewpoints as expressed in their scribblings, they are causing confusion, especially in the minds of young intellectuals and among some workers. In our country, the Trotskyists are now calling for the revision of Marxism and Leninism. One Richtman and company, are now trying to revive the bankrupt theory of Mach which Lenin pulverized in his "Empirio-criticism." Some of our journals are offering hospitality to such types as the surrealist Marko Ristić, an intimate friend of the Parisian Trotskyite and bourgeois degenerate Breton . . . . Hospitality is offered also to Richtman who started by "rectifying" Engels and Lenin's dialectics and ended by slandering their best successor, Stalin. He also is defending Bukharin, Hitler's spy. Or else, let's take V. Bogdanov who in 1929 made shameful statements to the police and in court and is now attempting to revise the 1848 positions of Marx and Engels, a man who constantly and very cleverly pursues his destructive work at the expense of the working class. These men and their ilk of whom we shall say more as the need arises, are carrying out their destructive activities under the guise of literary creation . . . (Josip Broz, "Trotskyism and Its Helpers," *Proleter*, May 1939).

This text and another like it ("For the Purity and Bolshevization of the Party," April–May 1940) were reprinted in volume IV of Tito's *Collected Works*, published 30 years later together with the following comment written by him for this publication:

Unity of the Party and the whole revolutionary-democratic movement was the more indispensable as our country was facing an imminent fascist aggression and the danger of the introduction of totalitarian rule, along the lines of fascist countries, coupled with the revival of the worst aspects of the sixth-of-January dictatorship. For this reason, any *disbelief in socialism* jeopardized the unity of revolutionary ranks and *objectively served the enemy*. We therefore conducted an energetic struggle for Party unity, we qualified such manifestations as ignorance of the Party's basic tasks on the eve of the revolution" (Josip Broz, *Collected Works*, vol. 4, p. 9, emphasis added).

The first thing that strikes the eye is the total disproportion between the virulence of Tito's prewar attack and the tone of the later comment. On the eve of World War II, Tito even used accusations taken from the Moscow trials. Tito's ideological retrospection contains a milder category of "objectively serving the enemy"; whereas before the war the tone was suited to those who allegedly deliberately served the enemy. But we may well ask who objectively served the enemy more: was it those who, like Tito, consciously pushed Stalinism into culture, or was it those persons who opposed this?

Tito's argument later also makes use of the need to preserve the "unity of the Party and the whole revolutionary-democratic move-ment." However, it is well known that in genuinely democratic movements unity is not imposed but is built up through free com-munication. Moreover, would not unity based on antidogmatic posi-tions rather than a primitive totalitarian cultural policy be more suit-able for a "revolutionary-democratic movement"?

The target of Tito's attack was not the supposed "disbelief in socialism" as he subsequently stated, but rather the attitude to art, science, psycho-analysis, philosophy. Tito also asserts that his attack was not only understandable but also justified *in the light* of the YCP's preparations for the antifascist and revolutionary struggle. Even several decades later, Tito assumed that men had to believe in the canons of dialectical-historical materialism and socialist realism in order to be truly prepared to fight fascism and capitalism. However, it is impossible to adduce any kind of logical or even only psychological necessary connection between these two matters. Furthermore, are someone's chances to marshall fighters against fascism and capitalism the more effective the more radical is his sectarian ignorance of art, science, psychoanalysis, or philosophy?

We must also test Tito's "logic" by applying it to the original Sta-linism in the USSR. It would then turn out that there also the imposition of diamat and socialist realism was justified because it was indispensable to have unconditional unity in face of the fascist danger. However, why would this also not hold true for the forcible collectivization of farms, the Moscow trials, and even the liquidation of a considerable number of Yugoslav communists in the USSR? After all, this is no polemical construct of mine—the Stalinists in the USSR as well justified their policies by invoking the danger of fascism.

But to go back to the Yugoslav situation. If we assume that Tito's prewar attitude to culture was necessary due to the preparations for the National Liberation Struggle and the revolution, why was it necessary to perpetuate such an attitude even after the communists began ruling the country? Then, too, everything that came from the USSR was adopted: Lysenko, the attack on the Leningrad group of writers, the campaign against Western philosophy, the forcing of diamat and socialist realism. Even after the publication of the Cominform Resolution against the YCP, at its Fifth Congress in 1948, Tito's prewar assaults on the free-thinking left-wing intellectuals were reaffirmed.

As Tito's retrospective arguments clearly lead into new difficulties, let us attempt to reformulate and strengthen his argumentation. Here is one such thesis: had Tito not sharply attacked the nonparty intellectual left-wing, Stalin would have disbanded the YCP and the Yugoslav communists would have been unprepared during World War II for the role they played in it. But let us sharpen this thesis to its logical conclusion: only an unconditional adherent of Stalin, as Tito was, could survive at the head of the YCP at that time and as such reach the position in 1948 of being able to turn his back on Stalin. In this way, the whole previous Stalinism of the YCP would be viewed as indispensable and justified precisely *in the light* of the break up in 1948. A philosophically-versed reader will here recognize the application of the notion of the "ambiguity of history," as in M. Merleau-Ponty's book, *Humanism and Terror* (1947), which I criticized long ago (my book II). However, even had Tito known how to seek support from Merleau-Ponty's book, this would not have been of any vital assistance to him. It is not a question of deliberate and foreseeable consequences of Tito's prewar activity, but only of its unintentional and unforeseeable outcome (1948) which, in the best event, can be assessed by the expression "it turned out well." But what if it had turned out badly? If we were to *commend someone* for the unintentional and unforeseeable positive consequences, then we would have to *blame that person* for all the negative consequences.

But, consistently followed through, Tito's position would have destroyed itself. Let us assume that before Hitler's attack on the USSR in 1941, and not only in 1948, Stalin had demanded that Tito be replaced and that a group in the YCP had carried this out in a disciplined manner with the conviction that the "unity of the Party and the whole revolutionary-democratic movement" was indispensable due to the imminent antifascist war and the anticapitalist revolution. In keeping with Tito's "logic," such a group would be entirely in the right—on condition, of course, that it had really launched an antifascist war and revolution.

Koestler's Myth in the Light of Tito's Renegation

The view that Koestler's novel, *Darkness at Noon*, is a masterpiece has prevailed too long. Today, so long after the official Soviet confirmation that the confessions by the convicted persons were extracted by torture, it would certainly be superfluous to argue that Koestler's interpretation of the Moscow trials is factually erroneous. Nonetheless, I shall once again discuss this literary-historical construct, ultimately in the context of Tito's break with Stalin. A further reason for my discussion is philosophical and literary; that is to say, Koestler's example shows how ideology can destroy a historical-literary creation by rendering it *psychologically* unconvincing. My opinion (of this book) is the opposite of that proffered by the late Sidney Hook, who reiterated the claim about the novel's "psychological plausibility" (see the July-August 1983 issue of *Encounter*, devoted to Koestler's life, work and death). Joseph Conrad once wrote that the human longing for narrative is "greater than that for loaves and fishes of this earth." This explains why the influence of

Koestler's *narrative*-ideological text was incomparably greater than similar *discursive*-ideological interpretations.

Koestler did not believe that the accused men really committed the deeds for which they were convicted, namely, for spying for foreign powers, conspiring to kill Stalin and his closest associates, preparing the dismemberment of the USSR, and the like. However, according to Koestler, this does not mean that *as Bolsheviks* they were not *guilty* and that they had not *voluntarily* confessed and thereby rendered a last service to their Party.

They were allegedly prompted to confess by the original logic of Bolshevism. The hero of the novel, Rubashov, finally capitulates during the investigation before the demands of his own "internal consistency" and "logical necessity." Rubashov reflects on his generation in the Party in this manner: "They were too deeply entangled in their own past, caught in the web they had spun themselves according to the laws of their own twisted ethics and logic: they were all guilty, although not of the deeds of which they were accused themselves" (*Darkness at Noon*, New York: Macmillan, 1954, p. 253f).

While Koestler as a communist earlier believed that Bolshevism would *inevitably* triumph and create the foundations for a communist utopia, he as author of *Darkness at Noon* wanted to show that the Stalinist negative utopia was the *inevitable* result of Bolshevism's internal logic. Such a rigid determinism pervades both Koestler's former communist ideology and his later anticommunist ideology. In *Darkness at Noon* he presented a distorted picture of historical reality. This objection of course would be irrelevant regarding a work of fiction if such a work did not aspire to presenting the truth and was not received as such.

Still, such a super-Stalinist as Lazar Kaganovich actually insisted that a "Bolshevik must be ready to sacrifice for the Party not only his life but also his self-esteem and sensibility." However, not one of the founders of Bolshevism (and Rubashov is portrayed as precisely such a founder) would agree with this. The abstraction of "commissar" frequently used by Koestler disregards the essential differences between the Stalinized and unstalinized Bolsheviks. In fact, much terror directed also against the original Bolsheviks was needed for their *revolutionary dictatorship* to be transformed into *Stalinist totalitarianism*.

Koestler's is a deformed picture also because he presents the accused in the Moscow trials as actual and active fighters against Stalin. In reality, they were former opponents who had politically capitulated to Stalin years before their arrests, while some of them had even served him and praised him to the skies.

A third significant distortion was committed by Koestler when he turned the historical responsibility of the actors upside-down. Thus Koestler does not deal with Stalin's guilt and that of the other political malefactors, but only with the alleged responsibility of his victims for their earlier opposition to him, for destroying the Party's unity and damaging the "revolutionary cause" as well as for objectively helping the counter-revolutionary forces. But in fact no one caused greater damage to the "revolutionary cause" than Stalin himself and his faction. It goes without saying that the Bolshevik opposition also bears a historical responsibility, not because it opposed Stalin earlier, but, on the contrary, because it established the structural, institutional, and cadre basis for a possible and even very likely stalinization of Bolshevism.

The original Bolshevism and Stalinism were not bound by an iron-clad continuity, as Koestler asserted, but neither by an abyss, as Trotsky insisted. In my view, Stalinism was both the *realization of and the alienation from* the original Bolshevik intentions, program and policy. If it is correct to assume that the original Bolsheviks could not have foreseen the danger of the transformation of their intentions, program, and policies into totalitarianism (as it was a new historical phenomenon), we nevertheless cannot forgive them for installing a *ruthless revolutionary dictatorship which then gave rise to Stalinist totalitarianism*.

Counter to his own intentions, Koestler played into Stalin's hands by contending that the accused voluntarily confessed their guilt because they were guided by the internal logic of Bolshevik convictions. Koestler also distorted historical facts regarding the opposition to Stalin and its consequences and finally by turning upside-down the question of the responsibility of the historical actors. If someone endeavors to prove that Stalinism was the *sole* logical consequence and *only* true realization of Bolshevism, even if Stalinism is repugnant to him, such a person objectively propagates Stalin's monopolistic interpretation of Bolshevism.

Had the official version of the Moscow trials not presented to the world a rank and enormous lie but only a somewhat distorted picture, than a "sophisticated" literary construct such as Koestler's would perhaps merit some justification. The lie, however, should have been totally revealed and an artificial interpretative tale should not have been thought up.

Ultimately, had Bolshevik convictions even possessed a kind of iron logic which was Koestler's point of departure, the logic of *life* would have still completely gainsaid his story. In order to follow through his thesis to its conclusion, Koestler had to dematerialize the main hero by turning him almost into pure consciousness as regards consistency. Rubashov had become a virtually bodiless revolutionary, who takes upon himself the guilt for uncommitted crimes so as to perform his last service to the cause he devoted his life to.

In view of this contradiction between a virtually pure spirit and a body there follows an implosion of Koestler's literary edifice. It crumbles because of the tension between the basic ideological thesis and occasional accurate insights. Thus the Stalinist investigator Gletkin is well aware that the reason for Rubashov's confession does not lie in a kind of allegedly irresistible Bolshevik logic. So he proffers a different explanation as simple as it is convincing: "It is all a matter of constitution" (p. 240) referring to the fact that Rubashov became physically exhausted by being prevented from sleeping. After all, the novel also mentions the prisoners who were tortured and threatened with the lives of their families, tricked with false promises and the like. It is as if Koestler wanted to destroy his own construct by "transmitting" Rubashov's reflections before his execution: "But when he asked himself, For what actually are you dying? he found no answer" (p. 260).

In real life our reasoning does not consist only in drawing logical consequences from our convictions but also in a revision and sometimes in a complete abandonment of convictions if the consequences are unacceptable. If, for the sake of argument, we were to accept the mistaken thesis that Rubashov fully shared basic convictions with the Stalinists, it would be much more convincing for us if he had denied the accusations than, according to Koestler, admitting them voluntarily—of course on the assumption that *he could have had a choice.*

This is precisely what Tito did in 1948, even though he was not even an *original Bolshevik* but a pronounced and proven *Stalinist.* This takes us back to my initial thesis on the varieties of Stalinism.

When Stalin boasted that he could topple Tito with a flick of his small finger, he overlooked the key difference between *Stalinism in one country* and *Stalinism in a number of countries,* and even more the difference between communist countries in which he had *physical (military and police) control* and the communist country (Yugoslavia) in which he had only a decisive *ideologico-political influence.*

Stalin attacked Tito in order to complete the stalinization of communist countries, to make Stalinism fully uniform in those countries and turn all their leaders into obedient servants whom he would sacrifice from time to time and replace them with other servants. Even before Stalin's assault, Tito wanted to behave as much as possible as an *independent Stalinist.* But this introduces us to the topic of the genesis, development and fate of Titoism as a kind of *independent communism* and no longer simply as a *subspecies of Stalinism.*

Two

The Birth, Rise, and Fall of Titoism

The Titoist Ideal-Logy

After Tito's split with Stalin, the Yugoslav leaders and ideologists, mainly *Kardelj and Djilas*, sharply criticized social reality in the USSR and in Eastern Europe. Their common denominator was the rejection of Stalinism as a "new class society" in which the "bureaucracy" ruled the working class and the whole of society, by means of terrorism. Stalin's precept regarding the necessity to strengthen the class struggle and the repressive functions of the state in socialism was resolutely rejected.

Tito, however, was considerably more restrained and moderate in criticizing the USSR and the East European countries, both because he wanted to normalize relations with those countries as soon as feasible and because he feared the repercussions at the internal Yugoslav level. Stalin's death early in 1953 provided him with an additional argument in this context.

Among the supreme leadership of the YCP, Djilas alone did not accept the milder criticism but even applied it to domestic circumstances. His challenge to Tito ended in the well-known way. Would Tito have reacted so sharply to Djilas's "lack of discipline" had Stalin still been alive? In any event, at the time they boasted of their "humane and self-governing socialism," Tito and other close "comrades" of Djilas saw to it that he spent a total of nine years in prison. What else could other Yugoslavs expect if they were to set out along a critical and dissident path, when Djilas was being so heartlessly treated.

If we compare the political destinies of the three leading Titoists—Kardelj, Ranković, and Djilas—a good deal can be learned regarding the various faces of Tito. The draconian punishment meted out to Djilas shows that with his communist "liberalism" and "democratism" (which fairly quickly grew into genuine liberalism and democratism), Djilas was furthest away politically from Tito, although until the break he was closest to him emotionally. Much later, Ranković also fell away but he did not spend a single day in prison. Kardelj, dispatched from Moscow to Yugoslavia together with Tito, remained the second-in-command in the country until his death.

Tito's resolute denial of the accusation of domestic *Stalinism* (as a totalitarian, mass-terrorist, and super-despotic order) made it difficult to criticize *statism* as well as a system in which a group of people exercises the monopolistic structural control over the state and through it over other fields of social life (I shall return to statism defined in this way in Chapter 7); that is, a system whose only most extreme form constituted Stalinism. This is why in Yugoslavia the concept of "statism" was officially understood to mean only the increase of the state apparatus and its intervention in the economy and in other fields of social life, namely, something much more "innocent." Moreover, the Yugoslav officials constantly initiated criticism of domestic "statism" as well, so that foreigners sometimes wondered how it was that a ruling party could behave as though it was an opposition party.

But if "statism" was only that which the Yugoslav officials criticized, then our problem would not have been a very specific one, as huge bureaucracies and their interventionist activities can be found everywhere in the world. In such a case, many Western societies would be now "statist," now "antistatist," depending on the party in power. Consequently, it might be said that in Yugoslavia also, the situation constantly "essentially" changed: when the government froze prices, it was called "statist" and when it de-froze them then it was described as "antistatist."

What did Titoism, in the programmatic sense, oppose to Stalinism and statism? There was a gradual crystallization of the ideas which were finally summarized in the YCP's Program adopted at the 1958 Congress. In this Program, the trademark of Titoism was the "withering away of the state and the development of the worker self-management and social self-government," that is, "direct democracy." The principal ideological support for this was found in Lenin's *The State and the Revolution* and in Marx's *The Civil War in France*. For Tito's *ideal-logy*, from Lenin our communists borrowed the ideas of the withering away of the state and the development of worker self-management and social self-government, while for *practical* purposes they retained Lenin's "dictatorship of the proletariat."

I have used the notion of "ideal-logy," my old coinage, wherewith I signify a dimension or phase of ideology. It refers to a set of ideals which social groups utilize, at the cost of truth, to justify their own actions and discredit those of their rivals, opponents and enemies. In Chapter 7 I shall again deal with the communist ideal-logy (in the section on "The Decadence of Ideology").

The Program of the YCP is a masterly-worded manifesto of Titoist ideal-logy. What happened with this Program shows how lofty socio-political ideals can be misused for the purpose of ideological apologies. Our Marxist humanist intellectuals, including the present writer who was at that time a young university teaching assistant, were also impressed by the antidogmatic declarations and visionary messages contained in the Program. It was incomparably the most attractive programmatic text in international communism of that day. It was adopted by two-fold victors: they had brought a triumphal end to the enemy occupation of 1941–45 and were triumphant in their conflict with Stalin. One must not disregard either the fact that the Program was fiercely attacked by all the other communist parties, something that also contributed to its uncritical reception in Yugoslavia.

In opposition to a *status quo* ideology, a revolutionary ideallogy such as the YCP Program called for the transcendence of the existing situation in the name of a radically conceived future. This made it difficult for intellectuals as well to determine its apologetic potential and function. It was proclaimed that the withering away of the state represented the "basic and decisive issue in a socialist social system" (published in *Komunist*, Belgrade, 1962, p. 28). Here then is an excellent example of a utopia which by *drawing attention away* from real problems and the ways to resolve them, indirectly contributes to the preservation of the existing status and rule. And the real problem was the monopolistic structural control by a group of people over the state and through it over other fields of social life. *This statism (the Party state or the state Party)* was never officially questioned. Moreover, the one-party system in Yugoslavia was pronounced in the Program as being the form of a socialist democracy (p. 128). The Program rejected all the measures known in the history of liberal and democratic theories, and the practical struggles against monopoly rule.

This pretentious and arrogant utopianism rejected the rule of law in a pluralist and democratic state, preferring rather the idea of the withering away of the state and of law. The whole problem with the worker self-management and social self-government was perceived from a utopian perspective of the withering away of the state and not from the realistic perspective of trying to put an end to the monopoly of one group over the state. That is why no question was raised as to whether worker self-management and social self-government was possible in the face of such a monopoly or whether there was to be only some kind of participation in management at the work place and at other lower levels of social organization. The beginning of the withering away of the state was proclaimed in an ideological manner, but this never was nor could ever have been a Titoist or anybody else's genuine action program.

There were other more reliable indications of the operative goals involved in the Program. Thus, at the 1958 Congress not only was the Program adopted but so was also the Statute. It was symptomatic that the Program proclaimed the most radical goals of social development while the Statute did not transcend the framework of a typical ruling communist party in a single organizational or action precept. Besides, the then Constitution of the country nor any subsequent Constitution, nor the laws, decrees or current policies questioned the issue of the Party's monopoly. On the contrary, the Program explicitly protected the monopoly from "anarchist and pseudoliberal attempts to weaken the state and thus undermine the very leading role of the socialist forces and in this way to set the stage for antisocialist forces" (p. 93).

The YCP Program defended the Titoist policies in all its phases: "The Yugoslav communist understood on time the historical necessity to promote changes and acted toward removing the obstacles that prevent socialist development. They did not only oppose the tendencies for the restoration of bourgeois political forms and various hopeless petty-bourgeois anarchist manifestations, but they prevented the state from strengthening and elaborating its functions, its increasingly greater penetration into the societal life, the growth of administration, the more pronounced tendencies toward bureaucratism and economic privileges, by gradually turning the state into a power above society, into a master over the people. In this way, the Yugoslav communists cut the roots of the tendency to conserve the present relations and to halt the socialist development of the country" (p. 86).

It was exactly in this Program that the criticism of Stalin's USSR was fully mitigated, and this was accomplished in the following way: "The Communist Party of the Soviet Union, and the Soviet working class during Stalin's rule, succeeded in preserving the achievements of the October Revolution, in consolidating them through successful industrialization and by raising the general cultural and technical level of the country, by maintaining and developing the Soviet Union as a reliance for all socialist and progressive movements and against the stubborn pressures by the forces of capitalism and imperialism. However, Stalin did not for objective and subjective reasons oppose the bureaucratic statist tendencies, which stemmed from the huge concentration of power in the hands of the state apparatus, from the merging of the party and state apparatus, and from one-sided centralism. Just the opposite, it was he who became their political and ideological bearer" (p. 37).

Tito's pretentious belief that he could effectively influence the conflicts within the Soviet leadership, also softened the criticism. He supported the Soviet military intervention in Hungary in 1956, among other reasons because he wanted to support Khrushchëv in his quarrels with those who were an even worse lot than he. On that occasion, Tito "naïvely" relied on the official Soviet promise that Nagy and his group could safely leave their refuge in the Yugoslav Embassy and go home. How strange, if we bear in mind that Tito himself for two whole years before the Stalin's onslaught on him, avoided invitations to go to Moscow!

Another reason for Tito's support of Khrushchëv's intervention against the Hungarian revolution was his wish to extract the maximum for himself by occasionally relying on the USSR and not only on the USA.

The Program and policies of the LCY (League of Communists of Yugoslavia) experienced most serious *immanent* challenge from the student movement that culminated in the June 1968 demonstrations in Belgrade. That was an exceptionally significant year in the world. The critical youth movement in the developed capitalist countries had swelled and its cultural opposition proved to be more far-reaching than the political one. In addition, the reformist movement of the Czechoslovak communists under Dubchek reached its apex that year. But its fatal handicap was that the changes in the USSR under Brezhnev acted at the same time in the opposite direction.

The Czechoslovak reformers set their ideal of *"socialism with a human face"* against the existing system, while the Soviet and East European rulers were imposing the preservation of *"real socialism."* Everyone was told, thanks to their military forces, that there could be no question of any other socialism apart from the model existing under their control.

By analogy, I would say that our democratic socialist university movement criticized *real self-management and self-government socialism* in the name of *true self-management and self-government socialism*. The critically oriented students, and their professors who supported them, arrived at the conclusion that the hitherto progressive reforms of the system in Yugoslavia had exhausted their strength, and that the reforms had to be much further advanced. Their fundamental principle was *self-management and self-government from the bottom to the top of the social pyramid*. Besides their socialization and the real political influence of the professors on them, an important reason for their action was the intuitive feeling of the students themselves that it was most promising and least dangerous if as criticism from the inside, they could hold forth in the name of the LC Program. The movement did not, of course, pose the demand for a multiparty system and a "civil society" but it was doing something that was banned in the existing order—taking the opposition into the streets, striking, and demonstrating against the authorities. And when the demonstrations and the strikes were over, not all action committees in the university ceased functioning nor did all the students hail Tito after his speech in which he craftily stated that the "huge majority of the healthy forces" among the students and teachers were in the right.

It is also important to emphasize that this movement advocated a predominantly Yugoslav orientation. The nationality issues in Yugoslavia were not in its field of vision. The enthusiasm that prevailed in Belgrade at that time did not pay sufficient attention to the internal rift in the university movement in Zagreb nor to the fact that the pro-Yugoslav disposition there was attacked and suppressed. This was, in fact, an unnoticed prelude to the widespread national movement that was to break out in Croatia only two years later.

The 1968 student movement was *democratic* as much as it was *leftist*. The top rung on the ladder of values that it espoused was equality, while freedom, particularly economic freedom, was subordinated to it. Only later was it recognized that the statists could more easily manipulate the ideal of equality than that of freedom. The movement attacked the tendency to revive private ownership, market competitiveness, the profit motive. It was characterized by economic dilettantism. What else could one have expected when

44

these viewpoints characterized even the nucleus of the "Praxis" group of professors[1] who wholeheartedly supported the student movement. After all, economic dilettantes in some sense predominated even among the professors of economic studies, not to mention the state officials and the leadership. Likewise, the bulk of the people had no experience of the capitalist economy from prewar Yugoslavia.

Tito's first reaction to the movement was a manipulative one that then became more and more repressive. We Praxis professors endured a good deal, but the students were hardest hit, and especially their leaders, who were sentenced to prison terms. In order to quieten the university and arouse patriotism the regime also made use of the fear caused by the Soviet intervention in Czechoslovakia.

Charismarch(y)

Tito was born in Austro-Hungary of a Croat father and a Slovenian mother. He was a citizen of that empire for 25 years, up to its downfall. One of the politically formative factors in his life was his wartime service on the side of that empire and, for a period of time, against Serbia in World War I.

The following stratum in Tito's political personality was Stalinism. His swift rise in the Zagreb communist organization in 1928 and his later prison term coincide in time and politically with the victory of Stalin in the factional struggle in the Bolshevik Party and in the Comintern. The result of these events was the replacement of Sima Marković, then secretary general of the YCP, because of his *Yugoslav* orientation. That is to say that the Comintern had decided to use all its available means, mostly violent ones, to crush Yugoslavia as a "greater Serbian" and "Versailles" creation. In origin and by upbringing in a Croatian environment, in which the longing for their own state had existed "since always," Tito gladly accepted the at-

---

1. They were: Zagorka Golubović, Trivun Indjić, Mihailo Marković, Dragoljub Micunović, Nebojsa Popov, Svetozar Stojanović, Ljubomir Tadić, and Miladin Životić.

tacks on Yugoslavia and the communists who stood for its preservation. The decisive significance in Tito's political biography was his
rapid advancement in the party hierarchy leading him to the position of secretary general of the YCP at the time of the harshest Stalinist terrorism and general Stalinization in the USSR and in the
Comintern. Tito's exact role in the persecution of the Yugoslav
communist-émigrés in the USSR has not yet been fully investigated.
His role in the elimination of his predecessor, Gorkić, also remains
to be precisely established.

The third fundamental political dimension of Tito's personality,
one that is in contradiction with the previous two, is his role as
renovator and leader of the new Yugoslavia. In this context, Tito as
a Stalinist and a ruler was characterized by the full instrumentalization of the pro-Yugoslavia position, no less than his earlier instrumentalization of the nationality issues for the purpose of crushing
Yugoslavia.

However, as time elapsed, the formerly subdued Austro-Hungarian, Croat and Comintern attitudes toward Yugoslavia emerged from
out of the depths of Tito's being. There was a growing contradiction
between those attitudes and his stand as a creator and ruler of second Yugoslavia. Although in 1964, at the Eighth Congress of the
YCP, he identified himself as a Croat, it cannot be said either that his
Croat identity was not contradictory, because up to his last days he
firmly insisted that he was Yugoslavia-oriented. It is likely that he
really believed he could instrumentalize and control the impact of
the nationality problems. But when he died, the spirit of nationalism
flared up to such an extent that it finally put an end not only to
"Tito's Yugoslavia," but to Yugoslavia itself.

Nothing in Tito's nationality policy, starting from the mid-60s to
the end, can be understood unless we take into account his political
squaring of accounts with two groups of leading Serbian and one
group of leading Croatian communists.

After the short-lived support extended to Ranković in his dispute
with Kardelj, in 1966 Tito decided to remove Ranković. Tito was becoming more and more suspicious with age, so concerned for his
life-time power that he undertook "preventive" cadre blows at

Ranković and his collaborators. True, at that time rumors were rampant among political and other functionaries that Tito would soon retire and that Ranković would succeed him. A no less significant reason was the resistance Ranković and his circle offered to Tito's intention to introduce confederal elements into the Constitution. Seventeen years later, in 1983, when some one hundred thousand people attended Ranković's funeral in Belgrade, it was already possible to foresee what would be the fate of the Titoist order as codified in the 1974 Constitution.

In the early 70s Tito had difficulty in eliminating from the political arena another group of Serbian leaders, composed this time of liberal communists and led by Marko Nikezić. Tito removed this group because it wanted a more modern and freer economic, cultural, and political order in Serbia. That group also advocated that Vojvodina and Kosovo should enjoy considerable autonomy as Serbian provinces but they were against their becoming de facto separate republics, independent of Serbia and even above it in rights. This did in fact happen in line with Tito's wishes after Nikezić's group was removed in the fall of 1972. Early in the 70s Tito made preparations for radical constitutional changes in Yugoslavia and Serbia, and he therefore could not tolerate a strong and half-independent Serbian leadership. Being a very deft politician, however, he did not want a second conflict within a few years with the Serbian communists regarding the nationality issue and the state order of Yugoslavia and Serbia, so he accused the Nikezić group only of "liberalism." Because of the nationality-state issues Ranković had already been removed but this was not given as the reason (it was invented that Ranković organized the tapping of Tito's residencies, offices, and telephones).

Tito's sympathies were on the side of the national-"liberals" around Mika Tripalo and Savka Dapčević-Kučar in Croatia and not on the side of the Nikezić international-"liberals" in Serbia. That was why he tried to eliminate the latter *before* removing the former. In a speech held in early May 1971 in Sarajevo, Tito criticized the Serbian leadership, but he had to retract temporarily because he had come up against a wall—all the important Serbian leaders at the federal and republican levels resisted him. Of course, Tito was well aware that in this way his inviolability would be questioned, so he spent the rest of the time, up to the fall of 1972, in fomenting discord among the Serbian leaders.

Following upon his previous intervention (practically extorted from the pro-Yugoslav cadres in the political, army, and police sectors) against the mass Croatian national and nationalistic movement and the communist leadership in Croatia at the end of 1971, which until then he had supported, sometimes out of his convictions and sometimes manipulatively so as to achieve the intended constitutional changes—Tito was in a hurry to set up a repressive symmetry in Serbia and a balance of power(lessness) of the leaderships of the two strongest republics. This he considered as being indispensable for the preservation of his autocratic rule in the country.

It was symptomatic of the Croatian "liberals" in their national prejudices to feel that their main danger came from Nikezić's alleged unitarist group. That group, however, was highly conciliatory, even cooperative, vis-à-vis the Croats. And yet, the Croatian prejudices to the effect that the Serbian leaders could be nothing but unitarists obsessed Tripalo and Dapčević so much that Tito manipulated them till the very end.

He did remove them from political life but, in collaboration with the rest of the Croatian leadership, led by Bakarić, he implemented practically all their ideas and demands for restructuring of Yugoslavia. A fairly large-scale repression that followed in Croatia was also a bad omen, as some future leading secessionists were imprisoned, thus gaining the authority of martyrdom. The replaced Tripalo and Dapčević were to play important roles in the secession of Croatia from Yugoslavia in the beginning of 1990s as well as in the newly independent Croatia. The degree of Tito's inconsideration is evident even in his choice of Karađorđevo, a rest center in Serbia, as the location where he replaced the Croatian leadership.

In contrast to the resignations of Tripalo and Dapčević, the resignation texts of the Serbian "liberals" were not made public at that time. The former had pledged their loyalty to Tito while the latter submitted purely formal resignations which by themselves could have been interpreted as protests. It is a pity, however, that Nikezić and his associates did not grasp this opportunity to formulate clearly their political disagreement with Tito. Some very influential people in that group (above all Koča Popović and Mijalko Todorović) were unwilling to go "so far." For this reason, I would submit that this political group was more important by its potentials rather than by its achievements. Their political and intellectual possibilities were considerable, especially Nikezić's who seemed like a possible Yugoslav Berlinguer. But Nikezić did not have the luck to become that because he arrived at the head of Serbia prematurely, in the period of the inviolable charismarch.[2]

In summing it all up, it becomes understandable why the first and strongest criticism of Tito and Titoism emerged from the Serbian community. In that community, the earliest and swiftest transformation of Tito's positive into a negative charisma occurred. Yet, I must add that in this context there has been a good deal of simplification and exaggeration, particularly since the collapse of Yugoslavia. The common denominator of such attacks is the assertion that Tito harbored the diabolical intention of destroying Yugoslavia. Such an accusation, however, does not distinguish between consequences and intentions in Tito's nationality policies as pursued during the past fifteen years or so. I do not believe one can prove, for instance, that Tito's measures designed to reduce to a minimum the Serbian share in the state power were motivated by a deliberate wish to scrap Yugoslavia and enable Croatia and Slovenia to secede. Why would Tito have wanted to dismantle Yugoslavia when it had made him a celebrated personage? It is more likely that he wanted, through constitutional changes as well, to strengthen his life-time personal power, ensure his influence after his death, and thwart the revision of the new Constitution since such a revision would require the agreement of all the federal units. Tito knew that the Serbs in some sense had played the decisive role in bringing him to power. But he

---

2. The expressions "charismarch" and "charismarchy" I coined and started using long ago. To make them more understandable I offer an analogy with "monarch" and "monarchy."

also feared their influence that could limit or even totally restrict his powers. Tito's contribution, for instance, to the statehood ambitions of the Albanian minority in Serbia at first could be explained by his desire to create a Balkan federation under his leadership, but how else can one explain the continuation of such a policy after Stalin's assault and Enver Hoxha's pronounced enmity, except through fear of Serbian strength.

It would seem that the accusers I have in mind equally assess Tito's attitude toward Yugoslavia and Kardelj's, who did indeed hope for and prognosticate that Yugoslavia would simply be a "transit station" of constituent nations on the road to independent national states. Before and after a brief period of falling out of Tito's favor in the early 60s, Kardelj played a decisive role at Tito's side. Tito's patient and would-be "heir" died before Tito, although he was a much younger man. Kardelj always sided with Tito at all the crossroads and conflicts in the Party. As the charismarch was unable to create ideology, Kardelj was always at hand to offer "theoretical" explications. If it happened to be a question relating to a repressive course of action, Kardelj expounded in its favor—and if the issue was renewed liberalization then he was in favor of that since he knew quite well that Tito wanted the world to see in him a ruler who was essentially different from those in the USSR. One of Kardelj's "famous" ideologems was, for instance, the assertion that the Yugoslav system was not in fact a one-party system, an accusation leveled against it in the world. In any other language except in Kardelj's ideological language, this would have had to mean that there was more than one party in Yugoslavia or at least that there were no parties there at all.

Tito started life as a peasant boy who went out into the world in search of a livelihood but filled with the irresistible desire to live a life of luxury. When he entered the service of the Comintern he found a good pretext for his *bon vivant* habits in the need to assume a mask. That this was more of a rationalization than a real reason was obvious because as soon as he began ruling he moved into the "White Palace" in Belgrade and began a regal existence. His funeral in 1980 exhibited the same pomp. As a ruler he offered the other communist hierarchs a clear example of how to live an extravagant life. In a possible typology of communist revolutionaries and rulers, as a boundless hedonist Tito would represent one extreme end, the other extreme being a complete ascetic. Communists who have grown up in an impoverished and envious environment, like Tito, are most often inclined to enjoy material privileges and a high life-style. Communists from well-to-do families usually endeavor to "redeem" themselves by despising material comforts and benefits.

The generational relationship within the leadership of the YCP is also of interest to us here. During the war and after it, Tito gradually became the inviolable charismatic leader. However, even prior to this he was in his own circle a kind of communist patriarch. One of his far-reaching acts in this regard was the choice of much younger men as his closest associates and especially the leading trio Kardelj-Ranković-Djilas. The way they addressed him—"stari" meaning "the old man"—reveals a patriarchal relationship.

As he grew older, Tito was confronted more and more by the prospect of dying. Some "undesirable" archetypes dating from his youth became increasingly influential, such as the one formed by his religious upbringing. That was why toward the end of his life he publicly boasted of never having signed a death sentence. This was blatant hypocrisy as he ordered not only individual death sentences but also a system of wholesale executions during the war and for a period after he assumed power. But he always had others sign such sentences. It was as though he wanted to delude God as to the re-sponsibility for the death of his victims. There was a good deal of idealistic self-sacrificing on the communist side but incomparably more were others sacrificed ruthlessly. Every individual—especially a leader—must ask himself at life's end what he spent his life on as well as the lives of many others. As a rule, leaders issue directives for the violence committed, but they take great care to see that they give no personal practical example of this. If Tito was really convinced that the terrorism perpetrated on the Cominformists imprisoned in the "Bare Island" camp, why did he never pay it a visit. It would appear that he believed in a strict division into those of "clean hands" who give "the orders" and those who carry out the "dirty business."

Djilas's description of a conversation between him and Tito is well-known. After the funeral of Boris Kidrič, one of the leading Titoists who died young, Djilas bemoaned the fact that "There is nothing after death," to which Tito retorted sharply "How do you know there isn't!"

I suspect that for this reason Tito commanded that there should be no communist symbols on his tombstone. His stubborn worshippers should not regret that communist insignia have been removed from our national flag and from other official places as Tito was the first to start this fashion.

Yugoslavia's problems in the 70s should also be examined in the light of an aging man's charisma. Tito had already entered his 80th year, but it never crossed his mind to retire, nor did anyone in his entourage dare to suggest such a step. Just the opposite. Queried by foreign experts as to any possible constitutional guarantees against possible abuses of the position of a lifelong President, officials would reply that for this the exceptional personal qualities of Josip Broz were enough. It is no wonder that this reply was always met with disdain.

After having removed the most capable and most liberal associates in a series of successive political purges, it was sad to watch Tito alienate even his own wife and remain alone despite the large number of flunkeys around him. Death came upon him at a time when he could not stay long in one residence but constantly wandered from one of his palaces to another.

People are still talking and writing about his masterful handling of the position as ruler. However, this is an exaggeration. The most interesting question for researchers is not the functioning of Tito's charisma once it had been established, but rather its original formation. Tito started his career as a relatively small communist apparatchik, a Comintern agent, who returned to Yugoslavia with a mandate from the Comintern. At that time, of course, he still had no *personal* charisma, but as the leader of a communist party, the *collective* Comintern charisma had rubbed off on him. He jealously kept his personal radio contact with Moscow throughout the war in his private possession. That is why I am not convinced by the assertions that the leadership of the YCP almost replaced him during the war. That leadership had not chosen Tito as leader nor could it replace him without the agreement of Moscow. The membership of the YCP was for a long time mystified as to who was the person who had come to be the new secretary general of the Party. And for the young intellectuals in his entourage there was the mystery of a "worker" who was standing at the head of their Party. They were conscious of their "littleness" before the man not only because he was representing the Comintern but also because as a "working-class man" he knew how to act forcefully in contrast to what was allegedly the behavior of wavering and tender-hearted intellectuals.

The methodology of Tito's political way of gaining the better of his opponents was not essentially new. There were only some communist specificities in this as when, for instance, he was in the minority at the meeting called to remove the Nikezić group and when he threateningly stated that the "numerical ratio between the minority and majority" was irrelevant because the important thing was who "represented the historical interests of the working class." In asserting this he, of course, did not rely on his arguments but rather on the army, police, and propaganda apparatus. He therefore banned all information about that meeting from being publicized except what he had stated in his introductory and concluding speeches.

People often exaggerate when they point to *spontaneity* in the formation and sustainability of charismatic rule. That *well-organized* efforts by the Party apparatus were of major importance soon became apparent after the death of our charismarch. As soon as the support of the power mechanism, the propaganda, the falsifications and suppression of historical truths disappeared, Tito's charisma began to fade rapidly. It became evident how great was the illusion harbored by the guardians of "Tito's name and achievements" with the use of the slogan "After Tito—there will also be Tito."

Tito was practically obsessed by the wish to eliminate critical intellectuals from the public life of the country. In addition to his attacks on Dobrica Ćosić, in Serbia he especially came down upon the eight of us Praxis professors, in part because of our close association with Ćosić. In his attacks on us he was wholeheartedly assisted by Kardelj, who had a special reason for resenting us. Kardelj nurtured pretensions to a dominant position in Marxist theory and social criticism. I shall be speaking more of the Praxis group in the last chapter of this book. At this point, I shall only enumerate some of the main events in this conflict in which I personally participated.

The conflict began as soon as a Zagreb-Belgrade group of professors issued the *Praxis* journal and organized international meetings of intellectuals under the name of "Korčula Summer School." The conflict became even more acute when Ljubomir Tadić, at a meeting of the Faculty of Philosophy in Belgrade in 1967, criticized the constitutional provision exempting Tito from the mandate of the President of the Republic limited to eight years. Present at that meeting were the other members of the group of eight Praxis professors, at which I presided as chairman. An inquiry was immediately instituted by order of the Office of the President via the City Committee of the YCP. The Faculty had a good deal of trouble with all this but it maintained an honorable stand and managed to defend Tadić. All this, however, did not deceive Tito, especially when the eight of us and mainly Dragoljub Mićunović stood up in the forefront of the ranks in support of the 1968 student movement. After this, Tito publicly demanded our removal from the university.

In order to resist the wave of repression in culture in 1969, the ban on certain films, theatrical plays, books, etc., we organized a meeting entitled "Socialism and Culture" in the Philosophical Society of Serbia, at which I again happened to preside. One thousand intellectuals attended this gathering. The Yugoslav leadership responded to it by a massive media campaign against us.

In the Korčula Summer School in August 1971, I again "indebted" Tito with an analysis and criticism of the charismatic communist leader. This text was published a year later in the domestic and international issue of *Praxis*. Of course, I did not mention Tito by name but readers and Tito himself easily recognized whom I had in mind. Here follows what I stated on that occasion:

Unfortunately, even when charisma has exhausted all the internal possibilities it had for coping with social problems, it can still remain a formidable source of power. I am referring to the extremely humiliating situations in which a society can find itself, as for example in the USSR, during the last years of Stalin's reign, when the members of the party and state hierarchy were concerned only with surviving the leader's arbitrary whims, while together with the people they both feared his death and desired it secretly. Can a socialist revolution, this real flight to freedom, degrade itself more than by surrendering to the determinism of chance—and a chance of a *biological* nature at that? This confirms splendidly a thesis about the positive social and moral functions of death. . . .

A particular problem for the social scientist is the behavior of the charismatic leader of the postrevolutionary dictatorship when it enters the process of liberalization. If the decisive role of the charismatic leader is not made clear, it will be impossible to understand why the liberalization of a postrevolutionary dictatorship as a rule follows a zigzagging pattern. It is true that liberalization inevitably subverts the power of charisma. Although this may seem paradoxical, it is also true that the charismatic leader can compensate for this loss precisely by acting as the initiator and champion of liberalization. This, of course, can be his *genuine* role only to a very limited extent, for, the stronger the democratic institutions, the weaker the charisma, and conversely, the stronger the charisma, the smaller the chances are for creating and maintaining democratic institutions. This is why the tides of liberalization regularly alternate with counter-attacks by the charismatic leader, who appeals to the principle of monolithic unity. To maintain his charisma at such times, the leader resorts, among other tactics, to "leftist" demagogy: although he lives in abundance, the leader nevertheless leads the egalitarian political campaign.

Social scientists since Weber have often drawn attention to social crises and the efforts to resolve them as the most favorable condition of the appearance of charismatic leaders. But they often failed to note that the cause sometimes reverses direction, and that the charisma can play an important part in creating social crises. In this process, too, we should differentiate between *spontaneous* effects and *deliberate* efforts. Systematically obstructing the process of liberalization in a postrevolutionary dictatorship, the charismatic leader inevitably leads the society into a crisis. Although this may again seem paradoxical, the charismatic character of the leader is renewed in times of crisis owing to his monopolization of the savior's role. One of the consequences of such a renewal of charisma is the widespread feeling of uncertainty and fear about a future in which the charismatic savior and guide will no longer be present.

The charismatic leader is aware that democratization would gradually deprive him of his power unless he secures for himself the savior's role. He may, therefore, occasionally even instigate disagreements, tensions, as well as conflicts in the party and state hierarchy, and thus in society as a whole. A crisis created in this way will then be energetically resolved by him, thus refreshing his charismatic prestige. However, the leader is also aware that too strong an attack on one part of the hierarchy will make him dependent on the other, thus preventing him from exercising his role as arbitrator. In other words, he will refrain from resolving too radically the disagreements, tensions, and conflicts, i.e., the sources of eventual future crises within the hierarchy, since only in crisis can his charisma be renewed and refreshed (*Praxis*, nos. 3–4/1972, pp. 378+).

In that same year of 1971, in a Tuzla courtroom, I was called as an ethics expert to testify at a trial of a man against whom a tape had secretly recorded his words of abuse of Tito. On that occasion, I assisted Judge Radulović in presenting arguments against the use of such evidence. This was successful so that the accused was freed. Tito was furious about this and publicly attacked the "judges" who cling to the legal paragraphs as a "drunkard holds on to a pillar."

Tito continued increasing pressure for us to be eliminated. However, even the new Serbian leadership, enthroned after the removal of Nikezić's group, lost more than two years in the endeavor to have us removed from the university through the "self-governing" procedures. But the resistance made by us and our colleagues in the Faculty of Philosophy was both extensive and skillful. So much "lost time" in the conflict with us can only be explained by Tito's wish to preserve some semblance of a liberal communist leader. It may not be sufficiently known that Tito yearned to be awarded the Nobel Peace Prize and that this helps explain why there were a number of temporary truces in the public campaign against us.

The real question is not why Tito and Kardelj, not to mention the lesser functionaries, steadfastly persecuted us, but rather why they at least tolerated us prior to the above-mentioned remarks by Tadić in 1967. I believe they were under the delusion that in our social criticism we would stop short of their personal inviolability and that for the sake of the international *image* they would exploit the existence of our group of free-thinking Marxist intellectuals in Yugoslavia.

Many people even today are wondering why we in Belgrade suffered a worse fate than our like-minded colleagues in Zagreb, even though they were more important in initiating the publication of the *Praxis* journal and the Korčula Summer School. One reason was that we in Belgrade were more direct in our political activities and criticisms, not sparing even Tito. Another reason was that the Zagreb Praxis members were very active in criticizing nationalist attitudes in Croatia, so that it was awkward for the Party hierarchy to have them also removed from the university together with the nationalists.

With us, the authorities tried everything except imprisonment: there were threats of prison sentences if we failed to resign; our passports were taken away; we were visibly followed by the police and our telephones were tapped; rumors were circulated that there were police informers amongst us; attempts were made to make us retire by heaping "compliments" on us; efforts were exerted to corrupt us with offers of diplomatic posts abroad; minimum salaries were accorded us; efforts were also made to discredit us morally by requiring us to shut our eyes to the persecution of our students. . . . But the authorities made no attempt to blackmail us, not out of benevolence, but because they had nothing with which to do so.

Knowing only too well who our opponents were, we remained true to our agreement not to cede one inch on matters of principle, because the least sign of cowardly self-delusions would lead our persecutors to launch a final assault on us in the hope of their victory. The firmer we were, the more our persecutors were secretly respectful of us. I cannot say that we never used some tactics, but only to the extent that would not call into question our principled resistance. We were assisted in our successful opposition by political experience and the collective wisdom based on such experience. It is regrettable that neither we nor the general public still do not have available the stenographic notes of our individual talks with the officials of the Serbian government, practically every December in the second half of the 70s. In these talks we not only resolutely declined employment outside the university but, to the amazement of those officials, we offered detailed critical analyses of the situation in the society and in the state.

When the authorities in the beginning of 1975 and in the face of the domestic and international public had to remove the mask of "self-government" by removing us from the university by means of direct outside intervention, we had a breathing spell because we knew that in losing the administrative battle we had morally won the whole war. It was precisely in order to avoid this that the holders of power spent six years in the effort to get rid of us by "regular procedural methods."

The Balance Sheet

The first and most important success of Yugoslav communism was leading the National Liberation Struggle in World War II. This was the antifascist and patriotic basis of its legitimacy which future analysts as well will not be able to deny even when taking into account major relativizing moments which we discussed in the previous chapter. This differentiated it from the East European communism that was installed by the Soviet army. True, that war victory created a mythic picture of the struggle as waged exclusively against the occupying forces and their hirelings and relegated to the background the inter-nationalities, inter-religious, and civil dimensions of the war and the fact that a much larger number of the Yugoslav population lost their lives and suffered hardships in these mutual conflicts than in the struggle against the occupying forces.

Ahead of many other people, Tito realized the significance of what is now called an *image*. That is why he deliberately augmented data relating to the number, strength, and casualties of his army and those of the occupiers, especially the German troops. From then on, the deliberate propaganda exaggerations, to use a milder term, up to the collapse of the regime, remained one of the essential features of Titoism. Otherwise one cannot understand why there was such amazement and even astonishment in our country and abroad that Titoism should have collapsed so "suddenly." One of the Titoist myths was the belief that the Yugoslav partisans liberated the country all by themselves and thus gained control over it. This was only partly accurate since it was the Soviet army that initially participated in the liberation of the eastern parts of the country, while Great Britain as well and subsequently the USA supported Tito and renounced their support of Draža Mihajlović. The Western Allies and some prewar politicians at the Allies' directive, contributed in no small measure to the legitimacy of the new rulers in Yugoslavia.

During the war an image of moral purity among the Partisans was also created and disseminated. Yet Tito as supreme commander and his staff throughout the war enjoyed significant privileges, while collectivism, egalitarianism, and asceticism were reserved for the lower officials and the rank-and-file of the army. The *Partisan morality* operated much longer in some Partisan groups that were cut off from the Supreme Command. Only toward the end of the war, when these groups were integrated into the larger units of the National Liberation Army, were they, too, subjected to strict hierarchical distinctions in the matter of supplies, clothing, accommodation, and the like. On orders from the top, the "Partisan spirit" was abandoned in favor of the system in the Red Army and Stalin's criticism that "uravnilovka (leveling) was a petty-bourgeois principle."

THE FALL OF YUGOSLAVIA

The Yugoslav communists re-created Yugoslavia out of the wartime ruins. The state even annexed some regions that had not been given to Yugoslavia in 1918, and about 10 years after World War II some more territories were added to Yugoslavia. This was a further reason promoting the legitimacy of the new authorities, particularly in Croatia and Slovenia. I must mention here one more specific basis for the legitimacy in Croatia: had there been no communists, Croatia would probably have been treated like Hitler's Germany and exposed to forcible mass denazification and compelled to pay war damages to the victors as well as to the domestic victims of the Ustashi genocide.

The communists made an end to the bloody inter-nationalities conflicts in Yugoslavia and made tremendous educational and propaganda efforts in behalf of the policy of "brotherhood and unity." But at the same time they created a myth about having definitively resolved the nationality issue. The noble ideal-logy of "brotherhood and unity," however, concealed the contradiction between loyalty to Yugoslavia and loyalty to particular nationalities. The nationality question, as a long-standing factor in history, was gradually to undermine and finally destroy not only this ideal-logy but also Yugoslavia as a state. But the creation of that state, its collapse and its renewal after World War II, its reorganization under the communists, and finally its definite disintegration three years ago, will be treated in the following chapter.

A significant stronghold of Yugoslav communism in the eyes of the groups who stood to gain from it, were the measures that radically increased the vertical social mobility and the generally altered professional, stratificational, and class structure of our society. I here mean the militarization, the agrarian reform, the colonization, the confiscation and nationalization of private property, the industrialization, urbanization, the mass literacy campaigns among the population, the free education and social health insurance, etc.

Unfortunately, there was forcible liquidation of the "civil society" (underdeveloped) dating from prewar Yugoslavia and with it the last remnants of political pluralism. This was accomplished much more radically than in the other East European countries. And finally, even those political parties that had accepted the communist hegemony in the National Liberation Front were eliminated, in some instances by ruthless persecution with which Tito was still trying to placate Stalin in 1948.

For the above reasons, and especially due to the obedient attitude toward Moscow, patriotic support to the communist authorities in the early postwar years began rapidly to decline. The population felt that Yugoslavia was in fact becoming a part of the USSR and that its leadership wanted formally to annex the country to the Soviet Union. It was then that Stalin's "salutary" assault occurred.

Tito greatly boasted of his split with Stalin, "forgetting" that previously he had been most "deserving" in his subservience to him. He had even wanted to be a greater Stalinist than Stalin himself. For this reason he fully aggravated his relations with the West by his engagement in the civil war in Greece, by downing some western aircraft, by endeavoring to annex Trieste and the like. As a result, his relations with the West were at the lowest ebb at the time of his conflict with Stalin; that West in fact upon which very soon his survival was literally to depend. It is not true that it was Tito who broke with Stalin, as Tito constantly reiterated. It was *Stalin who was the first to break with Tito*. Tito did break with Stalin, especially on a psychological level but only gradually and later.

There is no gainsaying that every break with evil is a positive matter, but if that evil resulted from someone's deliberate activity, as in Tito's case, then in his self-appraisal he should be much more modest and moderate. Otherwise it would seem that to renounce an evil done, even a very big one, should be valued more than the nondoing of evil. In the history of Titoism, a good deed is interpreted as the outcome of one's own options and engagement, and evil committed as the result of the impact of unfavorable circumstances. In keeping with this train of thought, the conflict with Stalin was depicted as the result of Tito's choice, while the Stalinist characteristics of his policy before and afterwards were treated as the consequences of difficult circumstances. What is more, the Titoists even denied they had ever had anything to do with Stalinism. But, then, why did they break with Stalin?!

This does not mean that the successful independence of Yugoslavia from the USSR did not revive and expand the patriotic support for Titoism. Even the anticommunists, both the foreign and domestic ones, supported Titoism as a lesser evil than a possible Soviet occupation of the country. Unfortunately, in its struggle to survive, Titoism again resorted to mass repression and terror.

Soon after Stalin's death, there followed a slow-down of intended reforms in Yugoslavia. That is why it can be said that from the standpoint of Yugoslav development, Stalin died prematurely. Of course, from the perspective of events in the USSR, and in Eastern Europe, it was a good fortune that he died in 1953 and not later, because he would have inflicted much more harm.

In the second half of the 50s and during the 60s, there was nevertheless a certain economic, cultural, and even political liberalization under Titoism. This buttressed its legitimacy in the eyes of a large section of the population as well as in the anti-Soviet West. Undoubtedly, the achievements I shall now enumerate seem much less important when taken by themselves, but not in comparison with the previous Stalinization in Yugoslavia and the then situation in the USSR and in the other East European countries. This is a good illustration of the strength of so-called negative and comparative legitimacy.

At first persecuted by the forcible "buy up" of his farm produce and then pushed into "work cooperatives," the Yugoslav peasant was left in peace by the state only after Stalin's death. For this, Yugoslavia did not experience any serious food shortages afterwards, which cannot be said of the other East European countries. Titoism was to profit considerably from the more liberal attitude to the peasantry in the economic, political and legitimacy sense.

Given some experimenting with market practices also in industry, Titoism became a specific type of communism in this respect as well. It was, of course, a market for goods and services only, excluding labor and capital markets, so that such a market was unable to offer even a semblance of results that could be attained in a capitalist system. Despite this, Yugoslavia in the 60s had a very high rate of economic growth. This was achieved, of course, at the expense of profitability due to which to this day in the (former) Yugoslav territory, there has been no shift from extensive to intensive development.

It should also be emphasized that Titoism stimulated the participation of employees in management at the work place. In the current ideology of that time this was mythically presented as a *"new self-management direction, one between capitalism and statism."* Our self-management was intended to serve as a substitute for democracy. The ideology of official talk about self-management probably reached its apex in Kardelj's assertion that it had been introduced way back in the National Liberation Struggle.

Domestic and foreign critics were also wrong in insisting that there was a *dualism of statism and self-management* in the Yugoslav system. In actuality, Titoism was simply a *special kind of statism*. One of its specific characteristics dates back to the 50s when the employees' participation in the management was introduced. Another specific characteristic is of a later date: Yugoslav statism was divided into eight national-territorial units which negotiated among themselves, while at the same time paralyzing each other. A part of Chapter 8 is reserved for some other self-management experiences in Yugoslavia.

Under Tito, the Yugoslavs enjoyed a fair amount of freedom to travel abroad and find employment there. By abandoning the respective Stalinist dogma, the regime benefited as this reduced unemployment and social tensions and was probably also the result of Tito's youthful experiences of traveling and working abroad. Still, one cannot fully credit Tito for this because previously he had deprived Yugoslavs of the freedom of movement, which before the war had been a routine possibility.

After the split with Stalin, our country opened itself up fairly widely to the world in the fields of scientific and artistic activities, in the transmission of information, and in the translation of books. Creative individuals obtained some important freedoms but (unlike those in the prewar Yugoslavia) their freedoms were limited to those who did not encroach upon the government, the system, or the official ideology.

One should also not forget the successes of the Yugoslav foreign policy of nonalignment. I do not think that at the time I am referring to our country could have had a better and more realistic alternative. It is quite another matter that as far as Tito's pretensions were concerned, Yugoslavia was too small a country for him so that he devoted most of his attention and energy to the world's affairs on the pretext of leading the nonaligned world. He completely disregarded the fact that our country was primarily a European state. Moreover, the nonalignment policy could assuredly have been more useful and of greater moral weight had it cost us less financially. Besides, too much attention was paid to purely political relations and too little to promoting the economic ones. Even a myth about Yugoslav nonalignment was concocted by deliberately glossing over the degree of Western military, political, and economic support. Generally speaking, Tito's global ambitions were absolutely disproportionate to the political, military, economic, cultural, and scientific strength of Yugoslavia and its position in Europe.

It was typical of the Titoist regime to alternate periods of liberalization with periods of repression. Toward the end of the 60s Tito again introduced an oppressive policy that lasted until his death and even after it. Our rulers were seriously frightened by the student movement of June 1968 as well as by the Soviet military intervention in Czechoslovakia. It was as though our charismarch had so exhausted all his energy and daring in the conflict with Stalin that he could no longer undertake similar bold actions. There is sufficient proof that Tito feared Brezhnev and that he let him do what he had previously not conceded to other Soviet leaders. Tito though did make use of Brezhnev's threats, real and fictitious, so that the other leaders would be obedient to him, as was the case with his handling of the Croatian and Serbian leaders in 1971 and 1972. All in all, in the 70s there was a fair degree of parallelism between the "period of stagnation" under Brezhnev and Tito's conservative and repressive course.

Our official policy at that time was marked by the rejection of a multiparty system as a possible solution for socialism and at the same time by support for the Eurocommunist pluralistic orientation.

This, however, could have been a noncontradictory policy only on condition that the democratic transformation of the Western communists was really interpreted as pure tactics and as one of the ways that would ultimately lead to a monopolistically conceived socialism. In other words, it was not in fact a case of Yugoslavia's not yet being ripe for political pluralism but that Italy still had to become ripe for political monism!

The re-imposition of dogmatic Marxism in the social sciences, in education, and in public life and the persecution of the so-called "pessimistic wave" in literature and in art generally, was partly motivated by the desire of the Titoists to take their revenge upon the disobedient intelligentsia for what it had done during the previous liberalization period.

The highly restricted self-management in the enterprises introduced during that period was now atomized and paralyzed by the division of the enterprises and institutions into "basic organizations of associated labor," so that this inevitably required intensified statist intervention.

With the so-called delegates' system, finer filters for the cadre (self-co-option and supervision) were introduced, and the first independent representatives in the workers' councils and municipal, provincial, republican, and federal assemblies were eliminated.

The "consensual economy," through "self-management accords," set back the market-oriented and entrepreneurial tendencies. Under the name of a "self-management economy," republican nationality-statist economies practically usurped all that which the enterprises from other parts of Yugoslavia had invested on "their soil." This was the road to the confederalization of enterprises and the state. But this very limited and truncated market still gave us some advantages over those of the other communist countries. For a time, the high rate of economic growth continued but at the cost of steep loans from abroad, which were kept secret from the public. As soon as Tito died, foreign creditors knocked on the doors of the central government (although the federal units and even individual enterprises also borrowed money at will) and the Yugoslavs suddenly woke up from their consumerist sleep.

Up to the end, one of the props of the regime was the statist paternalism known also to the other communist countries. By this is meant a system in which the population, if not acquiescing to it, at least tolerates the monopoly of a group over the state and through it over the rest of societal life; in return, this group gives the people social security in the form of permanent jobs irrespective of output achieved, as well as free schooling, health and social insurance, and the like. This paternalism in our country even evolved into wastefulness based in good part on the illusion that we had unlimited resources and supported by abundant financial remittances sent by Yugoslavs employed abroad. Huge consumerist appetites were stimulated by the country's accumulated foreign and internal loans. Titoism corrupted the people with the self-management at the work place, with the "nationalities economies and states," and the heightened standards of living.

Tito and Titoism can be positively evaluated thanks to the big "No," one directed at Hitler and the other at Stalin. But the National Liberation Struggle had long since lapsed into pure (inexperienced) history not only among the young generation but also among the overwhelming majority of the general population. This had also been the fate of the patriotic prestige as revived in the conflict with Stalin.

The final outcome, even before the collapse, was more negative than affirmative, more spectacular and short-lived than solid and far-reaching. It was, to be exact, primarily a policy of negation: antifascism, anti-Stalinism, antistatism, anti-centralism, nonalignment. . . . Both Yugoslav Stalinism and Titoism were combinations of professionalism and dilettantism. The professional communist revolutionaries were very skillful in destroying and applying nihilism as a policy but after gaining power they immediately proved to be dilettantes through their efforts to create a new society and state *ex nihilo*, after having demolished all the inherited fundamental institutions. With time, and as conditions constantly changed, more and more creative political, economic, and cultural professionalism was needed. But the petrified and aging Titoism was unable to provide this. Arrogant incompetence and the unwillingness to adapt to the modern world, to its market economy and political institutions, all largely contributed to the downfall of Titoism.

Because Titoism was never tested in democratic elections and because there was no free public opinion polling, we shall never know with certainty how large a section of the population really supported Titoism. But from the fact that it was only 10 years after Tito's death that Titoism irretrievably collapsed as a social and state order, we can conclude that sincere support for Titoism was considerably smaller than was thought both in our country and abroad.

Tito gambled away the opportunities offered by Yugoslavia that he himself had enhanced by breaking away from Stalin. Unfortunately, in order to preserve his autocracy, to the end of his life, Tito obstructed the introduction of liberal and democratic reforms. His place in history would have been enhanced had he died before he inaugurated the repressive and disintegrational policies in the 70s.

After Tito, we were left with first-rate problems and second and third-rate leaders to solve them. The 70s were lost and the 80s willfully misspent. The latter decade laid the ground for the collapse of the social system and the state. When a country, especially a small and developing one, loses 20 years in preventing needed reforms, it is no small wonder that the consequences are disastrous.

After the death of its founder, Titoism required only 10 years to perish as an ideology, a social system, a state, a foreign policy. . . . This clearly means that the founder was a successful ruler but poor statesman. This is also evidenced by the visits to his grave—people have long since stopped going to see it!

Part Two

The Disintegration
of Yugoslavia

Three

The Break-Up of Yugoslavia from Within

Yes, Bosnia is a land of hatred. That is Bosnia. And by some strange contrast, but which in fact is not so strange and could easily be explained given careful analysis, it could also be said that there are few lands where there is such solid faith, such sublime strength of character, such tenderness and passion, such depth of feeling, devotion and staunch loyalty, such a thirst for justice. But under all that there lie concealed, in the turbid depths of the storm of hatred, whole hurricanes of shackled and serried hatreds that are coming to maturity and awaiting their time. . . .

Anyone who lies awake at night in Sarajevo can hear the sounds of the Sarajevo night. The clock on the Catholic Cathedral rings out hard and sure: it is two o'clock in the morning. More than a minute passes (seventy-five seconds to be precise—I counted) and only then does the clock from the Orthodox Church ring out somewhat less strongly, but piercing the night, and it too rings out *its* two o'clock. Shortly after, the clock tower of the Imperial Mosque strikes with a husky, distant sound, and that strikes eleven o'clock, ghostly, its time à la turque, according to a strange calculation of distant, foreign regions of the world. . . .

And that difference is, sometimes visible and open, sometimes invisible and insidious, always similar to hatred, often even identical to it.

(Ivo Andrić, "A Letter from 1920")

A Nonsynchronized and Contradictory State

Those prophetic words written by our Nobel Prize-winner should be extended from Bosnia to the whole of Yugoslavia, and from Bosnia's religious traditions to national and state-constructive or state-destructive traditions. The great writer and intellectual was singularly gifted in spotting "factors of long duration" in history.

From its coming into being in 1918, Yugoslavia was a *nonsynchronized and contradictory state creation*. It was created mainly by Serbia and Montenegro, countries that were victors in the First World War. The Serbian nation's human and material sacrifice invested in Yugoslavia was unparalleled, convinced that it could best solve its national question in a broader southern Slav framework. Besides, a broader state framework was necessary to fulfill the ambitions of the Serbian royal family and the victorious army, as well as those of Serbian political and other elites.

The other two then recognized state-constitutive nations, the Croatian and Slovenian nations, also entered Yugoslavia voluntarily, but from a different, vanquished state, Austria-Hungary; and this was, of course, also true of the Serbs living there. In that way those nations passed over onto the winning side in the war and saved some territories toward which Italy and Austria aspired. But, unlike the Serbs, a large number of Croats immediately expressed dissatisfaction at the common state and demonstrated a virtually obsessive aspiration for an independent state, all the more so as Yugoslavia was a unitary and not a federal state.

There can be no doubt that because of their number (some 40 percent) and strength, central location, and the fact that they were spread throughout almost all the country, as well as their state-protection inclination, the Serbian people were, and remained right to the end of Yugoslavia, the main "impediment" (an anti-Serb expression used by Croatian separatists) in the way of the break-up of Yugoslavia. The other Yugoslav separatisms, at first weak but since recently very strong, were also inherently anti-Serb oriented.

Nonetheless, it is erroneous to think that there did not exist close mutual similarities, links and other good reasons for the unification of the southern Slav peoples. The first such factor was identical, or very similar, ethnic origin. In addition, the marked majority of the population had a common, Serbo-Croatian language, and the two other main languages, Slovene and Macedonian (the latter officially codified only after the Second World War) are very close to that majority language. It was on this that close cultural links were founded. However, the Yugoslav ideologists of the time went to such extremes in their enthusiasm for the new state that they proclaimed that Serbs, Croats and Slovenes were three tribes of the same nation, although it was already a question of three formed nations. The Serbs from Serbia and Montenegrins wanted to help their southern Slav brothers, and particularly the Serbs who lived on those territories, to free themselves from Austria-Hungary, while the Croats and Slovenes (and the Serbs who lived there too) went over from the losing side to the winning side in the First World War. In any case, a larger state was a far better protection for security and borders: of the seven Yugoslav borders at least five were brought into question (with Italy, Austria, Hungary, Bulgaria and Albania). Many inter-national marriages also certainly made up a connective tissue for the two Yugoslavias, and there were over one million of them at the end of the 80s. Finally, the highly complementary nature of the economies in our region and the advantage of a larger marker should be recalled.

This does not, of course, mean in any way that violence did not play a huge role in the creation, maintenance, destruction and renewal of Yugoslavia. Let us start with Serbian military power, which in a certain sense carried out unification over the "barrel of a gun," as many Croats and Slovenes had taken part in the war against Serbia and Montenegro on the side of Austria-Hungary. Furthermore, King Aleksandar I Karadorđević suspended Parliament in 1929 and introduced personal dictatorship in order to save Yugoslavia from breaking up. Unfortunately, it was held together more by military, police, political, and administrative power than by economic, religious, cultural, and civilizational links. In both Yugoslavias *state* integration was stronger than *social* integration. Capitalism was not well developed, particularly in the central and eastern part of the country; the western regions were economically considerably more progressive, while Serbia dominated in the military, political, and administrative respect. Contrary to the broadly accepted idea of the tradition of democracy in the western parts, only Serbia in the east entered Yugoslavia with a democratic-state inheritance. In the 23 years of the existence of the first Yugoslavia, Serbia (and Montenegro) did not really succeed in lessening economic lagging, not to mention transforming the noneconomic hegemony into an economic one. This, however, was no surprise, as it had suffered irreplaceable human and material losses in the First World War.

Yugoslavia was renewed by the communist-victors in the Second World War. Here are another two elements from the history of communist Yugoslavia: Tito came to the conclusion that the Croatian national and nationalistic movement in 1970–1971 was threatening Yugoslavia to such an extent that he crushed it with repression; the Albanian separatist movement in Kosovo was repelled by force several times, and the situation remains the same right up to the present day.

The tenacity and acuteness with which the national question kept on renewing itself in Yugoslavia for over seven decades is actually understandable as Yugoslavia emerged, disappeared, and rose again in two world wars, and as, on the territory of Yugoslavia, those wars were (also) marked by inter-national, inter-religious, civil, fratricidal, and even genocidal conflicts.

Although, in my opinion, internal factors were more important than external ones for the final disintegration of Yugoslavia, this does not in any way mean that we should underestimate the role of foreign factors in the creation, maintenance, renewal, and break-up of the two Yugoslavias. First and foremost: Yugoslavia was created with the decisive support of France, the USA, and Great Britain, the three western allies of Serbia and Montenegro in the First World War; and it was occupied and dismembered in 1941 by Germany (and Austria that had been annexed to it), Italy, Hungary, and Bulgaria. It was renewed in 1945 with the support of the USSR and the same three western allies. Throughout Yugoslavia's entire history much has depended on whether the decisive countries have incited the contradictions in Yugoslavia or its cohesion. That is why our eminent scholar Jovan Cvijić noted with resignation: "No one but ourselves is to be blamed for our having built our house in the middle of the road." And we have already seen that our two writers, Andrić and Ćosić, masterfully use the metaphor of domestic clocks that do not keep time either with one another or with standard world chronometers.

After their coming to power and the renewal of Yugoslavia, the communists triumphantly continued with the defamation of the former Yugoslav state and claimed that the national question had been solved once and for all by their coming to power and through federalistic organization.

Tito spoke of the "three rotten pillars of old Yugoslavia" that had been torn asunder mainly by the national and social issue, as well as by dependence on foreign powers. The Kingdom of Yugoslavia was indeed not a solid state primarily because of the aggravated national antagonisms that were (also) fueled by the centralistic system. From its very beginning it had many dangerous enemies: the fascist and other irredentisms of neighboring countries, as well as internal separatisms, shook it from the beginning, and later that was compounded by the Nazi danger, from outside and inside (the "fifth column"). King Aleksandar I Karađorđevic himself was to die in 1934 at the hand of a separatist. But, nonetheless, Yugoslavia did not fall in 1941 because of internal antagonisms but under the blow of a multiple and far more powerful external enemy that had prior to that also occupied far stronger states, and was somewhat later to bring even the USSR to the brink of catastrophe. We can, by the way, ask ourselves how many "rotten pillars" Tito's Yugoslavia had when it broke up in 1991 mainly from within.

Titoists also estimated the economy of the Kingdom of Yugoslavia as being a mere bagatelle, turning a blind eye to, among other things, the damage wreaked on the eastern parts in the war between 1914 and 1918, as well as the fact that the world economic crisis had been underway for half the time that state had existed. For their own economic failures, however, Titoists were to use all possible justifications: the blockade introduced by the USSR in 1948, the economic recessions in the West, the oil crisis, etc.

As a factor of state integration, the initial enthusiasm of the Yugoslav communists was combined with the suppression of the national question by means of education, propaganda, and force. According to that ideology, "the new Yugoslav society" was in the national sense essentially a nonconflict one. And when it was not possible to deny some evident inter-national problem, then it was claimed that it was in no way a consequence of the new system but only a "remnant of the old society" or a consequence of "counter-revolutionary activity." It was believed that remaining silent about what had happened among the Yugoslav nations during the Second World War would truly contribute to the recovery and promotion of their relations. Ideologists "explained" everything with the syntagma of the "People's Liberation Struggle of the Yugoslav nations" and "occupiers and their henchmen." That Yugoslav form of internationalism was in many ways repressive: it was as if a radical solution to the national question presupposed the concealment, and not the perception, of its roots. In any case, what could pretentious Yugo-Stalinists, who had rejected all deep psychology, know about the consequences of the suppression of human trauma?

They never seriously posed the question of where all the hatred, the war crimes, and even the genocide that revealed itself during the Second World War had actually come from. Nor did they wonder why the People's Liberation Struggle (PLS) was considerably later and weaker in some national circles. In the first chapter (the section entitled "Yugoslav Stalinism and Antifascist Patriotism") I mentioned in passing that myth of socialist realism according to which all the Yugoslav national milieux had given a proportionally equal contribution to the PLS. Let me add another two things here: in the spirit of Yugoslav leveling exactly eight "heroic capitals" were proclaimed, one in each of the republics and autonomous provinces, and it was proclaimed that all the Yugoslav nations had liberated themselves mainly with their own forces. In fact, few national milieux had managed to do that without the decisive assistance of large military units from other parts of Yugoslavia. Besides, a considerable part of the country (for example, Zagreb) had experienced liberation only after Hitler's suicide and Germany's final defeat. The YCP leadership endeavored to conceal all that, as well as many other things, not only from the mass of the population, but also from other communists. And these did not in any case have access to the truth about the history of the relationships of their own leadership toward the national question and Yugoslavia as a state.

If my statement about the first Yugoslavia being in many ways a nonsynchronized and contradictory state is correct, what then can be said about the second Yugoslavia that endeavored, by keeping silent, to fill in the fatal fissure opened in Jasenovac and other places of execution of Serbs in the so-called Independent State of Croatia?

Was Yugoslavia Possible after Jasenovac?

Much has been written in the world about the phenomenon of Auschwitz, but little about Jasenovac. For example, Zygmunt Bauman gave a brilliant analysis of Auschwitz (in the essay "The Modern and the Holocaust") linking it with the inherently destructive potential of *modern* science and technology placed at the service of bureaucracy and the rules of *depersonalized* rationality. However, Ustashis killed Serbs in Jasenovac and in other places in a *premodern* way, *face-to-face*.

The communist victor in Yugoslavia never seriously looked into Ustashi genocide as an issue or a problem. Instead of carrying out denazification through education (see again the section on "Yugoslav Stalinism and Antifascist Patriotism" in the first chapter), he limited himself to the liquidation of captured Ustashis. It is true that Pavelić and the other main criminals had, however, fled abroad, and the new authorities did not endeavor to organize their trial (at least in absentia) like the one in Nürnberg, although they more than deserved it. The karst pits into which Serbs were thrown alive by Ustashis in Herzegovina remained concreted over, and their relatives were not allowed to take out the bodies and bury them. These "concreted pits" have become a metaphor for the communist illusion that enforced silence is the best way to deal with terrible crimes among nations. Perhaps that was why, not only due to his personal nonchalance, Tito never visited Jasenovac!

As I am criticizing others, I am obliged to admit that neither I, brought up as a child in the spirit of Yugoslav brotherhood, nor my wife, a Serbian from Croatia who had just managed to flee from there in 1941, spoke to our sons about what had happened to their mother and her family during the Second World War. When they saw on television the bones from those pits in Herzegovina being exhumed and buried on the eve of the Serb-Croat war in 1991–1992, they reproached us bitterly for our silence. For me, that scene was a turning point in the sense that I firmly decided to devote my full moral attention and my research to Jasenovac in the future.

With the wholehearted support of the other communists, and there again mainly Serb communists (in the illusion that it was "internationalism"), the leading Croatian communists did not even dream of launching a discussion on Ustashi genocide, as they took as their guide the comfortable ideological premise that their contribution to the PLS had expressed the *substance* of Croatian tradition, while the Ustashi movement was just an *accident* in it. Thus, communist totalitarism "solved" the potentially most acute problem of the renewed Yugoslavia in one monopolistic-essentialistic move. The genocide perpetrated against Serbs (and Jews and Gypsies) was relativized and placed under the general category of "crimes committed by the occupiers and their henchmen," instead of being treated as a separate category on account of its monstrous nature. And as the Ustashi movement was not classified as a kind of Nazism, which it doubtlessly was, no official denazification was implemented like the one in Germany.

The nonchalance will be remembered with which the greatest Croatian writer and longtime communist Miroslav Krleža "explained" what had happened there in April of 1941 with "a few truckloads of Ustashis" that had returned to Croatia from political exile abroad. That period of Croatian history has been approached in a far more responsible way by, for example, Lasić, Šneider, or Zafranović. I quote Stanko Lasić:

> It would be most necessary today for the very people who emigrated in 1945, who still exist, who have in part re-turned to the country, to take a most critical look. . . to see and examine their sin—that would give great impetus and lead toward a democratic climate. . . . And when I say that it was a great sin, I know what I am saying, for I experience that state as my own sin, although I fought against it. How can that sin be purged with a phrase ("I was on the other side of the river") when I know that not a small part of my nation took part in it (interview in the Split *Nedeljna Dalmacija*, quoted by the Belgrade magazine *DUGA*, 2–6 July 1993).

Lasić is not prone to misusing the truth about the nonexistence of the *collective responsibility* of the Croatian nation to avoid the quite legitimate question of *collective shame*. Even if his conviction that the Croats who fought against the Ustashis should participate in the common shame is debatable, this is certainly not so in the case of those Croats who identify themselves with *pride* with the whole of their national heritage, for the right to pride implies the obligation of shame.

There are a large number of excellent discussions on the (im)possibility of literature and philosophy after Auschwitz. Our intellectuals, unfortunately, have not even tried to "impose" on the world the question of the sense of literature and philosophy after Jasenovac. A few years ago I posed the question in writing as to whether Christianity as well is possible after Jasenovac. True ecumenicalism, in my opinion, presupposes an honest discussion in the Catholic Church, first and foremost with itself, but also with the Serbian Orthodox Church. Why has no Pope ever visited Jasenovac to pay homage to its victims? Why has this not even been done by a

Croatian cardinal? And it is known that the role of part of the Catholic Church in the Independent State of Croatia was shameful. The Catholic Church will not be able to find a convincing excuse for that avoidance retroactively even by claiming a symmetry of crime in the war of Serbs against Croats in 1991–1992.

The deliberate Ustashi state policy—kill one-third of the Serbs, expel one-third, and Catholicize one-third—cannot be explained, for example, by some kind of historical resentment on the part of the Croatian population due to the privileged position of the Serbian military border (march) soldiers in Austria-Hungary. The gaping disproportion between the reasons mentioned and the genocidal "ethnic cleansing" of the territory shows that it was to a great extent a case of intrinsic, and not only instrumental, criminality. A deep chasm also separates that genocidal racism from the "greater Serbian hegemonism" in the first Yugoslavia that is usually given as its explanation. The Ustashi never mentioned the number of losses on the Croatian side inflicted by that hegemonism, because their number would have seemed grotesquely disproportionate to their "reaction." Had not the killing of Radić in the Yugoslav Assembly already been "canceled out" by the murder of King Aleksandar Karađorđevic? In the case of almost absolute evil such as Jasenovac, the researcher cannot but be shocked by the abyss between the alleged motivation and explanation on the one hand, and the depth and proportion of the crime on the other hand.

The YCP leadership headed by Tito, who sought the cure for "greater Serbian hegemonism" in a federalist state system, did not allow the Serbs in post-Jasenovac Yugoslavia to have influence on the determination of inter-republican "borders." The self-deified victor drew the borders without asking anybody anything. The question arises as to *whether the renewal of Yugoslavia was possible after Jasenovac, and, if it was, then what kind of Yugoslavia?* It is interesting to note for informed comparison that on the occasion of the creation of the first Yugoslavia there were farsighted people who doubted its solidity on the basis of its having been created by nations from different sides in the 1914–1918 war.

The Break-Up of Yugoslavia from Within

From Paralysis to the Break-Up of the State

Many people divide postwar state development into that before and that after the passing of the 1974 Constitution. For me, the key moment came with the death of charismarch Josip Broz in 1980.

For the entire time a small group around Tito, and with his absolute domination, had made all important decisions for the whole of Yugoslavia, which its executive bodies in the republics and autonomous provinces implemented in a disciplined manner. In any case, that same group also passed the original decision on the formation of federal units and even determined the "borders" between them. The multinational composition of that group cannot give us the right to consider the Yugoslavia of that time as a truly federalistically organized state. It was a centralized, communist party state that only posed as a federation.

With the constitutional changes in the first half of the 70s the state order was *formally* so decentralized that each republic and autonomous province gained the right to block the passing of important decisions on federal level. Thus Yugoslavia was, *according to the Constitution*, transformed into a *confused, contradictory, and even self-destructive mixture of federation and confederation*. However, our federalism-confederalism right up to Tito's death was more apparent than real, as the "immobile mobilizer" could always, through his intervention, put an end to the paralysis and impose decisions. Then Tito would dictate a "consensus" to the discordant republican and provincial authorities. Thanks to that, the impression was gained that the constitutional system was functioning, while in fact it was an autocrat that was functioning.

But what in the 70s was a constitutional decoration for Tito's autocracy became after his death a *real* system of decision-making that quickly succumbed to complete paralysis, due, among other things, to the hypertrophied principle of the consent of the federal units, and even their right to prevent by veto the passing of practically all federal decisions that did not suit them.

There follow the ways in which the republics and autonomous provinces were protected at that time against outvoting on the fed-

eral level. First: parity representation regardless of size of population. Second: their representatives had virtually only an imperative
mandate. Third, not only did the federal units have the right of veto
as they felt fit, but their active agreement was required for decision-
making. Fourth: there did not exist any kind of constitutional way to
change anything in the Constitution unless *all* the republics and
provinces voted in favor.[1]

André Malraux visited Belgrade in the middle of the 70s and on
that occasion gave the following warning: "Your country has a national policy that is trifling with the state." (I quote from the *NIN*
weekly of 14 December 1986 that published part of a hitherto un-
published conversation between Živorad Stojković and Malraux 11
years earlier). Some fifteen years later that "trifling" even cost us the
common state.

This is a good opportunity to remember how Tito's leadership
had "trifled" irresponsibly with Yugoslavia as soon as it came to
power: initially it had wanted to include Yugoslavia in the USSR, and
then, in the form of a Balkan federation, practically speaking, to add
Bulgaria and Albania to it, as if there were not enough inter-national
domestic problems. That part of the intelligentsia also "trifled" with
the state that propagated the official claim that it was "withering
away," although it was quite evident that the Yugoslav state was
ruled by the autocrat Tito, and that in his shadow "republican and
provincial statehoods" were being prepared. Those politicians and
intellectuals who advocated the "withering away" of the state on a
federal level, and its parallel strengthening on the republican and
provincial plane—were not embarrassed by their inconsistency.

Having already mentioned "trifling with the state," I have to say
that the "international community" has recently also "trifled" with
Yugoslavia. And why not, when so many of our own protagonists
had already done so? However, the next chapter is reserved for an

---

1. The advocates of this kind of state system gave unreserved support, for
example, to the project of those fighting against the white racist regime in South
Africa that was based exclusively on the principle "one citizen—one vote," as if
inter-racial conflicts are not even graver than inter-national conflicts.

analysis of the role of the decisive western countries in the tragic break-up of Yugoslavia.

I was one of those intellectuals who sought a solution to the paralysis of the federal state in a maximally decentralized, a democratic-pluralistic, legal, and solidaristic federation, but one that was at the same time viable. Such a state could have been a favorable framework for the creation of a highly integrated Yugoslav market (with unhindered movement of workforce, capital, and goods throughout the entire territory) included in the European and world market. I warned of the destructive consequences of the *mono-organization* of a federal state constituted exclusively on a national-territorial principle. I pointed to the danger of the complete discrediting of the Yugoslav experiment with the so-called veto-community and the consensus notion of sovereignty and law as compared with the traditional notion founded on hierarchy and coercion. That would, I thought, be a great shame as the principle of consensus, if implemented moderately, is an important means for protecting the minority from the majority, which is one of the unavoidable components of a contemporary democracy. Since statesmanship consists in the skillful use of different, and even opposite, organizational-institutional principles, I persisted in repeating that our state crisis could not be overcome without the combination and balancing of two forms of representation and decision-making on federal level: civil and national.

I suggested that our nations should continue to have multiple guarantees against outvoting. That was why I said a new Constitution should also set up in the Federal Assembly a Council of Republics composed on a parity basis as well as a Council of Citizens elected on a proportional basis. That Constitution would, I suggested, codify national rights that could not be brought into question by any kind of voting, and a constitutional court should protect that reserved sphere of collective rights. Furthermore, representatives of the federal units would retain *the right of veto, but reduced to a smaller number of issues essentially relevant for the preservation of national equality,* while in other cases decision-making would be done on a two-thirds or simple majority basis, depending on the importance of the issue. Finally, I criticized the fact that virtually all the most important federal institutions were situated in Belgrade, and suggested that some of them be moved to the republican capitals. I also suggested a way to check the principled nature of those politicians and intellectuals who were obsessed by the danger of unitarianism and outvoting on the federal level. There would be the introduction of a Council of Nations in the republican and provincial assemblies that would (like the Council of Republics in the Federal Assembly) also prevent outvoting in issues that impinge essentially upon national equality.

My ideas were unacceptable both for the confederalists (covert separatists) and for the re-centralists (covert unitarians). I did, however, continue with contacts and discussion, particularly with intellectuals in Slovenia and Croatia who were advocating the further independence of the republics and autonomous provinces, but I became more and more aware of the absurdity of the position I found myself in by pointing to the *objective* interests of their nations.

Nonetheless, I tried again, that time with the idea of *Yugoslavia 1992*, by analogy with the integrative transformation of the European Community (EC) into the European Union (EU) that had been announced for that year. At that time the need for inclusion in the EC was being greatly stressed in our country (the Yugoslav authorities sought the status of at least associate member), as if the EC were looking forward to having us together with our economic (huge foreign debts, recession, high unemployment, hyperinflation) and political crisis, permanent attempts at mutual agreement and the blocking of federal units, "republican and provincial economies," etc. I expressed the opinion that no single nation that did not want at least the same degree of integration in Yugoslavia as the EU would achieve, had the right to prevent others from integrating, although it should not be forced to unify itself. I posed the question as to how those nations that did not consent to the federal political and legal institutions essential for the functioning of an *integrated market*, but only wanted a *common market*, had the right to make use of the advantages of the more or less integral economic area in Yugoslavia without the payment of compensation. I considered that the introduction of such duties would be a good opportunity to compare the efficacy of the economy of the Yugoslav scale with small-scale economies, and finally thus establish to what extent the more developed part of the country was really economically more efficient than the other parts, and to what extent it was under an illusion because it was using the advantages of that integral economic area.

But it was all in vain, both for me and for other Yugoslav-oriented intellectuals who were prepared to compromise; the process of the break-up of Yugoslavia was gaining increasingly in momentum. I must admit that right up to the last minute I neither believed nor anticipated that it would break up and therefore, practically speaking, I did not give up on it.

The leaderships of the republics and autonomous provinces were ever more taking the stand that Yugoslavia was "what they agreed to" and that the "federal state was nothing other than a service for the federal units"—just as if Yugoslavia's history had started with those leaderships. And it was not even enough for them to have vetoed any change to the federal Constitution and the passing of new federal laws and decisions, but they also began voting in their own laws and measures that were contrary to the federal ones.

Serbia, with the help of the central authorities and the Yugoslav Army, responded to the Albanians' national and nationalistic movement in Kosovo with repression—the Slovenian leadership and numerous intellectuals in Slovenia supported that movement—Serbia replied to them with a trade boycott—Slovenia demanded that the federal bodies force Serbia to halt the boycott, although it continued to pass its own laws itself and to implement only those federal constitutional and legal provisions it agreed with—etc., etc.

Slovenia increasingly became the "avant-garde" of the policy of confederalistic fait accompli, but at the same time vehemently opposed any suggestion that the federal Constitution be altered without its agreement. A war of words erupted among the mass media under the control of the republican and provincial leaderships. The most prosperous republics, Slovenia and Croatia, accused the underdeveloped republics of spending the resources of the Federal

Development Fund irrationally, and demanded that they should be drastically reduced and even placed under the direct control of those republics that were financing that fund, but they received the reply that this would be in contradiction to the "sovereignty" of the federal units, upon which those very two republics were insisting the most. The erosion of the common state also went deeper when Slovenia and Croatia turned to the international regional integration "Alpe-Adria," and with the dissemination of the stand that they, unlike the other Yugoslav republics, belonged to "Central Europe."

The separatists did, of course, maneuver right up to the free elections in 1990, concealing their ultimate goal behind the formula of the need for the reorganization of Yugoslavia into a "loose federation," "asymmetric federation," or a "confederation."

It was to turn out that one of Josip Broz's greatest "statesmanlike" illusions was that the League of Communists, which was itself rather fragmented nationally and territorially, could hold together a Yugoslavia in which the republics and autonomous provinces had the prerogatives of independent states. That was the expression of Tito's metaphysical faith that the federal-confederal system of a *communist party state* would not *essentially* affect the character and policy of the *state communist party*. Here is a list of some previous utopian ideas and experiments in this region: Yugoslav unitaristic utopianism founded on the (self)delusion of the Serbs, Croats, and Slovenes of being "one nation made up of three tribes"; the utopianism of the definitive settlement of the national issue in a centralized communist state; the utopianism of a Balkan federation.

After Tito's death, national and nationalistic aspirations *openly* encompassed not only state, but also communist party bodies. That cluster of *national and nationalistic communisms* was already in many ways a proto-multiparty system. Before the multiparty elections and referendums in 1990 some communist functionaries were carried away "with the preservation of Tito's name and achievements," while others had concluded that he was dead once and for all and that they had to search for new strongholds in their national milieux. In this way the national-communists markedly outweighed the Yugocommunists, and then there also developed competition among the former as to who would demonstrate the most radical possible nationalism and separatism. They did, of course, present that as their liberalism, their democracy, and even anticommunism.[2]

As far back as three decades ago I wrote that democratic socialism is unthinkable without the freedom of party organizing, but then and later I warned that the institutionalization of political pluralism in a country such as Yugoslavia should be approached gradually and wisely. I feared that we would repeat our history in which political parties were primarily national-confessional, which even state communities far older and sturdier than Yugoslavia would have found hard to survive. Sensing that after Tito's death developments would go quickly in that direction, I immediately asked the League of Communists of Yugoslavia to permit the creation of a League of Socialists of Yugoslavia. Those two organizations would divide power, but in such a way as to guarantee communists in advance 51% seats in the federal and other assemblies.[3] And as that would not have represented a sufficient protection against state-political fragmentation along national-confessional lines, I asked for elections to be held first on the level of Yugoslavia, and then in the federal units. Finally, when my idea of a League of Socialists of Yugoslavia was completely outdated by the establishment of a real multiparty system, I proposed the legalization of only those parties that had members and organizations in all national milieux.

At the end of the Second World War the *united* Communist Party of Yugoslavia renewed Yugoslavia as a very centralized state under the name of a federation. That party had, in fact, for a long time attacked the centralism of the Kingdom of Yugoslavia and incited national-separatist passions to destroy it. Although it was a rather

---

2 . Fukuyama was wrong when he predicted that we had entered once and for all into the era of the universalization of the liberal-democratic paradigm. The only thing that has happened is that, during the disintegration of communism and the emergence of postcommunism, nationalists and separatists opportunistically felt the need to present themselves to the West as liberals, democrats, and anticommunists.

3 . Polish communists and the Polish opposition were to try something similar to that at the end of that decade.

marginal force right up to Germany's attack on Yugoslavia[4] and the USSR, the YCP had nonetheless contributed considerably to the creation of those inter-nationality relations that were to cause it so much trouble in the fratricidal war of 1941–45. At the end of 1990 the *fragmentized* League of Communists of Yugoslavia (LCY) disintegrated when the Slovene delegation (headed by Milan Kučan) left its Congress, and when other LC republican and provincial organizations did not support the demand of the League of Communists of Serbia (that was already dominated by the arrogant Slobodan Milošević) that work should continue as if nothing important (!) had happened. My pro-Yugoslav stand was at that time stronger than my capacity to recognize reality, and so I did not see that Yugoslavia was really falling apart.

Wars between Secessionists and Antisecessionists

In the second half of the 80s it seemed that the Croatian-Serbian conflict was being pushed aside from the central place in the history of Yugoslavia by the conflict between the Slovenes and Serbs. That was a great surprise. It is true that many people still remembered the so-called road affair of Stane Kavčič in Slovenia and his removal from the political scene by Tito and Kardelj, but that did not have a visible anti-Serb aspect. However, what quickly came to light after Tito's death was to be something new in the relationship of Slovenes toward Serbs and Yugoslavia.

The great majority of the Slovene nation was even to support Slovenia's endeavor to secede from Yugoslavia, and that immediately, regardless of the consequences on the other nations. The newly elected multiparty Slovenian Parliament was to pass a declaration on independence on 25 July 1991. The Yugoslav authorities

---

4. What would have happened if Hitler, after the fall of the Yugoslav government (27 March 1941), which had concluded an agreement with him two days earlier, had overcome his anti-Serb fury and virtually ignored and circumvented Yugoslavia from a military point of view in his Drang nach Russland? I do not believe that under those circumstances Yugoslav communists would have had the opportunity to come to power.

responded to this with military intervention, but with highly limited purpose, dimension, and resoluteness. The aim was the re-establishment of federal control on Slovenia's proclaimed state borders. Frightened by the prospect of a conflict with the Yugoslav Army (YA), the Slovenian government agreed to a suggestion from EC envoys to suspend secessionist steps provisionally, but did not fulfill the obligation undertaken. The "international community" did not react, and, what was most important, the Yugoslav authorities and YA soon decided to give in where Slovenia was concerned. That was because Slovenia's secession, when considered in isolation from other factors, did not give any intimation of catastrophic wars, due to Slovenia's rather homogeneous national composition. To put it simply, the Slovenes did not have a problem that would be analogous to that between the Croats and Serbs.

Relationships between Croats and Serbs had been of crucial importance for Yugoslavia from the time it came into being. Jasenovac (for me also the metaphor of overall Ustashi genocide) attained the culmination of crime in that respect, but that rift was covered by silence and repression. It is true that the volcano threatened to erupt again when the Croats' national and nationalistic movement broke out at the end of 1970 and in 1971, which revived the mass consternation of the Serbs, but Tito "handled" that too with force. For nearly the next 20 years Croatian nationalism and separatism was to "struggle along" in hiding, waiting for a new opportunity.

But as it came to the fore again in 1990–1991, and that time with incomparably greater force, the *Jasenovac fissure* was to grow deeper and widen into the violent break-up not only of Yugoslavia, but also of Croatia itself, and, somewhat later, Bosnia and Herzegovina too. A war was to begin for Croatia's secession from Yugoslavia, or for preventing its secession, depending on the point of view, but it was soon to become transformed into a war of the Serbs for separation from Croatia and a war of the Croats to prevent them. So, in a certain sense, the roles changed: the initial separatists became antiseparatists, and the original antiseparatists became separatists.

As soon as it came to power, the Croatian Democratic Community (CDC) annulled with a new Constitution the constitutive-republican status of the Serbs in Croatia that they had won for themselves in the Second World War and enjoyed under the communists. The new authorities had assigned the role of a national minority to the Serbs, but they did not want to accept it, claiming not only the status hitherto, but also the fact that Croatia was not satisfied in Yugoslavia even with the right of veto but wanted to become separate at all costs. Croatia decided to retain only the republican "borders" from the communist Constitution. For that reason, the intermediator of the "international community" in Yugoslav conflicts, Lord Carrington, was to state that with its new Constitution, Croatia had kindled the conflict with the Serbs. These decided in a referendum to secede from Croatia and form the Serbian Republic Krajina (SRK) in just the same way as Croatia had done regarding Yugoslavia. (Let me just recall that Krajina—like Dalmatia and Slavonia—had not been part of the province of Croatia in Austria-Hungary.) Nonetheless, Croatia tried to force those Serbs to stay with it, although it had resolutely resisted such endeavors of the part of Yugoslavia when it was involved itself.

The new authorities did many other things as well, to alienate the Serbs radically: they adopted a state symbol that reminded the Serbs of the Independent State of Croatia (the more precise name would have been the Nazi State of Croatia); they changed the names of places, institutions, streets, etc., in the spirit of nationalistic, even Ustashi, tradition; Serbs were dismissed from their jobs; their expulsion from Croatia ("ethnic cleansing") was tolerated and even encouraged; endeavors were made in regions where Serbs make up the majority to change the national composition of the police by force—not to speak of preparations for the physical liquidation of the Serbs that was secretly announced by Defense Minister Spegelj, and that was filmed and made public by YA intelligence.

Serbian resistance passed through two phases. The first was led by the very moderate President of the Serbian Democratic Party (SDP), the late Jovan Rašković, who had been educated in Croatia, had worked there and lived there with his wife, a Croat, and his family. President of the Croatian Assembly Stipe Mesić, who openly vaunted his contribution to the break-up of SFRY while he was President of the Yugoslav Presidency, later admitted: "When I now recall what Rašković sought, I realize that he did not even want a tenth of what the constitutional law on the rights of national minorities now provides" (interview published in the Ljubljana daily *Dnevnik* on 7 August 1994).

As the Serbs were not offered even minimal *autonomy*, but only a *unitary* Croatia, with the help of Serbia and the YA they achieved the SRK by war, and men such as Rašković were pushed aside. Even those Croats who continued openly to support the Albanians' secessionist movement in Kosovo, giving precedence to their numerical domination over the Serbs' historical and state counterarguments, completely reversed their argumentation to oppose the self-determination of Serbs in Krajina. The outcome of the mutual war waged twice (in 1991 and 1992) was to demonstrate that Croatia does not have the strength to subjugate the "rebel Serbs." Its ruling elite had underestimated the resolution and the power of the Serbs, although it must have known that they (together with the Serbs in Bosnia and Herzegovina) are deeply aware that they were the greatest victims and, at the same time, the main victors in Yugoslavia in the Second World War.

But even if other Croatian separatists made that fatal mistake, why did Tudjman make it? For Tudjman knew the Serbs better, dating back to their common struggle against the Ustashis. But perhaps it is not so puzzling as he believed that the mass of the Serbs, and not only Serbian communists, would accept the official explanation according to which the Ustashi dimension in Croatian history was a short-lived *accident* (about which I spoke in the second section). An additional explanation should be sought in Tudjman's complete obsession with electoral triumphalism, but also in the desire to retain at all costs the support of ultranationalistic circles. In any case, Tudjman has not gone to Jasenovac to pay homage to the victims, but, on the contrary, has taken advantage of any opportunity drastically to lessen their number, and he has even boasted publicly that he is happy his wife is not a Serb or a Jew. It is true that he later apologized to the latter, but not to the former! Unfortunately not even he can resist the negative fixation with Serbs.

Why have many Croats explained their desire for a separate national state more by mentioning the alleged characteristics, conduct, and policy of Serbs than by giving their own intrinsic reasons? The extremes to which this definition of national identity by counterpoising with Serbs can be seen in this testimony: "In answer to my question as to what they would do if the Serbs were, by some miracle, to adopt the Croatian language type, with all its newly invented and exhumed 'distinctive' words, an eminent Croatian linguist replied curtly: 'Then we would have to invent some new differences'" (Pavle Ivić, "Contemporary Serbian Literary Language," quoted in the Belgrade daily *Novosti*, 11 April 1994). It is true that Serbs belatedly reconciled themselves to the fact that the overwhelming majority of Croats wanted to secede at all costs, and that Serbs had wasted time and energy preventing them instead of concentrating immediately on their own self-determination.

The fear (frequently unconscious) of a possible Serb collective vengeance must have played a large role in the Serbophobic secessionism in Croatia. That is perhaps why there was such a desire to separate from the victim, but at the same time to retain the territories on which the victims make up the majority. It is true that an explanation, although not, of course, a justification, of the unscrupulous war extremism on the Serbian side (too) may be sought in the shame at the silence over Jasenovac and the awoken fear of history repeating itself.

It is on account of the support of a not so small number of Bosnia and Herzegovina Muslims to the Ustashi authorities and genocidal crimes, and even their active participation in them, that the fissure between them and the Serbs, long suppressed and concealed under a layer of civilized behavior, opened up to its full width and depth as soon as the Muslims expressed the intention to separate Bosnia and Herzegovina from Yugoslavia. And while on the subject of the unhappy history of mutual relations, it has also to be said honestly that some Serbian Chetnik units killed in retaliation not a small number of innocent Muslims during the Second World War.

Further, throughout the long Turkish occupation, Muslims were a privileged and ruling population that treated Serbs (and Croats) as rightless Christian Turkish subjects and these in return called them (and still call them) abusively "Turks." It was not until 1878 that the Berlin Congress gave those territories to Austria-Hungary, which for its part formally annexed them 30 years later. That was to arouse the anger of the Serbs that culminated in the assassination of the archduke Franz Ferdinand in Sarajevo on the 28th of June 1914, thus setting into motion a series of reactions and counter-reactions that ended in the First World War.

When Yugoslavia's disintegration began at the beginning of the 90s it was completely unrealistic to expect that such a statequake (earthquake) would halt at the "borders" of Bosnia and Herzegovina. It is not clear why the Muslim leaders nonetheless hoped that they would be able to keep the Serbs within the seceded Bosnia and Herzegovina, when the far stronger Croatia had failed to keep them in Croatia. This is especially strange as there are far more Serbs, both absolutely and relatively speaking, in Bosnia and Herzegovina than in Croatia. And it should, after all, have been expected that Serbia and Montenegro would assist those Serbs no less abundantly that those in Croatia. It was also already visible that Bosnia-Herzegovina Serbs were successfully taking over from other Serbs entire units, armaments, and equipment from those parts of the YA that had previously been stationed in Bosnia and Herzegovina or had withdrawn into it from Slovenia and Croatia. That, among other things, is why the Serbs entered into the conflict with the Muslims with a large military advantage.

The communists did not make Bosnia and Herzegovina into a separate republic in the SFRY for it to be dominated by Muslims, but rather in order to avoid a conflict between Serbs and Croats over that territory and over the national identity of the Muslims ("Serbs of Muslim faith or Croats of Muslim faith?"). Our communist rulers knew well that a political balance had to be maintained in that republic among the three national groups. Of course, consensus, as a form of decision-making in Bosnia and Herzegovina, did not have a democratic character, but rather involved only agreement of the national communist oligarchies.

As soon as multiparty organization was allowed at the beginning of the 90s, the huge majority of Muslims, Serbs and Croats joined different political parties. And these were, in fact, three mass national and nationalistic movements. These also won at the elections and formed a new government that continued for a time to function according to the principle of the consensus of the three national representations.

However, when Slovenia and Croatia made it known they were quitting Yugoslavia, the Muslims found themselves faced with a grave dilemma: to stay in it despite the fears of possible Serb domination, or to try to separate Bosnia and Herzegovina as a whole with the help of Croats, the Muslim world, and the "international community" in general, particularly as a demographic projection indicated a forthcoming majority over Serbs and Croats taken together. They decided on the latter by a huge majority. It is true that a minority of Muslims under the leadership of Adil Zulfikarpasić desired an agreement with Serbia on remaining in Yugoslavia, but the majority did not want to hear of it. Zulfikarpasić had wisely taken into account everything that Izetbegović had neglected in his electoral triumphalism, and also the fact that there were incomparably more Slav Muslims in Serbia and Montenegro than in Croatia. Later, Izetbegović was to lament aloud: "Perhaps we made a mistake by leaving Yugoslavia." And how could he not lament when he has lost the war with the Serbs, waged war against the Bosnia-Herzegovina Croats too, and even gone into battle with a quite large group of Muslims in western Bosnia who proclaimed autonomy under the leadership of Fikret Abdić.

In a referendum, the Muslims (together with the Croats) gave a solid vote for Bosnia and Herzegovina to be separated from Yugoslavia. At a separate referendum the Serbs living there decided the contrary, and then proclaimed their Serbian Republic (SR). Let us note: Muslims (and Croats) resorted to outvoting even though they themselves had not had it imposed on them in Yugoslavia. Under the excuse of a "civil state," the Muslims tried to impose a *unitarily* organized Bosnia and Herzegovina on the Serbs (and the Croats), although even the Yugoslavia they had abandoned had been a mixture of federation and confederation. Such a Bosnia and Herzegovina did, of course, prove to be utopian (that should be added to the series of state utopias mentioned in the previous section).

The first larger-scale battles for mutual demarcation in Bosnia and Herzegovina erupted in fact between the Croats and Serbs (in Herzegovina and the Sava valley). The Croat-Muslim alliance was, however, only temporary in character. It is surprising that the Muslim leaders rely on them so much, when they know that many Croats consider them as only religiously Islamized members of their own nation. In any case, that is the way they were officially treated in Pavelić's Independent State of Croatia. The most important thing for the leaders of the Bosnia-Herzegovina Croats and their supporters in Croatia was to break up Yugoslavia as much as possible with the help of Muslims, and to cut the Serbs west of the Drina off from Serbia and Montenegro, as well as to cut the SRK off from the SR. After that they would attend to the separation of the territory they call Herceg-Bosna from Bosnia and Herzegovina, and perhaps also subordinate the Muslim part to Croatia. In the capacity of special adviser to the President of Yugoslavia at that time, Dobrica Ćosić (about whom I shall speak in detail in the fifth chapter), I was present at negotiations in Geneva in autumn 1992 when Tudjman repeated to Vance and Owen, the co-chairmen of the Conference on Former Yugoslavia, that the Croats in Bosnia and Herzegovina would accept nothing less than a confederation of three national states, but stressed that even that solution would be short-lived as the Croats would join Croatia, and the Serbs would join Serbia, while the Muslims would be left with a small national state between them.

Under pressure from the USA and Germany, Tudjman recently agreed to a federation of Croats and Muslims in Bosnia and Herzegovina, which will, however, be able to establish a confederal relation with Croatia. Few people well acquainted with the state of affairs there believe in the future of a Bosnia and Herzegovina organized in this way, due, among other things, also to the opposition of the Croats there, particularly those in western Herzegovina. Agreeing to such an arrangement, however, Tudjman has exposed himself to the danger of the SRK seeking the same such relationship with Croatia. How would Croatian separatists feel if Croatia had to agree to the SRK becoming a federal unit of it, to a representative of SRK rotating as Federation President with the representative of the Croatian federal unit every two years, and, in addition to all this, the SRK entering into a confederal relationship with Serbia? But if he returns to his original insistence on Bosnia and Herzegovina being a confederation, Tudjman will find himself in an even more difficult position toward SRK concerning his argument.

Whatever it may be, there is one thing about which there can be no doubt: in Bosnia and Herzegovina, no less than in Croatia, it is a question of a fratricidal war in the literal sense of the word. The unitarian ideology of the first Yugoslavia was based on the assumption of "one nation consisting of three tribes." This was not quite erroneous, as Serbs, Croats and Slovenes do originate from the same people (southern Slavs). This is also true of the Slav Muslims, who were first recognized by atheist communists as a separate nation, primarily defined by religion (another irony of history).

In the fratricidal war in Yugoslavia, Muslims have to date fared the worst. Their losses deserve great regret and sorrow, as indeed do the losses of the other two national groups, but nonetheless they do not give Muslims the right to cast the blame on others completely, unprepared to recognize the catastrophic mistakes that their leadership has made, but they themselves have made too when they supported their leadership en masse.

Of course, each side, secessionist and antisecessionist, used the possibilities of a Yugoslav combination of federalism and confederalism in opposite ways. If the Serbian side had really dominated Yugoslavia, as Slovenian, Croatian, Muslim, and Macedonian separatists claim, then their secession would have been thwarted. On the other hand, however, if Yugoslavia had been a confederation only, as their Serbian opponents bemoan, then the other republics would have seceded more easily and even taken with them the Serbs west of the Drina, and, in any case, the greater part of the Yugoslav Army would not have passed so quickly into the control of Serbia and Montenegro.

It has turned out that the Serbian question in some sense was more fateful than the Croatian question, both for the creation and 70-year survival of Yugoslavia, and for the way in which it was to finally break up. It is unlikely that Yugoslavia would have been created and that it would have broken up so tragically if there had not been so many Serbs on the other side of the Drina. As demonstrated by the Serbs' struggle not to be taken out of it even at the cost of mass death, Yugoslavia was also in their national *interest*, even though many of them think that their forefathers decided on a common state first and foremost out of *generosity* to their southern Slav brothers.

It is self-explanatory that the Serbs' right to state self-determination cannot be any justification whatsoever for war crimes and robbery, the torturing and killing of prisoners, rape, ethnic and cultural "cleansing.". . , which, by the way, the other two warring sides have also committed. . . . Not even in a civil war are people allowed to do absolutely everything they want, although in such a war it is undoubtedly far more difficult to control the participants (who also include paramilitary groups, people seeking revenge, criminals, foreign fanatics and mercenaries, psychopaths) than is the case in a war between states.

It should also be self-explanatory that those barbaric acts of war cannot, however, be equated with the genocide during the Second World War. It reflects credit on the Austrian philosopher Rudolf Bürger that he drew attention to this back in 1992, when Serbs were already being selectively satanized in the world. He called for a "disarmament of concepts" (*Abrüstung der Begriffe*) so that the Yugoslav tragedy could be perceived in its historical dimensions and proportions. As an illustration he put forward the claim about "destruction camps" (*Vernichtungslagern*), through which, he considered, the impossible "associative bridge with Auschwitz, Majdanek, Treblinka, and even Jasenovac" was established. He concluded by saying: "Those people who speak of genocide—do not know what they are talking about." He further said: "What is happening there is war, secessionist and civil war, that we can encounter over and over again in history" (Bürger's interview in the Vienna magazine *Profil*, 11 September 1992).

The suspension of human considerations in Yugoslav wars should be regarded not only from the standpoint of "instrumental rationality" but also from that of humanistic morality. An example of the former is the indication that such destruction of Vukovar and Sarajevo (the mass media barely mention the Croatian razing of Mostar) was not at all necessary for the Serbs' war efforts. This is not to mention the catastrophic consequences on their image in the eyes of the world. However, a good image is an important precondition for turning military successes into peace in the current constellation of forces. The same is true for the Yugoslav Army. True, so much destruction inflicted by it can partially be explained (but not justified) by the fact that a great number of untrained, inexperienced, and panic-stricken conscripts were involved.

But such criticism has little worth if it is not accompanied by resolute condemnation, and the demand for those who perpetrated the crimes to be punished most severely. In doing so the critic can refer to both international moral and legal norms and to the tradition of the Serbian army and its command, particularly in the First World War. As I said, those who share national pride do not have the right to exempt themselves from national shame. It seems that it is because of that glorious reputation as well, that the world expected and demanded more from the Serbian side than it did from the other two sides in our war conflicts.

As a moral critic too, Patriarch Pavle of the Serbian Orthodox Church has excelled. Naturally, the extent to which his *saintly* criteria can realistically be applied to the mass of the population, and what is more in a civil war, is open to discussion, but those Serbs who claim that they belong to a "*celestial* nation" certainly do not have the right to question them. And it goes without saying that it is better to go too far than not to go far enough in setting up moral standards, as evil is powerful enough to impose itself spontaneously, while we have to apply ourselves to good incessantly.[5] In that context I shall only mention those people who, through their extremism in war, try to "prove" their Orthodoxy and Serbian identity, although until recently they had not cared about them at all. It is also extremely important that Pope John Paul II, during his visit to Zagreb in September 1994, spoke in a genuine ecumenical spirit in his sermons about the Serbian Orthodox Church and the Serbs (about the Muslims too, of course)—which shocked Croatian warmongers.

However, what can one say about practical political steps, particularly on the part of the Serbian side, to put an end to the Yugoslav tragedy?

This is what I said about the conflict between Serbs and Croats over Krajina:

---

5. In the inquiry entitled "The Clergy and Politics" in the Belgrade daily *Borba* (20 March 1992), I said the following about the "trials of the Church in politics":

> In the spirit of the principled separation of the Church and the state, the clergy should not participate in political party life, and even less in party struggles. This does not mean that the Church does not have anything to say and should not speak of politics on another, more principled level. Here I am thinking of the resolute effort to contribute to the definition and realization of ethical principles and moral footholds that must be contained in all politics that has democracy and humanism at heart.
>
> It is not, of course, easy to achieve that spiritual measure that avoids the temptation and sin of party manipulation, on the one hand, and indifference to the political fate of the moral community, on the other hand.
>
> In any case, the language of the clergy, when speaking about politics, and about everything else for that matter, should be quite calm and collected, and not nervous and quarrelsome; it should inspire understanding and love, and not bitterness and hatred, modesty and not haughtiness. It should be something like the language of Patriarch Pavle of the Serbian Orthodox Church.

Serbian national interest should be conceived pluralistically and polycentrically. The interest of a Serb in Zagreb and in the Serbian Republic Krajina where it is extremely threatened, cannot be identical to that of a Serb living in Belgrade. There is little chance for all the Serbs in those areas of the Balkans where they are in the majority, being able to unite into one state in the near future. This, of course, is not just. It is not just for Slovenians, Croatians, Macedonians and Muslims to obtain the right to state self-determination, when Serbs cannot achieve that right. But that is how world circumstances dictate. Besides, it must be clear to everyone that not even the minimum of Serbian national interest outside the territory of FRY can be protected if Serbia and Montenegro founder. FRY is the mother country, it is a state, it is a support. And this means that both the Serbs in Krajina and the Serbs in Bosnia and Herzegovina must, when contemplating their fate—and great are their misfortunes—constantly bear in mind that it is in their interest to preserve FRY, and for it to overcome this catastrophic situation. Secondly, in the case of the Serbs in Croatia where they are in the minority, FRY must struggle and use all legitimate political means to ensure that their interests are protected according to the principle of the protection of human, national, and civil rights. In the case of the Serbian Republic Krajina, I cannot see any other realistic policy than to adhere to the Vance plan. . . .
So, the Vance plan exists, UNPROFOR troops exist, and the only realistic thing that can be expected, although it does not necessarily correspond to our wishes, is that UN troops will remain there for an unspecified length of time, as they have done, for example, in Cyprus, and that the Serbian population in those territories will be protected. Under such circumstances, Serbs should start reconstructing that part of former Yugoslavia—in the domains of economy, culture, education, and transport, and come to some agreement with the Croats, in the scope of the common interest that the Republic of Croatia must have with that population, if for no other reason than the fact that railway lines and other transport links pass through that territory. . . . That means that UN troops should remain for an unspecified length of time with the hope

that either state borders will become irrelevant through the process of European integration, or that Serbs be allowed self-determination in the form of a plebiscite (interview published in the daily *Borba*, 28–30 November 1992).

Not even today would I change anything essential in that position, but I would add a few remarks. The first concerns the self-destructive nature of secessionism: Croatia lost control over more than a quarter of the territory it claims; it is virtually cut in half, and it has even lost access to the greatest trans-European waterway, the Danube. Furthermore, the principle of the non-use of force in preventing its secession from SFRY, on which Croatia insisted so much when addressing the "international community," has rebounded against it, as now Croatia too is not allowed to use force to re-establish territorial control. Finally, through the way that it treats Serbs even outside those lost territories (tens and tens of thousands have been expelled or have had to escape), Croatia has done everything to alienate them forever. And if Croatia assumes that it is Croatia and Croatian citizens that are involved, and not an area and citizens belonging to another state (SRK), it would have to win them over itself, and not seek a solution to their state problem from everyone (Western powers, UN, Serbia) except "their own" Serbs.

On the subject of Bosnia and Herzegovina, the Serbs there, and the war raging there, I said the following on the same occasion:

> There can be no greater benefit for the Serbs in Bosnia and Herzegovina than for the war to cease immediately and negotiations to start, because a peaceful political solution must be found among the three nations. The international community, it seems, will not consent, and certainly not in the following years, to allow the issues to be solved by redrawing state borders. The international community will insist on the territorial integrity of Bosnia and Herzegovina. In my opinion, there is no better formula for Bosnia and Herzegovina than the formation of a United States of Bosnia and Herzegovina. The three nations (in those regions where they are majority) should

find some kind of common functions on the level of Bosnia and Herzegovina. But these cannot be "ethnically clean" states, nor would the international community agree to such a thing.

And recently I published the following proposal:

Instead of threatening, bombing, and blockading Serbs of Bosnia-Herzegovina and their Serbian Republic, it would be a good idea to offer the following measures, in return for their acceptance *in principle* (further negotiations would establish the concrete details) of the territorial division of Bosnia and Herzegovina in the ratio of 49:51 per cent:

1) The UN Security Council would order the warring sides to halt military operations; it would immediately introduce *safety separation zones*, and then extend them to encompass the entire territory of Bosnia and Herzegovina. It is well-known that the Muslim side will not agree to a cease-fire without considerable compensation, fearing the permanent loss of territories that it considers its own, but if Serbia were to undertake, before the United Nations Security Council, to adhere to the mentioned territorial division and the political solution to be dealt with shortly, this should be a sufficient guarantee for it.

2) Bosnia and Herzegovina would be defined as a confederation-federation of three nations and three states, which no side would be able to leave in the following three years without the consent of the others, and after which time each of them would vote in a UN-controlled plebiscite on whether to stay in Bosnia and Herzegovina or to leave it, whether the Serbs would join FRY, the Croats Croatia, and the Muslims would remain in an independent state between them, etc.

3) In the course of the three-year period, the member states would be free to enter into various arrangements with other states. I assume that the Croats would immediately openly strengthen their links with Croatia, and the Serbs with FRY, whereby they would be able

to obtain another citizenship from those states (thus gaining dual citizenship).

4) FRY would offer assistance to the Serbs who through the delineation were to come under the control of the other two confederal units, offering those Serbs the possibility of moving to FRY if they so desire or to the predominantly Serbian unit (SR). It goes without saying that Croatia could do the same for the Croats, and the international community (particularly the Muslim part) for the Muslims.

I do not believe that the Serbs in Bosnia and Herzegovina will start really to differentiate among themselves until they receive the above-mentioned or similar guarantees. Only then will the majority of them be able to overcome the fixation with *territory* (invoking the Ustashi genocide perpetrated against them, the principle of ownership, and the victories in the war to date), and concentrate on *time*, thinking first and foremost of the younger and future generations. The Serbs must know that they will not be safe enough until their neighboring nations are also functionally capable. The most dangerous thing for the Serbs is war triumphalism combined with martyr-like fatalism. Everything that they have gained to date, and even more, could be lost if they are not able to yield considerable territories in return for peace.

Of course, the Muslims too must rid themselves of the illusion that they can impose some kind of "Bosnian (geographical!) nationality" on the Serbs (and the Croats). Let me give just one comparison: the first Yugoslavia did not succeed in creating a "Yugoslav nation," and the second did not even try to do it. In addition, the Muslims must constantly bear in mind the fears of Serbs (and Croats) and of Europeans in general of the possible establishment of a fundamentalist-Muslim *state bridgehead* on the Balkans and in our continent (letter to the Belgrade weekly *NIN*, entitled "How to End the War," published on 30 September 1994).

Analysts of the Yugoslav tragedy do not devote sufficient attention to the fact that since the beginning of the break-up of Yugoslavia, *a war for control over the Yugoslav Army (YA)* has (also) been waged. Even less attention has been paid to the fact that the YA was in part even a factor *sui generis that was also waging war for its own survival*, depending, of course, more and more on Serbia and Montenegro, as well as on Serbs in Croatia and in Bosnia and Herzegovina. It was also a struggle to ensure state territories to which YA members and their families could withdraw from hostile and seceded environments. The extent to which this was decisive is shown by the case of Macedonia, where not a single bullet was fired because the secessionist authorities had agreed to the YA withdrawing peacefully to Serbia and Montenegro.

However, before I continue with an analysis of the YA, I wish to quote a worthwhile general observation on the relationship of social science to the armed forces:

> There is a further oddity about the sociological enterprise as it is practiced today. Opening any textbook of sociology, the reader will find there discussions of the most modern institutions—the family, class, deviance, etc. But it is very unlikely that he or she will discover any discussion of military institutions, or of the impact of military violence and war upon modern society. Much of the same is true of more rarified treatises on social theory, which concentrate on capitalism, industrialism, and so on. Yet who, living in the 20th century, could for a moment deny the massive impact which military power, preparation for war, and war itself, have had upon the social world (A. Giddens, *The Nation-State and Violence*, University of California Press, 1985, p. 22).

In my judgment, this is also true of our social science, all the more so as the YA was subordinated to Tito alone and completely closed to scientific research and the public. That is why our leading intellectuals, and even many politicians, met the break-up of their own state knowing virtually nothing about its army. Thus was their surprise all the greater at the degree of incompetence and, at the same time, the privileged state of that army.

If we take the YA isolated from other state institutions, then we can freely say that it did not have any major confederal characteristics. The republics and provinces in themselves had nothing to do with its organization, functioning and system of command, and the same is true of their Leagues of Communists. The Yugoslav Army had its own communist party organization formally subordinated only to the federal communist party leadership. This is one of the reasons why it not only broke up later than other federal institutions, including the League of Communists of Yugoslavia, but in a different way from them.

Knowing this about the YA, after Tito's death the separatists did everything in their power to bring about its confederalization. Slovene circles were "prominent" once again, and they demanded: that Slovene and Macedonian be introduced into the YA as languages of command, but they received the reply that this would lead to chaos (what would happen in civil aviation in the world if the various national languages were introduce instead of English?); that recruits should perform their military service in their own republics and autonomous provinces exclusively; that strict national parity be practiced in the officer corps; and, finally, that the massive territorial defense, which the YA had organized, trained, and armed, be placed under the sole authority of republican and provincial leaderships, which in any case already had sovereign authority over huge police forces.

The separatists attacked the fact that the YA did not have major confederal characteristics as a mark of Serbian domination in it and over it. And here are the facts:

At the time of the proclamation of the independence of Slovenia and Croatia in the summer of 1991, the composition of the YA (taken all together: recruits, officers and civilians working in it) was as follows: Serbs—32.9%, Croats—17.5%, Muslims—13.4%, Albanians—10.4%, Yugoslavs—9.7%, Macedonians—6.9%, Slovenes—5.4%, Hungarians—1.3%, etc. To serve as a comparison, there follow the results of the census of the population of SFRY in 1981: Serbs—36.31%, Croats—19.75%, Muslims—8.92%, Slovenes—7.82%, Macedonians—5.98%, and others (Yugoslavs, Hungarians, etc.)—18.64%. It is also important to note that at the time of secession of Slovenia and Croatia, by far the greater number of their recruits (93% of Slovenes and 77% of Croats) were doing their military service on the territories of those republics.

At that time the 10 most important positions in the Ministry of Defense, the General Staff of the YA and the military district commands, the Air Force and the Navy were held by: one Yugoslav (the minister of defense with a Serb father and a Croatian mother), three Serbs (the head of the general staff, the commander of the Skopje military district, and the naval commander), two Croats (the assistant minister for the rear and the air force commander), two Slovenes (the deputy defense minister and the commander of the Zagreb military district that covered the territory of Slovenia and Croatia), and two Macedonians (the commander of the Belgrade military district and the head of a department in the general staff). It might not be a bad idea also to recall that at the time of the break-up of the SFRY its President of the collective Presidency, prime minister, and foreign minister were Croats.

I do not have the data for officers under the rank of general, but I assume that Serbs were by far the most numerous, which was doubtless an important factor for the outcome of the break-up of SFRY in war. After all, Serbs in any way accounted for nearly 40 percent of the population; took proportionally greater part in the People's Liberation Struggle, which they passed on to their children as well, in the choice of profession; and, furthermore, the military tradition and the renown of the warrior is greater among Serbs. However, even when all this is taken into account, it is still not clear why and how Slovenia and Croatia managed to get only a small part of the air force and navy, those specialized branches of the YA in which national composition and tradition went in their favor at least as much as it did in that of the Serbs. It is true that the YA headquarters was in Belgrade, but that does not apply for so many planes, and especially not for ships.

The confederalists-separatists first used the circumstance that the eight-member SFRY Presidency (representatives of the six republics and two autonomous provinces), according to the Constitution, made decisions by simple majority, as the collective commander-in-chief of the YA. Those state breakers had previously wholeheartedly supported Serbia being split up into three parts, but that weakness of Serbia's was to turn into an advantage as soon as it succeeded in imposing compliant leaderships on its provinces, and thereby changing the ratio of forces in the SFRY Presidency too. Instead of the majority up to that time that had outvoted Serbia, there occurred a stalemate position (4:4): there was not a majority for introducing confederal changes in the YA, but neither was there one for proclaiming a state of emergency to thwart the secessionists.

YA was a *Yugoslav*-communist oriented army that followed Tito unconditionally, and after him transferred its loyalty to the Constitution and the collective commander-in-chief. Not only were Serbs thus oriented in it, but also many others. That army was not politically, psychologically, morally or professionally prepared for war among our nations, but for the defense of the country against an external enemy. Few of the key military officers were willing to make use of all available resources against the secessionist republics, especially without the consent of the SFRY Presidency. The YA did not, of course, have to seek its permission to defend itself when the secessionists began to surround and attack its garrisons. Some people, especially among Serbs, condemn the YA for not preventing the break-up of SFRY in its own name. But, was it really worthwhile keeping any nation in Yugoslavia by force? What kind of a state would that have been, and how long would it have lasted? I even consider that the YA made a mistake when it agreed to intervene in Slovenia, and that it would have been far better if it had warned that it would immediately withdraw from that republic if it was not allowed to re-establish federal control on the border in a peaceful way.

When the secessionist republics of Slovenia and Croatia withdrew their representatives from the Presidency, to be followed by Bosnia and Herzegovina and Macedonia—the YA continued to implement the decision of the diminished, four-member Presidency that continued to pass decisions upon the instructions of Serbia and Montenegro.

The separatists conducted a counterproductive policy toward the YA. They called too early on their compatriots to refuse to do their military service, and on officers and soldiers who were already in the YA to desert, and then they started to surround and attack the barracks and mistreat officers' families. During that time, the Serbs cooperated in everything with the YA. The secessionists' policy is an excellent example of a *self-fulfilling condemnation* of Serbian domination in the YA.

The present chief-of-staff of the Yugoslav Army, General Momčilo Perišić, has boasted that during the disintegration of SFRY three armies were created out of the YA: the army of the Federal Republic of Yugoslavia, the army of the Serbian Republic Krajina and the army of the Serbian Republic. In the first phase of the break-up of the SFRY its army defended the territorial integrity of the state and itself; when the Serbs took up arms to oppose the secessionist authorities first in Croatia and then in Bosnia and Herzegovina, the YA for some time did actually come between the conflicting sides, but that *objectively speaking* went in favor of the Serb side; and, as the break-up of SFRY progressed ever more, the YA became irrevocably Serb due to its national composition and its *consciousness.*

Albanian Separatism

Tito's policy toward the Albanian minority passed through two phases, to result in a complete fiasco only a few years after his death.

The first phase lasted up to the removal of Aleksandar Ranković. He had implemented Tito's policy, but that did not prevent Tito from putting the blame for the policy up to that time on "Rankovićism" or from taking the credit for the reversal. Until that reversal Kosovo had been ruled unquestioningly by *Serbian and Montenegrin* partisan cadres, with, of course, a scattering of Albanians who had taken part in the People's Liberation Struggle (PLS). One of the reasons given for that state of affairs was the low level of Albanian participation in the PLS. Also officially passed over in silence was the incomparably higher level of Albanian participation in nationalist-separatist and quisling formations, and these formations did, in fact, offer armed resistance to the People's Liberation

Army when Kosovo was being liberated and raised a rebellion against the new authorities. Those authorities introduced military rule, crushed the rebellion mercilessly, but also banned the return of the Serb inhabitants who had been driven from their homes during occupation. Pragmatic "internationalism" certainly served as internal justification, but there can be no doubt that the authorities practically speaking accepted the "ethnic cleansing" of the Serbs. Is it then any wonder that from 1966 onwards the Albanian minority has been placing increased pressure on the Serbs to move out of Kosovo?

Even before the reversal in 1966 Kosovo formally had the status of autonomous province, but that was in reality *pseudo-autonomy in the pseudo-republic of Serbia in the Yugoslav pseudo-federation*. I repeat: for the whole time a small group around Tito, with his absolute domination, made all the more important decisions for Yugoslavia as a whole, and these decisions were implemented in a disciplined fashion by the country's executive bodies in the republics and autonomous provinces.

I spoke of Tito's new course that began with the dismissal of Ranković in 1966 in the previous chapter, but more in connection with Tito's aversion to the influence and power of Serbian communists than in the direct context of Kosovo. Admittedly, these two things were closely connected as Tito considered that *Yugoslavia could only be strong if Serbia was weak* (as testified by Lazar Roliševski, a leading Macedonian communist).

It was no longer enough for Tito that only Serbia had autonomous provinces (even during the war he had rejected the suggestion of Moša Pijade, one of his closest associates, that an autonomous province should be established in Croatia because of the Serbs), but he replaced the indisputable domination of Serbian and Montenegrin communists in Kosovo with the complete supremacy of *Albanian* communists. Thus, Tito opened up the possibility, from a cadre point of view, for gradual and covert confederalization, which was to expand with the removal of Nikezić's group in 1972, and assumed codified form with the 1974 Constitution.

The provinces became transformed increasingly into "direct constituents of the federal state," even to the extent of having the possibility to veto unwanted decisions of "their own" republic. Their representatives took part in all the bodies of Serbia, while Serbia's authorities had virtually no say in what happened in the provinces. The consent of the provincial authorities was even required to effect a change in the Constitution of Serbia, but the reverse was not required for the provincial constitutions. That "remainder" of Serbia was de facto turning into a nonautonomous province of Kosovo and Vojvodina, and the autonomous provinces into some kind of super-republics (in authority over "Serbia Proper"). That is why the same description could be used for the Serbia of that time as I used for SFRY: *a confused, contradictory, paralyzed, and even self-destructive mixture of federation and confederation.* Of course—and I say this conditionally—since all the official bodies in the autonomous provinces, republics, and the federal state were in practice subordinate to Tito personally, then before his death there could have been no question of anything but pseudo-federation and pseudo-confederation.

When Serbian communists started seeking change in the constitutional-state system in the 80s, other nationality circles rejected it by pointing out that the Serbs had agreed to it.[6] This was true, of course, but it was no less true that the agreement had come from alienated power-holders, and not from the people. Neither Serbs nor any others had the possibility of declaring themselves freely with regard to the constitutional-state reform. That was implemented upon the decision of the inviolable charismarch Tito.

I do not believe that Tito wanted to break up Yugoslavia with those changes. It is more likely that he thought he would save it by weakening Serbia and de facto giving a republic to the Albanians.

---

6. Serbian lawyers on the whole acted in a cowardly way, and many even publicly supported that kind of system. The most important exception was Mihailo Djurić, professor at the Faculty of Law of the University of Belgrade, who, because of his public criticism (1971) of the constitutional changes, spent a year in prison. A small number of his younger colleagues from the faculty (Cavoski, Kostunica, Vracar, Stojanović, Basta), as well as Dobrica Ćosić, the Praxis group, etc., protested against his imprisonment.

This did, of course, turn out to be another in his series of misconceptions on the "settled national issue" in SFRY.

Not even elementary facts of *political geography* could weaken that faith: the communist leadership of a numerous and economically undeveloped national minority, which speaks a language that is completely foreign to the southern Slav population and is located next to the state border with the main part of its people, obtained far more than territorial-political autonomy in Serbia.

On the basis of the *economic-deterministic* conception and *homo economicus*, the Titoists believed that economic development, with abundant aid from the entire country, but mostly from Serbia, would prevail and cause the Albanians to become integrated into SFRY.

Nor did the Titoists expect the great *language* difference to have any major repercussions. Although (young) Albanians were obliged to learn only their own language in the schools, they were nonetheless expected to manage in communication with the southern Slav population and to find jobs throughout Yugoslavia. In fact, all the teaching in Kosovo, from primary school to university level, took place *separately* in two languages (Albanian and Serbo-Croatian), even in natural sciences and technical subjects.

The *religious* differences among Albanians, Serbs and the others were not considered to be particularly relevant either. This was probably because their leaders were atheists.

Although the Albanian working class was small in number and with a low educational level, and the population organized on the basis of *tribes*, the alleged internationalistic predomination of that class was not to be doubted.

The *density and population growth* in Kosovo was not a source of great concern to the Titoists. It was not only undesirable but even dangerous to warn of the exceptional birth rate among Albanians in Yugoslavia; that birth rate being the highest in Europe, even higher than that in Albania. Tito did in fact believe in the need for birth control in the Third World abroad, but not in his own Third World.

Communist policy suffered from u-chronia (timelessness), and this is in fact a characteristic of utopia. There was no national problem that it allegedly was not able to solve *quickly* if it so decided. Wise statesmen and thinkers consider national *equality* (that is far more than equal rights) to be the goal and possible result of a long period of development, but it was "achieved" in our country overnight by simply lowering the criteria. The Kosovo authorities decided, without prior thorough preparations, to make the university that was conducted in the Albanian language independent, and to equate it in all ways (even as to the right to award the highest academic titles) with the old Yugoslav universities. That mammoth university turned out on a mass scale an intellectual proletariat that had no chance to obtain corresponding employment in Kosovo, not to mention anywhere else. To be entirely truthful, it should be added immediately that some other universities in Serbia and in Yugoslavia as a whole came into being in a similar way.

Responsible countries take great care concerning their state symbols and foreign policy, while in SFRY a province was allowed to take the same flag as Albania, and to foster direct and close relations with that country without consulting republican and federal authorities. Why, then, was that province expected to behave toward Albania as it would toward any other foreign country?

Manipulation of concepts usually conceals underhanded intentions. In this respect a crucial mystification was perpetrated with the introduction of the special term *narodnost* (for Albanians and Hungarians) instead of the term *national minority* that had been used up to that time, and that the Titoists proclaimed to be insulting, although it is a customary and legitimate term throughout the world.

Only a year after Tito's death Kosovo was swept by a mass, partially violent, movement of Albanians under the slogan "Kosovo Republic." And the Yugoslav and Serbian state-propaganda machine continued to deceive itself that the same language that is used at home can successfully be used abroad. That was why it tried to label the Albanian movement "counter-revolutionary" instead of simply "separatist." The West was amazed: if the right to revolution exists, how is it that there does not exist the right to counter-revolution?

Not even Tito was willing to meet the demand for an *explicit* "Republic of Kosovo," so it is not clear what the leaders of that movement were counting on. It was only a question of time before the Serbs' power de facto predominated, and also essentially changed the situation *de jure*. Serbia was not so weakened that it could not prevent Kosovo's separation. Charismarch Tito had assigned some figures with roles and power out of all proportion to their intrinsic strength. But when he had gone, the hitherto mechanisms of power and their props disappeared, and the actors came out from the background in their "natural" size and with their natural relations of strength.

The most shocking surprise for the confederalists and separatists on the post-Tito political scene was the opening up of the Serbian question, and very noisily at that. Before that time many politicians had deceived themselves that the existing constitutional solutions were permanent. Instead of agreeing immediately to a certain correction of Serbia's position in their own interest, the power holders in the other republics and autonomous provinces resisted any change whatsoever for a long time, which provoked mass Serb mobilization and offensive and enabled Slobodan Milošević's breakthrough to leadership. I doubt that his political opponents could have done better if they had actually intended to help him. Through many years of political struggle and repression, Kosovo was first of all reduced to territorial-political autonomy, and then even that was de facto annulled.

At one time the Albanian movement practiced mass strikes, demonstrations, and even violence, but the authorities responded with far greater force. Many observers therefore predicted that the initial war in Yugoslavia would erupt in Kosovo, but they were wrong.

In the second phase, the leadership of the Albanian movement mainly abandoned offensive and violent means and introduced the total *boycotting* of official institutions, and the parallel creation of its own ("*separate* society and *separate* state"). This tactic has considerably improved its image in the world, but, in the final account, it has turned out to be pretty unproductive and, to a certain extent, counter-productive. Upon instructions, Albanian manual and office workers left their enterprises and institutions en masse, but that "self-dismissal" of theirs was welcomed by the Serbian authorities as it removed the nightmare of daily strikes and the subsidy of non-productive and hostile enterprises and institutions. Many Albanians were later to ask to return to their posts, but they were told that those posts had been filled or had become superfluous in the mean-time. Pupils, students and teachers also left the official schools and universities and organized teaching in private homes. As a conse-quence, the state no longer had to worry about Albanian young people constantly gathering and demonstrating, and those young people have for a long time already been receiving unofficial school and university certificates that no one recognizes outside Albanian circles. Finally, Albanians are boycotting all official elections, mu-nicipal, provincial, republican, and federal. They do gain something symbolically and psychologically from the "nonrecognition of the state," but they deprive themselves of powerful legal platforms for propaganda and political struggle, and even "cede" electoral victory in advance to Slobodan Milošević and his party.

There is no doubt whatsoever that the Kosovo Albanians wish to secede and unite with Albania. The Albanians in Macedonia want the same thing too, but in a more covert manner. There is, of course, nothing unusual or unnatural in that. Here is an imaginary discus-sion between an Albanian and a Serb on that subject.

(A) We are the autochthonous inhabitants of Kosovo, and you are newcomers. And, what is more important, there are incompara-bly more of us. That means that the demographic and ethnic facts speak decisively in favor of our right to self-determination.

(S) Your autochthonism is a myth. It is true that you make up the great majority in Kosovo today, but that territory is, historically speaking, ours, as the Serbian state and Serbian religious and cul-tural shrines have been situated there for centuries, and these make up an inseparable part of the Serbian national identity. In any case, you are a minority in *Serbia*, and you do not have the right to im-pose your solutions on the Serbian majority.

(A) But demographers predict that there will be fewer Serbs than others in Serbia as a whole in the not so distant future. It is therefore in your interest to let us separate as a state.

(S) Some time or other you are going to have to accept that the right to having children is limited by the same such right of others and by the community's ability to ensure a decent life for the newly born.

(A) How do you justify your support for the right of Serbs in Croatia and Bosnia and Herzegovina to secession and unification with Serbia, while at the same time denying us that same right?

(S) In SFRY the Serbs were a "constitutive-state nation" and you were and have remained a "national minority," and national minorities do not have the right to secession anywhere in the world. Existing states have the right to defend their sovereignty and integrity with all means.

(A) But Croatia and Bosnia and Herzegovina have for nearly three years been internationally recognized countries in which Serbs are a national minority.

(S) The decisive factor, nonetheless, is that at the time when those republics seceded from SFRY, Serbs, as a constitutive nation, had just as much right to self-determination as Croats and Muslims. And if you are in favor of a "Greater Albania," why then are you against "Greater Serbia"? Only when they achieve it will Serbs be psychologically and politically more prepared to meet you half-way.

(A) We have the support of the international community that has introduced a blockade against Serbia and will not lift it until our problem is solved too.

(S) You deceive yourselves expecting other countries to ensure your secession while Serbs west of the Drina are dying for their rights. In any case, the "international community" is not at all prepared for a principled solution of national-state issues in the Balkans (not to mention in Europe as a whole) that would be founded on the general right to self-determination, as that would bring into question the integrity of Albania, Macedonia, Romania, Bulgaria. . . . Why don't you give proof of your high principles and support the right to secession of the Greek minority in southern Albania? And where Macedonia is concerned, unlike Serbia, it certainly would not survive Albanian secession.

(A) We have built Kosovo, and you are preventing us by force from the sovereign enjoyment of the fruits of our labor and property.

(S) Serbia has invested huge financial and other resources in the development of Kosovo that you have to return before we even think of returning to you some territorial-political autonomy. Finally, even the Federation of American Scientists (FAS) proposed (in mid-1993) that you pay lease for Kosovo in order to obtain self-rule in return.

(A) We have sovereign right over all of Kosovo, and we shall never agree to "buying it back" or to its territorial division.

(S) SFRY does not exist any longer, and nor does its division of Serbia. That is why Serbia should detach all mainly Serbian settlements and the main Serbian religious and cultural monuments from Kosovo as an administrative entity and place them under its own direct administration, and only then negotiate about political autonomy with the other two thirds.

This constructed dialogue should show the extent to which the ultimate objectives of the two sides are irreconcilable. And if that is the way that things stand, then it is wisest to talk about pragmatic-functional measures for solving everyday problems, on the basis of common interests, leaving aside a comprehensive and ultimate solution. In doing so, each side (like the Palestinian and Israeli sides, for example) will publicly predict different final outcomes to the process being launched. But as life has to go on in the meantime, then it is better for the Albanians (too) to start out on a "Long March through official institutions" than to continue to boycott them. It is not true that by that very act they would be "recognizing the legitimacy" of Serbian control over Kosovo, as even enemies on a war footing do, in fact, negotiate.

In any case, there is the chance that European integration will one day render borders relative, even in the Balkans, by decreasing the practical differences between a "state" and a "territorial-political autonomy" in the framework of various regional and continental international arrangements and combinations.

The Break-Up of Yugoslavia from Within

Intentions, Elemental Forces, Circumstances

There is a great deal of rashness, simplification, lack of objectivity and evil intent in the interpretation of the Yugoslav catastrophe. Instead of entering into a complex analysis of cause and intent, there is usually mention of one or two factors. Some overaccentuate the importance of the leaders and their interactivity, while others claim that the violent break-up of SFRY was inevitable. There are many who put the main blame on foreign countries, but there are also a number who do not see any major foreign interference.

Very frequently the cause of the secession of Croatia (and of other republics too) is Milošević's inflexibility. However, not only is this inaccurate but also insulting to the Croatian nation if the protracted and deep-seated separatism in their ranks is in the final account to be interpreted as being due to the conduct of a Serb, particularly a political newcomer such as Milošević. He was nowhere in sight when the mass movement rose up nearly a quarter of a century ago, in which Tudjman had a role that was to ensure him incontestable leadership in the secession from SFRY.

The allegation is widely to be heard that Yugoslavia would not have broken up, and certainly not so drastically, if Milošević had accepted Croatia's (and Slovenia's) offer of complete confederal reorganization. But, what is a confederation if it is not an alliance of independent states that maintain sovereignty over their own territories and can withdraw from it at any time—and our wars have been waged over territories and state sovereignty over them. Even if he had wanted to, Milošević would not have had the power to impose such a solution, especially on the Yugoslav Army. It surprises me that this untruth is repeated when the already quoted Stjepan Mesić, former President of the SFRY Presidency and Tudjman's key associate in the break-up of SFRY, has long since "admitted" otherwise: "Gentlemen, Tudjman did not propose a confederation because a confederation was our objective. Of course not, a confederation was for us a means to achieve a state. We offered equality because we knew that Serbia cannot accept equality. That is why we gave them equality, so that they would not accept it, and not for them to accept it" (statement made at a meeting of the Croatian Democratic Community for Bosnia and Herzegovina in Siroki Brijeg—published by the Belgrade daily *Borba*, 4 February 1992).

I have to say that it is also not plausible to connect Milošević's rise as a leader to Tudjman, as the latter was far from power in Croatia when Milošević reached political heights in 1987.

But, as we are already speaking of leaders: why should a Milan Kučan, and especially an Alija Izetbegović, be "neglected"? There is no doubt that Kučan's leadership in Slovenia blazed the trail in separatism.

How did Izetbegović succeed in presenting himself to the world as a fighter for civil democracy, and not for Muslim rule? As the author of the *Islamic Declaration*, for which he was imprisoned under the communists,[7] Izetbegović could not be acceptable to the Serbs (and Croats). Here is what he wrote, and he has never renounced it: "The first and the most important of these conclusions is certainly the one on the incompatibility of Islam and non-Islamic orders. There can be neither peace nor coexistence between the Islamic faith and non-Islamic social institutions"; and "The Islamic movement can and should take over power as soon as it becomes morally and numerically strong enough—not only to destroy non-Islamic rule but also to create a new Muslim rule." Could there be greater proof of Izetbegović's Muslim fundamentalism? According to my judgment, his option, together with the Croats, to outvote the Serbs in Bosnia and Herzegovina was even more fatal, although he well knew that (despite the contribution of Muslims in the People's Liberation Struggle) the Serbs still have vivid memories of Muslim participation in Ustashi genocide and of the Muslim SS "Handzar" division. Why, then, does he wonder out loud at the renewed outbreak of so much evil among the inhabitants of Bosnia and Herzegovina since 1992.

---

7 . It is worthwhile noting that Dobrica Ćosić together with his intellectual circle attacked Izetbegović's prison sentence for "thought delicti," although Izetbegović's views were completely unacceptable to him, and demanded that he be set free. After his release, Izetbegović thanked Ćosić.

In Izetbegović, as in Tudjman, it is not difficult to recognize the rigidity of a political prisoner. This is not a new occurrence at all(we also saw it in Tito, Kardelj, Ranković . . .), but it is interesting that it has repeated itself in an authentic anticommunist such as Izetbegović and in an excommunist such as Tudjman.

The politically naïve who adhere to the myth (that is also Titoist) of an "internationalistic people" and "nationalistic leaders" are still large in number. It is high time to face the bitter truth: powerful national and nationalist, and in the majority also secessionist, movements developed in the republics of SFRY, and we cannot understand them if we overestimate the extent to which leaders can animate and manipulate "the common people." Horizontal conflicts among nations have erupted, and not a vertical rebellion against power holders. It is true, however, that the mass of the population had such a low level of political experience and political culture that they quickly succumbed to radically nationalistic and separatistic influences.

That does not, of course, mean that the role of leaders and the effect of "water always finding its own level" between them should be negated, but only that their influence is not comprehensible without the "factors of long duration," favorable domestic and international circumstances and the support of their nations.

Why is it that in our very case so many domestic and foreign observers have demonstrated the inability or the unwillingness to differentiate among: agents, conditions, and causes; latency and reality; necessity, chance, coincidence, and constellation; intentional and nonintentional consequences; subjective and objective responsibility; mistake in assessment and the desire to inflict evil; organization, spontaneity, and elemental powers; material and ideological factors. . . ?

In the context of the ideological factors of the Yugoslav tragedy, most frequent mention is made of the so-called Memorandum of the Serbian Academy of Sciences and Arts (SASA) of 1986. I say so-called, because SASA never actually adopted it, not to mention publish it, and there exists after all the right of authorship (copyright) and the obligation to honor it. If someone should bear the consequences for the publication of that draft, then it should be those circles (most probably journalist-police circles) who stole it and gave it to the press. Even if the group of Academy members who had worked on the analysis and assessment of the social state in SFRY had completed their job and decided to present it to the public without authorization, in the name of SASA, the blame would not have been able to fall on SASA because it had not examined it and adopted it collectively.

It is not true that the Academy members in that text, either explicitly or implicitly, expressed chauvinistic hatred and called on Serbs to settle accounts with the other nations and to break up SFRY. What is true is that they complained about the position of Serbia and the Serbs (which was at that time characteristic for all our national milieux) only, unfortunately, on the basis of a redistributive statist economy and calling for a redivision of power within the single-party system.

It is completely out of place to link Milošević's rise to power with the Academy members' Memorandum. As a high-ranking communist party official, he took part in the organization of a public campaign against SASA and "its" Memorandum. Milošević's main political sponsors for years were Ivan Stambolić and a group of older communists behind him. Milošević became the power-wielder in Serbia only after he had succeeded in dismissing Stambolić through skillful inter-party maneuvering and with the help of a rival group of older communists. However, neither SASA as a whole nor the above-mentioned group of Academy members had anything to do with that.

It is quite another matter to claim that a few of the Academy members who wrote that draft later offered great support to Milošević. We may wonder at their lack of caution and uncritical attitude toward Milošević, all the more as some of them had also been in conflict with someone such as Tito. Milošević's support of the demands of Serbs and Serbia should not have misled politically experienced intellectuals and made them fail to see that he was instrumentalizing the Serbian issue for authoritarian and careerist ends.

And if we are already talking about texts: why is so little attention devoted to Alija Izetbegović's *Islamic Declaration* when he is the leader of the Muslims and the commander-in-chief of one of the warring sides in Bosnia and Herzegovina? Even if we were to abstract the evident content differences between his *Declaration* and the so-called SASA Memorandum, the fact would remain that, due to the completely different roles and powers of the authors, these are factors of quite different orders.

Why is the so-called SASA Memorandum also mentioned far more frequently than the texts (with occasional anti-Serb and anti-Semitic implications) of Franjo Tudjman, President of Croatia, commander-in-chief of its armed forces and supporter of the Croatian side in the war in Bosnia and Herzegovina?

How is it that the influence has virtually been forgotten of a number of program texts by leading Slovene intellectuals in the Ljubljana magazine *Nova Revija* in the middle of the 80s, although their authors carried great weight in the Slovene separatistic movement, and some of them even have held important state positions in Slovenia after secession?

I am sure that these distinctions of mine would be confirmed by any team of neutral experts if they submitted the above-mentioned texts from the four decisive national milieux to comparative analysis. Speaking so much of these texts, I do not, however, wish to give the impression that I underestimate the effect of pop-ideology, both national and nationalistic, in favor of such "high ideology." Elite intellectuals, unfortunately, underestimate that "down to earth" ideology. It would be useful to examine national and nationalistic kitsch, and even to stage an exhibition of typical examples of such.

Those people who have been brought up as Yugoslav *internationalists* wonder at the fascination with *national* identity and belonging. A thorough knowledge of cultural anthropology, social psychology, science of language, history . . . is, of course, necessary for a scientific understanding of nation and nationalism, and this is what intellectuals and politicians in our regions are lacking.

Nationalists are those who give priority to the interests and rights of one nation before those of other nations, all other things being equal. In order to see if someone is implementing dual criteria in a nationalistic spirit, it is not necessary to know that person's nationality—otherwise it would seem that what is crucial is who has a specific stand, and not what that stand is. People can be nationalists not only to the benefit of their own nation, but also to its detriment. For example, if a Serb seeks less rights for Serbs than for other nations, then that Serb is a nationalist, albeit not Serbian but anti-Serbian, even if that person was moved by a specific type of national masochism, by "generosity," by the wish to show at all costs that he or she is not a Serbian nationalist, etc.

In connection with nation and state, the greatest confusion is felt by those who have considered themselves Yugoslavs, and these have been most numerous among the Serbs. For decades that nation lacked an analytical and critical relationship toward itself, its history, and its state issue. That is why even today a large part of the Serbian elite is not able to separate its stand toward the ruling regime from its relationship toward the state.

Tensions that have grown into grave contradictions have long been crucifying Serbian identity. I am thinking primarily of the contradiction between Yugoslav identity and Serb identity, as well as of that between hubris and a sense of extreme jeopardy.

The Yugoslav identity of many Serbs had reached the proportion of national self-negation. Such people have been in a state of complete confusion for several years. Yugoslavia no longer exists, and FRY cannot take its place; FRY is not exclusively a Serbian state either. This is because a good part of the Montenegrin population would not agree to that and, furthermore, one-third of its inhabitants are not Serbs; and there is also the question of where so many Serbs west of the Drina belong . . . Serb-Yugoslavs often react by attacking those Serbs who have never had that duality or who have overcome it.

By saying this, we have touched on one side of the second Serbian contradiction that was mentioned. Yugoslav-Serbs accuse the other Serbs of being responsible for the break-up of SFRY, not noticing that they are thus manifesting the hubris that is characteristic of the Serbian mentality. It is really megalomanic to accuse the Serbs of even being responsible for the evident wish on the part of the other Yugoslav nations to secede. Perhaps because their forefathers created Yugoslavia, many Serbs think that they could have saved it too, only if they had met all the demands of the other nations. Now, among the Serbs in Serbia, there is growing resentment against their brothers on the other side of the Drina, who, they say, are also destroying any hope in a renewal of Yugoslavia. However, if it was not good to try to force any nation to stay in Yugoslavia—and it was not—why then should the same not be true for the Serbs in Croatia and Bosnia and Herzegovina?

Serbs are a rare nation in that, besides hubris, they also have the feeling that they are constantly a victim. Here are some illustrations of that feeling:

The liberating character of Serbia's Balkan wars in 1912–1913 has been denied and an enslaving character ascribed to them, particularly in communist and postcommunist Macedonia.

The Serbs created Yugoslavia, putting into it two independent states, and, in return, they were accused of hegemonism. This went as far as the date of the creation of Yugoslavia (December 1, 1918) not being marked under Tito, although the communists relied on the international-legal continuity of new Yugoslavia with old Yugoslavia (and through it even with the Kingdom of Serbia).

Although incessantly accused of domination, other nations were taken from the Serbian national body, as some kind of mother body, and then proclaimed as separate. This refers particularly to Montenegrins, but also to a large part of Muslims and Macedonians. The tradition of statehood was not "sufficient" to make Montenegro a legitimate separate republic in communist Yugoslavia, but the ethnic particularity of Montenegrins was invented.

Others have been presenting themselves as the victims of the Serbs, although it was the Serbs who were by far the greatest victims in both world wars: only Serbian soldiers were taken off to prisoner-of-war camps; Serbian civilians were killed in great numbers exemplarily in retaliation for the early uprising against the occupiers; and this is not to mention the Ustashi genocide. Why is it that now their allies from the world wars wish at all cost to impose a territorial, state, political, and international-legal state of affairs on the Serbs that would be more fitting to the losers of those wars?

The separatist circles of Croatia and Slovenia launched the thesis on "Serbocommunist unitaristic rule" in SFRY from 1945 to 1991. However, no one's *national* unitarism existed under the communists.

Did the first and the greatest support to Albanian separatism in the 80s have to come from Slovenia? For, after all, many Slovenian refugees found the most selfless possible shelter among peasants in Serbia during the occupation from 1941 to 1945.

However, let us concentrate on intellectuals again. In my opinion, they should beware not only of nationalism, but also of a moralistic approach to it. If intellectuals only express antinationalistic stands and emotions, but do not at the same time try to understand and explain nationality conflicts—then they are not playing their role. This is especially the case if in so doing they entangle themselves in contradictions by calling for peace using the language of war and demanding international military intervention. In this way they perhaps retain an alienated image, but not the identity of true humanist intellectuals.

Moralizers also profane themselves ethically if they consent to the hypocrisy of foreigners who look down on us and take us to task, and, in doing so, "forget" the histories of their own nations. Besides, do those who support the break-up of SFRY have the right to single out and condemn only some consequences of that tragic process? How can we, for example, talk about what is happening to Sarajevo outside of the overall context of war and the catastrophes of other places, including Mostar? The moralizer who consents to that shows a lack of principle and insufficient sensitivity. Here moralism touches upon objectivism. The latter is suffered by those who approach war in a cold and reasoning manner, as if it were not a question of human beings but of objects. Intellectualistic explanation, understanding, quoting of facts, quoting from history, applying logics, reifying—leaves no room for the soul to express itself. If war, especially war among brothers, is treated exclusively through the prism of cause and effect, means and ends, the ratio of forces . . .

this demonstrates a lack of sensitivity. There is no such thing as "objective reality of war" independent of human suffering.

And when it is a case of a tragedy that is provoked by highly complex objective factors, as ours is, the humanist intellectual should point to possibilities and ways to limit the violence, even if it is rationally speaking no longer possible fully to prevent it. The realism of war imposes itself with its own force, and that little remaining humanity requires constant human care and support. In the purely cognitive approach to human misfortune there is, in any case, a fine line beyond which explanation and understanding leave the impression of moral indifference, and even the implicit justification of evil. Objectivism shows an incapacity for compassion, and moralism shows an incapacity to understand and explain.

National and state communities know little of self-destructive powers until the circumstances are ripe for them to show themselves. After Tito, and especially after the fall of communism in Eastern Europe and the first signs that the USSR itself was rocking, hitherto concealed national ambitions, and energies came to the fore.

The break-up of the USSR, one of the most powerful empires in history, can help us weigh up various factors in our country too, and test the claim that SFRY could have been preserved only if its leaders had wanted it. *So much violence* could probably have been avoided if we had had statesmen of international format at our head, and not provincial functionaries. But there was no room for such figures in the shadow of the charismarch Tito.

Many people ask themselves how it came about that the Czechs and Slovaks separated peacefully but the Yugoslavs were unable to do so. Czechoslovakia had certain things in common with Yugoslavia: it was also created as a consequence of the break-up of Austria-Hungary, international support, and the belief that there exists a "Czecho-Slovak nation"; it was divided by the Nazis who established a quisling regime in Slovakia; it was renewed by the communists in 1945, who had already before attacked "Czechoslovakism" (analogous to "Yugoslavism") as an ideological means of Czech domination. In that state, like in Yugoslavia, there was constant mutual accusation: the Czechs considered the Slovaks an economic

burden, and the latter considered the former as an economic ex-
ploiter and a state hegemonist—but that is where the symmetry with
the relationship between the Croats (and Slovenians) and Serbs
ends, for in Yugoslavia they experienced the Serbs not only as an
economic burden but also as a state hegemonist. The most important difference, however, is that in the renewed Czechoslovakia of
1945 there did not exist a genocide fissure. It is also important, although less so, that it was easier for the two republics (of Czecho-
Slovakia) to separate peacefully than for the six republics (of SFRY).

When in a state entity such as SFRY, with such a history of inter-
nationality problems, conflicts and extermination (a terrible *historical a priori*), there erupt mass movements that violate the hitherto
rules of the game and even consciously break up the state, then it is
no wonder that elemental forces and chaos ensue. The philosophical description of a war of "everyone against everyone" in a "natural
state" is not very far from the truth here. Thinkers who speak of the
"natural character" (*Naturhaftigkeit, Naturwüchsigkeit*) of the historical process could quote what is happening here as an illustration
and argument. An avalanche of fear, panic, fury and revenge has
destroyed the connective tissue in SFRY. The wars that emerged are
for the greater part in no way a "continuation of politics with different means" (Clausewitz), but rather the negation of politics as the
rational use of available resources for reaching set goals.

The slogan "nothing shall surprise us" was launched under Tito.
And it turned out: nothing . . . except the disintegration of the state
primarily through our own forces. On account of the justifiable hor-
ror at the sight of fratricidal wars, there is the increasing tendency to
assess Tito's rule retroactively as being better, or at least less bad,
than it really was.

We can estimate with certainty that there is no single nation that
has not paid a high price for the break-up of Yugoslavia. Is it necessary to prove this at all to the majority of those who have had so
many dead, crippled, refugees, displaced persons . . . ? Many mixed
marriages have been threatened or even destroyed, and children
placed in the impossible situation of choosing between their parents—can there be a greater sin?

The economic crisis of the 80s in SFRY incited separatism, but in the newly emerged independent states there has now been an even greater fall in production, the social product, and the standard of living. The severing of so much production, consumer, financial, personnel, transport . . . interdependence and complementarily such as exited in SFRY could not but result in catastrophe. The accelerated "brain drain" from all the national milieux is only one of the consequences.

Who is going to replace the thousands of international contracts supported and concluded by SFRY, and how?

The cultural, scientific, and sports links, brought about by the same or similar languages, were such that they cannot be replaced by turning to other nations and states.

In order to emphasize some specific consequences I shall take Macedonia as an example of the most underdeveloped republic, and Slovenia as the most highly developed republic in SFRY.

By seceding, Macedonia lost the huge material and all other assistance of the common state, and now it is having problems coping alone with Albania separatism. It may sound sarcastic, but its sovereignty is such that in international communications it cannot even retain its own name, but is called the "Former Yugoslav Republic of Macedonia."

Slovenia enjoyed all the advantages that the Yugoslav market provided for its products and services. The market was protected from external competition by customs duties and had, by the way, eleven times more consumers than there are Slovenes. In the SFRY that republic was constantly sounding the alarm due to alleged outvoting, although it was represented on a parity basis and not proportionally in the federal bodies, and it even had the right of veto, while the Slovene language was in compulsory official use in those bodies. Can Slovenia hope that it will also be treated in that way in the European Union if it is one day accepted as a full member? Is it possible to image countries such as Germany, Great Britain, France, Italy, Spain . . . agreeing to Slovenia having the same number of representatives and the right of veto? Is the Slovene language, the language of a small nation, less or more threatened now? And as concerns Serbo-Croatian, the Slovenes will have to use it again if they wish to do business in the region of former Yugoslavia. Finally, influential circles in Italy have already started to bring into question their border with Slovenia, since the so-called Osimo Accords were concluded with SFRY, and not with Slovenia. Furthermore, they are threatening to make Slovenia's integration into European Union dependent on border and other concessions from it.

Let me add in conclusion that although the separatist and other republics of Yugoslavia have paid a huge price for its break-up, this does not mean that it is possible to renew it. But a less ambitious type of reintegration is possible and useful. That is why I put forward (in the Belgrade press in the middle of 1994) the idea of a "Partnership for functional re(integration)," of which there follows the main part:

> The European Union, in my opinion, should offer the leading factors in the region of former SFRY an agreement on gradual *economic* and other *functional* reintegration. In order to avoid misunderstanding, let me say immediately that this is not another kind of *state-political* unification. . . .
>
> The settlement of existing political and territorial conflicts should be left as much as possible for the future, and the suggested partnership should immediately be offered to *those factors really responsible* for functional activities and services, such as the postal services, road, rail, river, and air transport, power supply, medical services, banking, culture, science and education, etc. Parallel to this, or immediately afterwards, the markets should be opened again and linked, the division of labor and other economic cooperation founded on it renewed, tourism reintegrated, etc. In that respect as well, our regions are more interdependent and complementary than those in the European Union.
>
> This would be an agreement not only among the protagonists in the former regions of SFRY, but also between them and the European Union, organized in phases, with abundant financial and other assistance from the European Union as well as the prospect that, if the mentioned

experiment were to succeed and then state disputes settled, the whole of that region would be accepted into the European Union in the foreseeable future. . . .

One of the results of this kind of mutual "Yugoslav" reintegration and its specific linkage with the European Union would, it seems, be the relativization of the most difficult types of disputes such as those over borders, sovereignty, and nationality. It is incomparably easier to re-link separated "civil societies" than to draw demarcation lines between states. It would be utopian to believe that anything of importance can be done without that pragmatic-functional change in approach.

Four

Western Triumphalism and the Yugoslav Tragedy

The Triumphalistic Temptation

Encouraged by the collapse of communism, and particularly that of the USSR as a state, the West has succumbed to a triumphalistic temptation. This triumphalism at times has even taken on the characteristics and proportions of self-deification.

Lord Acton provided us with an important insight: "Power tends to corrupt—absolute power tends to corrupt absolutely." On that and other similar realizations the liberal-democratic systems are based, in which position and opposition, checks and balances exist and government is divided among separate branches and levels.

Acton's warning is important for international politics as well. The West ought to draw lessons from it for its own world domination, especially because it is accompanied by the misleading and dangerous feeling of moral exclusivity.

Fukuyama's proclamation of the "end of history" was precisely an expression of that Western triumphalism. In accordance with Fukuyama's understanding at the time, liberal democracy had definitively defeated communism and all other competing conceptions of humans and society, and hereafter the political, economic, and cultural development of humankind would occur exclusively in the spirit and within the framework of the paradigm of liberal democracy. The critics of an ideological novelty have rarely had an easier task: having just been announced, Fukuyama's utopia of the "end of history" was already being refuted by the nationalism, chauvinism, and separatism unleashed under postcommunist conditions. The critics of that utopia did not even have to mention the antiliberal fundamentalism of a different type and of considerably older origin.

The sudden and harsh eruption of nationalisms, chauvinisms, and separatisms in Yugoslavia at the beginning of the 90s took Western politicians, intellectuals, and mass media by surprise, as it did us. It is almost as if everyone had taken Tito's propaganda about the final solution of the nationalities question in Yugoslavia at face value.

Following temporary support for the Yugoslav government of Ante Marković, which held that by means of market-oriented economic reforms it would be possible to eliminate the paralysis of the federal government, to prevent the disintegration of the country and to bring about its integration into the European Community, the West briefly played the role of a neutral mediator between the opposing Yugoslav republics and their leaders, only to wind up actively supporting the break up of Yugoslavia.

The Comintern tried, by stirring up nationalisms, chauvinisms, and separatisms, to break up capitalist states. Capitalism turned that weapon against communism. In fact, due to successful resistance against Soviet hegemonism, Yugoslavia was for a long time considered an exception by the West. Nevertheless, as soon as the Soviet Union began to fall apart, Yugoslavia became no longer necessary to the West, and so here too the West showed disregard for the Helsinki Agreement (1975) that guaranteed existing state borders within Europe.

In an imaginary world of equal rights the official Western characterization of the break-up of Yugoslavia would have been construed as only one among several persuasive definitions to be compared with competing definitions, and not to be taken as a *sui generis* factual statement, much less as a divine utterance creating facts ("*In the beginning was the Word . . .*"). But in the world such as it is, the Western *fiat* was sufficient for Slovenia's and Croatia's, and, then, for Bosnia and Herzegovina's, unilateral secessions to be proclaimed the "democratic outcome of the disintegration of the Socialist Federal Republic of Yugoslavia." The West *recognized* the breakaway republics as sovereign states, while it *defined* the antisecessionist intervention on the part of the remnants of the Yugoslav government, the Yugoslav Army, Serbia and Montenegro as "aggression."

The West acted in the same manner with regard to the war between Serbs and Croats in the Yugoslav republic of Croatia, and later with regard to the conflicts in Bosnia and Herzegovina between the Serbs on the one hand and the Slavic Muslims and Croats on the other. The West *decided* not to treat these wars as civil wars *inside* Yugoslavia, but rather as "defensive wars" of Croatia and Bosnia and Herzegovina against "external attack." Accordingly, the participation of regular military units from Croatia in the war inside Bosnia and Herzegovina is tacitly approved as the allegedly legitimate military cooperation of two sovereign states or, at the least, as the establishment of a Muslim-Croat military balance vis-à-vis the Bosnian Serbs and their allies in the Yugoslav Army, Serbia, and Montenegro.

Nonetheless, even were we to suppose that the West, through the *preventive recognition* of Bosnia and Herzegovina (prior to the outbreak of greater armed conflicts), produced a quasi-legal international basis for its characterization of that war, the same could in no way be applied to the wars in Slovenia and Croatia, since those broke out six months prior to the recognition of these Yugoslav republics as independent states. Actually, all these have been wars literally *among the citizens* of an internationally recognized state (SFRY) that began disintegrating.

Naturally, the definition of our wars as *civil* could not and would not conceptually prevent anyone from denouncing the warring sides and their allies. However, the West did not want to accuse Serbia, Montenegro, and the Yugoslav Army *merely* for aiding the Serbian faction in the civil wars in Croatia and Bosnia and Herzegovina, since the West itself had intervened countless times in civil wars far and wide. Moreover, the Muslim and Croatian sides also receive military and other aid from elsewhere, even from very distant countries. Finally, that could not have been a sufficient legal-international basis for the imposition of a blockade and other sanctions against Serbia and Montenegro.

Rather than the war in Croatia having put the Western governments extremely on their guard in Bosnia and Herzegovina, they even rushed to recognize this Muslim-Croatian secession as well. And as if such intromission in our conflicts were not sufficient for them, the Western governments even sought to impose a *unitary* state arrangement on the Bosnia and Herzegovina Serbs (and Croats). One is flabbergasted that it could have even occurred to them that Bosnia and Herzegovina could be a unitary state, when federal-confederal Yugoslavia was unable to survive as Bosnia and Herzegovina's state framework!

But why not? Those who conceive of themselves as possessing practically divine powers and divine rights know no bounds. If they feel so inclined, they will attempt to create even *ex nihilo*. Indeed, here we are dealing with an endeavor, via international recognition, to create a new state, and a unitary one at that, an endeavor that has produced nothing but catastrophic consequences. The West will not be able to escape the co-responsibility for the increase in war victims and for the illusion on the part of the Muslims in Bosnia and Herzegovina as to the West's readiness to help them, by military intervention if necessary, to impose a unitary solution on Bosnia and Herzegovina. The West is also unwilling even to hear of the separation of the warring factions along the existing front lines because it wants the Muslim side to increase the territory under its control. One is left with the impression that some circles in the West may be more bothered by the fact that the war in Bosnia and Herzegovina is being waged on an uneven playing field than that it is being waged at all!

In keeping with the belief that "divinity" (not only creates, but also) rends asunder as it sees fit, it has been ordained that the Federal Republic of Yugoslavia (comprising Serbia and Montenegro) be excluded, by *decree of nonrecognition*, from the map of the countries of the world.

Naturally, the "divinity" is not in the least bothered by contradictions, not even when they become obvious. Theologians try harder to eliminate their own contradictions, much more so than do the Western politicians, ideologues, and journalists when they try to impose a *new Balkan order* as part of the "new world order." Aside from those mentioned above, here are some other important contradictions in which the West has become entangled in its support for dividing up Yugoslavia:

A) The West has violated the principle that state boundaries can be changed solely by way of agreement, not unilaterally and much less by means of force. The first step down that unprincipled path was made by promoting the notion of "internal borders" (which international law does not cover or recognize). The second step was putting them on a par with "external borders" (the only ones covered and recognized by international law), and the final step was giving priority to the former "borders" over the latter *borders*. The world should somehow believe that international law is not broken by those who have unilaterally seceded from Yugoslavia, nor by the West that has supported them, but rather by those who have opposed their secession!

The hypocrisy of the "international community," whose dominant countries in no way recognize the right of their own constituent parts to secede, was hidden behind elections and referenda on the part of our secessionist republics, while the central government was not allowed to hamper them with elections or referenda of *all the citizens of Yugoslavia*. If the internal issues of the Western countries had been at issue, they would surely have rejected, with democratic disdain, the very thought of "street-populist" decision-making in haste, without careful preparations and rational public discussion, under circumstances where political passions are at the boiling point. Finally, what should be said about the treatment on the part of Great Britain of the separatist movement in Northern Ireland, or of Spain vis-à-vis the Basques, or of France in Corsica!

B) The secessions from Yugoslavia were recognized as the expression of the right of *nations* to self-determination, but, in practice, this was interpreted as the "right" of *entire territorial units of Yugoslavia (i.e. republics)* to separate from the state of which they were parts. It is well known, however, that such a "right" does not exist and that the United Nations has declared the exclusive right of nations to self-determination, and even that only when they are resisting foreign occupation, colonial government, or apartheid—which, in any event, was not the case in Yugoslavia.

Nonetheless, even the right of nations to self-determination has no absolute validity, but rather it depends on the consequences of the practice in each concrete instance. It is necessary to determine which group is included and which excluded by the prefix "self" in the principle of "self-determination." In other words, what remains to be defined on the level of meta-principle is where the right to self-determination of a nationality group ends and the same right of a different nationality group begins, i.e., what should be done when these two rights are in conflict.

C) The right to self-determination was recognized in the case of the Slovenes, the Croats, the Slavic Muslims, and the Macedonians and it is denied to the Serbs in those territories in Croatia and Bosnia and Herzegovina where they constitute a majority. Self-determination was deliberately interpreted as the right to secede from Yugoslavia, but not as the right to remain part of it.

D) The West has, following decades of support, rejected Yugoslav communism as illegitimate, but it has insisted that the internal territorial divisions of the communist Yugoslavia be transformed into international borders. However, Yugoslavia was not divided into republics strictly according to national or historical criteria; instead, the Yugoslav party state was made to reflect the organizational structure of the Communist Party of Yugoslavia (CPY) as a state party. Tito himself, on the occasion of the introduction of these administrative lines, declared—and subsequently repeated several times—that they were not genuine borders. Since the Politburo of the CPY implemented these divisions dictatorially following the Second World War, one cannot escape the impression that the West supported the self-determination in 1991–1992, but only on condition that the results of the original, fundamental *non-self-determination* be respected.

The apologists of Western policy point out that such divisions were constitutionally ordained in Yugoslavia, but do not mention that, in keeping with that same Constitution, no federal law could be adopted without the consent of *all* the republics, which even more should be the case in the event of the decision of any republic to secede from the common state. After all, in any country in the world the secession of any part therein without an agreement with the central government and the remaining constituent parts represents *casus belli.*

E) The European Union initiated its diplomatic-political intervention in Yugoslavia's internal disputes, promising impartial good services to all sides, but it was quick to start imposing secessionist solutions. The members of the European Union, for example, not only did not punish Slovenia, but instead recognized it as a sovereign state, albeit in violation of its obligation undertaken to the Union in summer 1991 that it again allow on "its" borders the federal army, police, passport, and customs control.

The European Union formed an arbitration commission of lawyers (the Badinter Commission) to set up the legal pretext for intervention in the internal affairs of Yugoslavia. But when that commission proposed the recognition of Macedonia and not that of Croatia, the European Union acted to the contrary, recognizing precisely Croatia, although its government even today has yet to control a fourth of the territory it claims. With the awarding of recognition to Croatia and, somewhat later, to Bosnia and Herzegovina, the European Union also violated the Montevideo Convention of 1932, which conditions the recognition of a state to the existence of an effective central government, its total territorial control, and a clearly defined populace.

The break-up of a state like Yugoslavia hardly represented such an insignificant danger for the West to dare to allow itself such a lack of prudence and principle, particularly when by so doing, they

also expunged the results of two world wars. History usually pun-
ishes such arrogance.

Instead of helping the West to free itself from self-contradictions,
even some of the better known intellectuals have succumbed to the
incongruities. Take for example, the following quote from a speech
by Vaclav Havel, an author and the President of the Czech Republic:

> An internationally recognized multinational state is being
> subdivided according to the dictates of fanatical warlords.
> Regardless of how well intentioned—and did not Cham-
> berlain have the best of intentions?—such behavior means
> sanctifying the idea of the "ethnically pure state" and
> giving up on the idea of the civic society. . . . The former
> Yugoslavia is the first great testing ground for Europe in
> the era that was initiated by the end of the Cold War. . . .
> Another one consists in how to deal with the temptation
> to open the back gate to the demons of nationalist
> collectivism with the apparently innocent emphasis on
> minority rights and the right of minorities to self-
> determination. At first sight, this emphasis would seem
> harmless and beyond reproach. But one real consequence
> could be new unrest and tension, because demands for
> self-determination inevitably lead to questioning the
> integrity of the individual states and the inviolability of
> their present borders, and even the validity of all postwar
> treaties (speech to the European Council, Vienna, 9
> October 1993).

Here the reader might think that Havel is criticizing the destruction of Yugoslavia and the Western support for its destruction, but in
reality he is alluding solely to Bosnia and Herzegovina. That is not
the first time that Havel has fallen into a contradiction when we are
at issue: he approved separatist decisions that targeted a multinational Yugoslavia, only to turn against the disintegration of a
multinational Bosnia and Herzegovina. But how can one reject the
consequence (the breakup of Bosnia and Herzegovina) and at the
same time approve of its cause (the destruction of Yugoslavia)?! After all, Yugoslavia had been an internationally recognized state for

over 70 years, while Bosnia and Herzegovina was recognized as an independent state only in 1992.

Havel also commits a factual error implying that a national minority (the Serbs) wishes to parcel out Bosnia and Herzegovina, when in reality there exists no national majority and, consequently, no minority either. I must add that Havel unforgivably relativizes Chamberlain's surrender of a part of Czechoslovakia to Hitler when he alludingly equates it to the Western European "appeasement" of the Serbs at the expense of the Muslims in Bosnia and Herzegovina. All in all, it would be incomparably more useful if Havel critically analyzed something with which he is much better acquainted, and that is the disintegration of his own country.

But, to return to Western Europe and the United States: their approach to the conflicts and wars between secessionists and anti-secessionists in Yugoslavia is neither principled nor realistic. It is an *unprincipled unrealpolitik*. Until now I have spoken more about legal, political and moral contradictions than about the failures of Western policy. I would like to add to that now. On the territory where they make up a majority, and even elsewhere where they do not, the Serbs have, in fact, seceded from Croatia. In Bosnia and Herzegovina as well they have effectively opposed the imposition of the pro-Muslim solution, so the West will, it seems, have to reconcile itself to some kind of a partition of Bosnia and Herzegovina. Finally, Serbia and Montenegro have seized control over the largest and best trained part of the Yugoslav military and have successfully supported the Serbs in Croatia and in Bosnia and Herzegovina to resist the policy of a separatist *fait accompli*.

The (Re)Actions of the Leading Countries

The US and other Western countries have actively wished that from the six Yugoslav republics would emerge an equal number of new little states. I was present when, at the beginning of March 1992 at the Institute of International Politics and Economics in Belgrade, the then American ambassador, Warren Zimmerman, openly presented that plan. The two of us argued a little on that occasion, and the ambassador finally "conceded" somewhat, allowing that Serbia and Montenegro could remain in a unified federal state, though by no means in the role of a successor to the Socialist Federal Republic of Yugoslavia.

The US administration has failed to take sufficiently into account that the manner in which a state was founded has to exert significant influence over the manner of its eventual dissolution. Since Yugoslavia was created in 1918 not by the linking of the six territorial-political entities alluded to above, it was not realistic to expect it to break up precisely along those lines.

There are many reasons why the US has been striving to attain exactly that end. The Milošević regime, which has explicitly declared itself in favor of the maintenance of political, administrative, economic, cadre-related, and symbolic continuity with the previous social order, could not count on the impartiality, let alone the magnanimity, of the US even regarding the continued existence of Serbia and Montenegro as a unified federal state, let alone the creation of a new state greater than the sum of Serbia and Montenegro. Let us imagine that the western Yugoslav republics emerged under the banner of continuity with communism, and that Milošević came out in favor of a definitive break with it. To whom would the Bush administration have lent its support then?

Furthermore: big powers prefer smaller states because they are more inclined to be obedient.

The concern of the United States that any change in Yugoslavia's "internal borders" would be setting a precedent for the former Soviet republics, particularly for Russia vis-à-vis the Ukraine, played a major role as well.

With regard to the US policy toward Bosnia and Herzegovina, I must again mention Ambassador Zimmerman.[1] When I asked him what their next move in Bosnia and Herzegovina would be, the ambassador answered that the West would recognize it as an independent state on 6 April (1992). I replied that the consequences would

---

1 . He gave a dinner party for my wife and me, along with one other couple, three weeks after the encounter with him I described previously.

be very serious, since the local nationalities had not resolved a single essential issue, and I added that I saw a chance for a peaceful settlement only in some type of cantonization or confederalization. I also cautioned that Alija Izetbegović, emboldened by the recognition, would probably withdraw his agreement to the recently attained Lisbon Accord regarding a tripartite cantonization, in reaction to which the Serbs would take up arms in fear for their own survival—not merely for their national self-determination. With respect to the Croats, I stated that they would continue with the support of the Muslims, but only tactically and temporarily. I also reminded him that on 6 April 1941 Hitler began his punishment of the Serbs by means of the barbaric bombing of Belgrade and the all-out attack on Yugoslavia. For that reason, the greatest possible insult that they could convey to the Serbs would be to choose precisely that date for the recognition of Bosnia and Herzegovina. (As if to spite the Serbs, that recognition was declared on exactly 6 April 1992). I also explained that on 10 April 1941 the Nazi puppet state of Pavelić was set up in Croatia, to which was subsequently incorporated Bosnia and Herzegovina, where the anti-Serb genocidal collaboration of Croatian and Muslim Ustashe occurred. Zimmerman did not agree with my "pessimism," convinced that the West, through an "authoritative recognition" of Bosnia and Herzegovina, would avert war among the national communities.

American economic, military, and political interests in the Muslim world have wielded enormous weight as well. Accordingly, the head of the American delegation, Lawrence Eagleberger, conspicuously reminded us, as participants of the "Conference on the Former Yugoslavia" in London at the end of August 1992, that there were more than a billion Muslims in the world. By supporting Alija Izetbegović and his followers, the US has believed that it could turn the Muslims away from the jihad-fundamentalist Islamic embrace and simultaneously improve its own image among the Muslim peoples.

The United States has constantly acted with the firm support of Turkey, to whom they have allocated the role of principal anti-fundamentalist exponent among those peoples. Thus they neglected the fact that Turkey was a centuries-old occupier of Serbia and of Serbs (and Croatians as well) in Bosnia and Herzegovina, not to mention the Turkish tradition of genocide against the Armenians and Kurds. Overcome by triumphalism, not even Turkey itself paused to take that into account. Therefore, the late President Turgut Ozal of Turkey set out to tour the surrounding countries with the explicit intent of "laying siege to Serbia."

The American effort toward a unitary order in Bosnia and Herzegovina is incomprehensible if one fails to bear in mind the political culture and ideology in the United States as well, in which the "melting pot" occupies the place of honor: all the citizens of the US, without regard to their national origin, are "Americans" who, by a majority vote, influence political decision-making. The very thought of a federation of nationalities, to say nothing of a confederation, must be quite alien to such a country. But, this is not the place for a discussion about which ethnic groups in fact dominate by means of that general "Americanism." However, it is the place to recall that, for all non-Serbian peoples in Yugoslavia, any program along the lines of the American "melting pot" ("Yugoslav-ness") would, beyond a doubt, represent an expression of "greater Serbian hegemony and assimilation." The official US has imagined that it can build a unitary nation state ("nation building") not only in trinational Bosnia and Herzegovina, but even in multitribal Somalia, as well.

What right does so many a politician, intellectual, and journalist from *national* states such as Germany, France, and Italy think they have when they arrogantly occupy a moral high-ground to reject the strivings of the national communities in Bosnia and Herzegovina for *national* self-determination?! The standpoint of such criticism are their own alleged *civic* states. Nonetheless, it is easy to be for a democracy exclusively of the type "one citizen—one vote" where 90 percent of the citizenry constitutes one's own nation, thus insuring that the nation's state-territorial integrity and sovereignty will in no way be called into question by the voting process.

Those west Europeans who readily condemn the Yugoslav wars as axiologically belonging to earlier centuries and non-European places suffer from an even greater hypocritical "amnesia." How quickly they have repressed the awareness that fascism and Nazism raged in the middle of our century and in the midst of Western Europe!

And it is hard to believe that the increasingly restrictive employment and immigration policy in the countries of Western Europe stems always from reasons other than the attempt to preserve their existing dominant *national* composition.

The Clinton administration, rather soon after assuming office, began criticizing the former administration and, even more so, the European Union and, most of all, Germany for its premature recognition of former Yugoslav republics (see Warren Christopher's interview in *USA Today*, 17 June 1992). As is widely known, in December 1991 the German government announced that it would recognize Slovenia and Croatia, even if it meant doing so alone. In so doing, Germany exerted the decisive pressure on the remaining members of the European Union to join it and to abandon their former position—wise, up to that point—ratified at the meeting of ministers of foreign affairs on 8 November 1991, in Rome, in accordance with which the matter of recognition for the new states on Yugoslav soil should be addressed only after attaining an overall settlement. Later, Germany introduced the recognition of Slovenia and Croatia as the argument for a rapid recognition of Bosnia and Herzegovina. It remained, nevertheless, unclear how the recognition of the first two republics, though extended only *after* a cessation of war conflicts therein, could serve as a valid formula for *preventing* the war in Bosnia and Herzegovina from breaking out!

The reunification of Germany brought about the triumphalistic self-assuredness of its politicians, mass media, and general public opinion. Many reasoned in the following manner: since Russia allowed East Germany to reunify with West Germany, then the Serbs have no right to retain the Croats, the Slovenes, and other nations within Yugoslavia by force.

However, right from the first glance that analogy between Russians and Serbs is unsustainable. To begin with, Slovenes and Croats joined the Serbs of their own free will to form a united country in 1918. And no serious person could characterize the situation in

Yugoslavia under Tito, or even 10 years after his passing, as "Serbian occupation." Moreover, by seceding from Yugoslavia, Slovenes and Croats just created their own states, and they did not (like the East Germans) return to their state of origin. Finally, should not one's opposition to retaining by force extend just as much to the Serbs in Croatia and Bosnia and Herzegovina?

In other words, if Germany wanted to be principled in its support for the self-determination of the nations in Yugoslavia, then it should also have upheld the secession of the Serbs from Croatia and Bosnia and Herzegovina, and not just that of the Croatia and Bosnia and Herzegovina from Yugoslavia.

It is simply astounding that, in their campaign against the Serbs, the electronic and print media as well as many politicians and intellectuals in democratic Germany have pulled out all the stops. One might have expected that they use a diffident tone in speaking about the Serbs since they are aware of the anti-Serb role of Germany in WWI and of the destruction of Yugoslavia and the crimes against the Serbs during WWII, as well as of its co-responsibility for setting up a genocidal Ustashe state in Croatia and Bosnia and Herzegovina in 1941.

This time as well the attitude of the majority of Germans toward the Serbs recalls for us the force of historical, religious, cultural, and civilizational factors. In almost every dispute between Serbs and, let us say, Croats, the greater part of the Germans instinctively side with the latter. Of course, the opposite is true for the Greeks, the Russians, the Armenians, and the Romanians. Accordingly, it is naïve to be shocked that Germany has not adopted a more balanced position regarding the break-up of Yugoslavia. Nevertheless, there were reasons to believe that this spontaneous anti-Serbian attitude would have been under greater control, owing to the collective-historical shame and critical-democratic public in Germany.

The explanation for the hysterical anti-Serbian campaign should also be sought in the political *revanchism* of millions of Germans who, as individuals or as family members, originated in Southeastern or Eastern Europe, having fled or been banished from there at the end of WWII. Many of them immigrated from or can trace their origins to Yugoslavia, particularly to the region of Vojvodina in Serbia.

The Catholic electoral constituency and its elite exerted an enormous influence on the position of the German government through the Christian Social Union (CSU) as the coalition partner of the ruling Christian Democratic Union (CDU). Together with Germany, the Vatican led an organized campaign in favor of a rapid recognition of the Yugoslav-seceding Catholic republics. Even much more numerous and powerful nations than the Serbs would have been stunned to have such influential world factors as Catholicism (and Islam) mobilized against them!

All this produced Germano-phobia among the Serbs, many of whom do not hesitate to accuse Germany of trying to create the "Fourth Reich." This will bring about even greater harm to the Serbian economy, science, and culture, which have long been tightly linked to Germany. Over the past 30 years many Serbs have lived, worked, and settled down in that country. Finally, the best road, rail, river, and air links pass through Serbia connecting Germany with Southeast Europe and the Middle East.

The Russian government has joined Germany and the West in its position toward the former Yugoslav republics. This has created additional hardship for the backers of Yeltsin, who have already come under serious attack on the part of the nationalist-communist coalition for being subservient to the West. Yeltsin is criticized as having an anti-Serb policy, and the explanation for it is to be found in his alleged indifference even to the fate of millions of Russians outside of Russia following the disintegration of the Soviet Union. Through its shortsighted pressure on the Russian government to conform unreservedly to its policy in the former Yugoslavia, the West has played into the hands of Yeltsin's opponents, making it easier for them to blame him for the threat to the interests, independence, dignity, and status of Russia as a superpower.

Of course, I do not mean to overestimate the importance of the Serbian question for internal Russian politics. The interests of the Russians in and around Russia naturally play a much more important role. This could serve as a good illustration of the assertion that the *procedural* legitimacy (democratic election success) is insufficient and that the *substantial* proofs of legitimacy are needed as well. Naturally, the less a government is capable of invoking social-economic successes, the greater is its need to use national, state, and international-status types of reasons to prove its legitimacy.

This is an appropriate opportunity to comment further on the comparison that is irresponsibly and unjustly constantly made anew by the superficial and the ill-informed, namely the comparison between Russians and Russia on the one hand, and Serbs and Serbia on the other. First: To reiterate, Serbia did not drag the other Southern Slavs by force into Yugoslavia, and therefore, equating its role with that of imperial Russia is totally inappropriate. Second: the Serbs did not constitute a majority in Yugoslavia, while the Russians in tsarist Russia and the USSR did. Third: if the Serbian elite dominated politically, militarily, and administratively (though not economically) in the first Yugoslavia (1918–1941), that was certainly not the case in the second (1945–1990). Finally, the Serbian diaspora west of the Drina river did not spring into being through Serbia's campaigns of conquest, but rather as a result of the Serb's fleeing from the Turkish conqueror. Due to these differences alone, it is not likely that any leadership of Serbia would dare to cut off completely its support for the national self-determination of the Serbs west of the Drina wherever they constitute a majority of the population.

After all, the Serbs would say, Russia has sufficient strength to rush to the aid of the Russians in her "near abroad" if they are threatened. Besides, there are incomparably more Russians than Serbs, so Russians can easily afford to indulge in a demographic-state "magnanimity" vis-à-vis other nations. And what is more important, the Russians outside of Russia, in contrast to the Serbs outside of Serbia, have not been subjected to genocide. That is probably one of the main reasons that they did not oppose the dismemberment of the Soviet Union into constituent republics.

THE FALL OF YUGOSLAVIA

The Ideology of Human Rights

The body of human, civil, and national rights has been playing a big part in the humanization and democratization of capitalism. Conceding that those rights should be enshrined in the Declaration of European Nations in 1975 in Helsinki (in exchange for guaranteeing the inviolability of existing interstate borders in Europe), Brezhnev and the other communist leaders in fact adopted a kind of *limited ideological sovereignty*. However, those rights have been applied by the West not only to criticize and destroy communism, but also to justify its own domination in the world.

I must say that the policy of the United States is less hypocritical than that of Western Europe, because that country quite openly accords priority to its own interests and rights when they come in conflict with those of the other countries, while the Western European states, as a rule, attempt to cloak their foreign policy in the guise of democratic humanist principles. On the other hand, when evaluating the national-religious civil wars in the former Yugoslavia, the former Soviet Union, and other parts of the world, from the *arrogantly moral high-ground*, it is as if many politicians, intellectuals, and journalists in the US forget the genocidal "ethnic cleansing" of the Indians, their brutal civil war in which paramilitary bands carried out crimes against the civilian population as well, and their slave-holding system owing to which an enormous number of Blacks perished even while being transported from Africa to the Americas.

The dissolution of Yugoslavia probably would not have assumed such tragic proportions had not the Western governments competed among themselves in imposing "human, civil, and national rights." The Western politicians, as a rule lacking in experience with our types of conflicts, and limited as to their perspective, but overcome with triumphalism, got their chance to decide the fate of over twenty million Yugoslavs.

No sooner had Gorbachëv consolidated his position in the USSR than interest for communist Yugoslavia on the part of the Western mass media waned. This was the reason why, at a decisive time, one

146

found so many second- and third-rate reporters there, some of them complete novices, eager for affirmation at any cost. How else to explain their spreading such utter nonsense as, for example, that of "thousand-year-old Bosnian statehood" or "hundreds of years of peaceful coexistence among the local national communities?"

Western mass media are the main hothouse of *pop ideology* of "human, civil, and national rights." Even more than their own governments, they suffer from a reckless superficiality in the name of those rights *when dealing with non-Western states*.

In the West a *presentism* increasingly predominates as the basic disposition of prosperous capitalism and its mass culture. I am referring to the fixation on immediacy and a total disregard for the past, particularly that of other nations. Thence the irresistible temptation to extrapolate the future merely from a *de-historicized* (D. Ćosić) here-and-now. What chance is there for such a world to grasp the world which is fundamentally characterized by *historicism*? It is in this light that one has to view the astonishment of Westerners at the nations in Bosnia and Herzegovina citing their mutually difficult "past," say, that of World War II. Compare that with the even greater astonishment of those nations as to how the Westerners overlook the fact that a numerous generation (not to mention its direct descendants) who participated in that "past" is still alive in that area.

The domination of the electronic media over that of print, of images over words, both reflects and strengthens this presentistic state of mind. The information-communications capabilities are today an inseparable dimension of all power: political, military, diplomatic, economic, cultural. The mass media with a planetary range, as is true of CNN, have no market counter-balance. Therefore, it is difficult for them to avoid the temptation to transform themselves from informers to partisan participants of world events. They even attempt to create what from their standpoint is desired reality by means of "informing"—let us call it *inform(cre)ation*.

I shall be saying nothing new if I state that the mass media in the West are highly commercialized, which means that for big money they link public relations agencies, even those hired by foreign governments, with their viewing and listening audiences and with their reading public. Quite a bit has been written in the West about the consequences for the future of democracy that profiteering may bring about, but not nearly enough has been said about its influence on the foreign policy of those countries.

Western mass media are much less pluralistic and critical with regard to the foreign policy than they are with regard to the domestic policy of their own governments. In the US there is even a tradition of general rallying around the President in the conduct of foreign policy, especially when deciding about American military involvement. That is why their criticism of the censuring of reporting on American military invasions (as was the case recently in Panama and Iraq) is rather rare, as is the criticism of the suppression of information regarding civilian victims in the invaded countries.

Though they know very well that the representatives of all three national groups that are destroying each other are predisposed to lie outright, the Western reporters and commentators rely incomparably more on the information and images (which are even more important) provided by the governments of Bosnia-Herzegovina and Croatia than on those provided by the Serbian authorities. The United Nations also bears responsibility for hushing up reports on the part of its representatives in Sarajevo as to who really perpetrated some staged and televised mass crimes against civilians.

How many more human victims and material destruction would there be, were the Western governments to succumb completely to the anti-Serbian, war-agitating pressure of the mass media?! Some of them continue to carry out actual anti-Serbian "ethnic cleansing" in their news and commentary and really conduct racist attacks on the Serbs as a nation. After all, with their support for the onerous international blockade they have inflicted considerable suffering on the population of Serbia and Montenegro.

We can only hope that the more independent and serious media, and perhaps some "watch" organizations, will critically investigate the reporting and commentary on the collapse of Yugoslavia and post-Yugoslav events. What would the professional and moral assessment of reporters and commentators (as well as that of the Western experts)—even those who have been given prestigious awards—be, if their reviews and evaluations were retrospectively compared with the actual causes, actors, duration, and results of the Yugoslav wars? Who will answer for the fact that the Western television viewer has constantly witnessed the destruction of Sarajevo, while not also seeing the annihilation of Mostar?

The Western governments are not, of course, blameless when it comes to the situation into which they have been led by the mass media. In fact, the initial impetus of the public campaign for military intervention against one of the sides (the Serbs) was given by the Western governments themselves with their decision to recognize the breakaway Yugoslav republics, while simultaneously trying to prevent, almost at any cost, the secession of the Serbs from those republics. Though these governments have increasingly been getting the information that what they are dealing with is essentially national-religious-civil wars, they have continued revolving in the vicious circle of a mass-media image that, in part, they themselves have deliberately provoked. How to maintain their credibility, while simultaneously continuing to insist on the validity of their false basic premise? How to stick with a diagnosis of "external Serbian aggression" when the Muslims and Croats for at least a year have been warring with each other and when their mutual crimes have also become public?

The Anachronistic Approach

The tendency to bid farewell to multinational states, particularly to those in which the national communities are territorially concentrated and separate is getting ever stronger. B. B. Ghali, general secretary of the United Nations, has expressed the concern that, if the current trend continues, within a few decades there will be around five hundred independent states.

To refer to what has occurred in the former Yugoslavia and the former Soviet Union, as well as in some other countries, we can use expressions (not only from the field of psychoanalysis, but also) from geology: fissures, faults, erosion, subterranean rivers, eruptions, earthquakes. The fact is that *beneath* the maps of the internal divisions of existing states and *beneath* the maps of the international state borders there lie *deeper suppressed maps.*

In order accurately to link space and time, an *in-depth cartography and an in-depth carto-analysis* are indispensable. I have in mind multilayered maps that would reflect the ethnic, linguistic, religious, cultural, economic, warring, genocidal . . . sediments. Presentistically disposed, the West overlooks these concealed, but latently more forceful, maps. Had it started out with such maps, the West would not have been so surprised that Yugoslavia was dismembered in a manner different from the West's wishes and plans.

This geopolitical myopia is enhanced by the fascination with the institution of "citizen" coupled with the resistance to the political expression and institutionalization of "nations." But what if the conceptualization and functioning of realistic democracy in multinational states with separate territorial concentrations of national groups demands that the principle "one citizen—one vote" be combined, amplified, and balanced by the opposite principle "one national group—one vote," including even the power of veto in order to prevent decisions that could essentially threaten national equality? But that goes far beyond the liberal-democratic readiness to guarantee the rights of "national minorities."

The conceptual fundamentals of Western liberalism such as "citizen," "voter," "civil society," "the buyer-seller" (homo economicus), in my estimation, are left without effective connection to the traditional, ethnic, religious, cultural, and civilizational characteristics and divisions in multinational states. Before individuals become "citizens," "voters," "members of civil society," "buyer-sellers" (homo economicus), they are socialized in the family and school, wherein language, religion, and awareness regarding ethnic, cultural, traditional, and civilizational identity and belonging are passed on to them.

The manner in which the United Nations and the regional organizations, such as the European Union and the Conference on European Security and Cooperation, react to inter-nationality conflicts and wars indicates how inadequate they are to the new circumstances and problems. As a rule, they adopt reactive, therapeutic, retrospective, negative, and punitive measures instead of active, preventive, prospective, positive, and rewarding ones. How is it that the Western world, that is internally very proud of its positive thinking and positive approach, imposes such negative thinking and such a negative approach on the rest of the world?

That B. B. Ghali is completely aware of these weaknesses was shown by his suggestions at the beginning of 1992 for modifying the work of the UN. In the summer of the same year, at a conference organized by the Stanley Foundation in the United States, I suggested that the general secretary establish an "Advisory Council for UN Development," as a forum of "collective wisdom" that would assist that organization in adopting a long-term, anticipatory, and positive approach.

Particularly in politics it is important constantly to draw a distinction between *static "realism" and dynamic realism*. The latter originates with diachronic knowledge and diachronic analysis. Since they knew little and wanted to know even less about the in-depth map of Yugoslavia, even many advisors to Western governments were shocked, for example, when the Croats and Muslims in Bosnia and Herzegovina turned their weapons against each other.

To put it mildly, the West is not supporting imaginative changes in the operations of the United Nations. A further illustration of this is again linked to the aforementioned Stanley Foundation and its constant vigil over the United Nations' activities. At one meeting on the possible responses of the United Nations to the Iraqi occupation of Kuwait, organized by that foundation in the fall of 1990 in Washington, D.C., I urged the utilization of all nonviolent methods before eventually undertaking military intervention: specifically the Security Council should have made the decision on the peaceful introduction of UN troops into Kuwait, and the Iraqi government should have been notified and warned that it would have to answer for war crimes if it attacked those troops. Those present at the meeting, all Americans except me, passed over my proposal with a telling silence.

The Ranking of Factors

It is highly unlikely that Yugoslavia could have been saved. This is primarily due to the internal reasons which I have outlined and analyzed in the preceding chapter. Since we were not the victims of external attack, occupation, and dismemberment, as was the case in 1941, it is fitting to search for the main reasons for the present-day dissolution (exactly fifty years later) within Yugoslavia itself.

Our principal fissures did not follow the "boundaries" between the republics that the "international community" sought to impose as international borders. They rather followed the lines that divide nations, religions, cultures, histories, civilizations. Still, the list of necessary and sufficient conditions for the tragic disintegration of Yugoslavia cannot exclude the catastrophic omissions and errors of the most powerful foreign nations. The collapse of our state did not have to be bloody (in any event not as bloody as it turned out to be), had the "international community" acted more cautiously, more objectively, more constructively, and more wisely. The Yugoslav tragedy demonstrates how self-deified human power can easily provoke hellish consequences. And that these are in fact hellish in the former Yugoslavia is hardly a matter of dispute anymore.

If Yugoslavia as a whole had been linked in a constructive manner to Western European integration, the tragedy of war could probably have been averted. In the mid-80s our country expressed the desire to become an associate member of the European Economic Community, but this was never seriously taken into consideration. Several years later Slovenia and Croatia would come to believe that that Community could hardly wait to have them as members as soon as they declared their independence. That illusion played an important role in their effort to secede, suddenly and at any price, from Yugoslavia.

The West has expressed ample understanding for the presence of former central government military in some of the former republics of the Soviet Union, patience with its gradual withdrawal from the breakaway Baltic republics, and even for its several-year-long pull out from Eastern Germany. Why, then, did that same West pressure the Yugoslav Army to withdraw instantly, and at any price, from the separatist republics of Yugoslavia? As a matter of fact, did not the West thereby encourage our republics to lay siege to and attack the garrisons of the Yugoslav Army, and bring about an increase in human victims and material destruction? Attaining their agreement with the Yugoslav Army on the unhindered relocation of its personnel and armaments from its territory, Macedonia showed how it was possible to avoid bloodletting on the occasion of Yugoslavia's collapse.

As soon as the first symptoms of our state crisis and collapse became apparent, the United Nations (but not the European Union) should have called a conference on Yugoslavia with the task of defining the rules for peacefully leaving the state as well as for peacefully remaining within it. The leaderships of our republics should have been informed that they would not be granted international recognition (preventive nonrecognition!) unless they first reach a mutual agreement, and that UN sanctions would be applied against those that attempt a policy of *fait accompli*. It is self-explanatory that the fate of the Yugoslav Army would have had to occupy the central place in that inter-nationality accord. When such a conference had not been held prior to armed conflicts in Slovenia and Croatia, why was it not organized at least to prevent the war in Bosnia and Herzegovina?

It was easy to foresee that the Serbs in Croatia and Bosnia and Herzegovina would offer armed resistance to those who wanted, at any cost, to take them with them out of Yugoslavia. Regarding their insistence on the existence of the inviolable inter-republic "borders," the Western countries could only offer one serious argument to the Serbs, namely that any changes in those "borders" would set a dangerous precedent, particularly for the apocalyptically armed Soviet republics.

Nevertheless, such an argument would be insufficient to deny the right of the Serbs in Croatia and Bosnia and Herzegovina to state self-determination, when it had already been accorded the Slovenes, the Croats, the Macedonians, and the Slavic Muslims. One could at the most ask the local Serbs—but in a constructive and not a selfdeifying tone—*consciously to sacrifice part of their right to state self-determination* for the sake of universal human interests (avoiding a precedent with eventual apocalyptic consequences).

Instead, the "international community" behaved in an extremely ultimatum-making and punitive manner. It is as if it were dealing with an indisputable choice between good (which it supposedly represents, insisting on the perpetuation of inter-republic "borders") and evil (which the Serbs supposedly embarked on by questioning those "borders"), rather than with the difficult choice between an irrefutable right on the one side, and a potentially dangerous precedent on the other. In actuality, we are dealing here with a very complicated comparison between a *rights* argument and a *consequentialist* argument.

As compensation for such a profound sacrifice, the United Nations should have offered the Serbs the guarantee of a very specific political position in Croatia and Bosnia and Herzegovina:

— a constitutional-state constitutive role with the right of veto over those decisions which could threaten their national equality.

— a great territorial-political autonomy in those areas where the Serbs make up the majority of the population.

— the absence of central government military and police in those territories.

— the presence of UN protection forces.

It should be recalled that Croatia and Bosnia and Herzegovina (as well as other Yugoslav republics) were within Yugoslavia in a much better position vis-à-vis the Yugoslav federal authorities than what the first two points above would accord the Serbs, and, despite that, the Serbs were not offered anything even remotely approaching such a position by the two seceding republics. It would appear that Western triumphalism has spread to them as well.

Understandably, it is difficult to demand rightfully from anyone to sacrifice an unquestionable right in order to avoid a precedent, especially if, by so doing they would feel physically threatened. No one wants to be treated as simply a means, albeit for avoiding (or establishing) important precedents. Who has the right to punish a nation if it does not accede to that? After all, the Croats in Bosnia and

Herzegovina have established the same precedent, and yet they have not been punished in any way.

In fact, border-related wars have already broken out on the territories of the former Soviet Union, and therefore any further reference to an eventual precedent is completely groundless. The Western politicians and mass media, however, concentrate their attention on our region and disregard those other wars. Could this, perhaps, be an expression of their Eurocentrism, not to say Euroracism, as well as of a political-military realism, since what is at issue is the "near abroad" of a superpower?

With the collapse of the Yugoslav state in which they felt secure and, even more so, with the pressure to become part of nation-states in which they had already suffered genocide, the Serbian people west of the Drina River found themselves in a "limit situation" (an existentialist expression). Therefore, they should have been approached with understanding and offered guarantees, rather than with denunciation and excommunication on the part of the "international community." Is there any greater right than that to freedom from fear of genocide? It is my conviction that the United Nations should extend a special kind of guarantee and aid for those nations that have been victims of genocide, such as the Jews, Armenians, Serbs, Kurds, Gypsies . . . .

If it is unwilling to go that far, at the very least the West should feel obligated to draw all the practical conclusions from the fact that it itself has considerably contributed to the Yugoslav and Serbian tragedy. *Morally,* that is all that the West is left with, when even James Baker, the architect of the Bush administration's foreign policy, has already acknowledged that the premature recognition of the breakaway Yugoslav republics was in fact an error. Prior to him, former foreign affairs ministers De Michelis (Italy) and R. Dumas (France) had done the same. And it is known that Perez de Cuellar, Lord Carrington, and Cyrus Vance had opportunely warned about the severe consequences of recognition prior to concluding an all-out accord. In the summer of 1993 Lord Owen stated that the war raging in Bosnia and Herzegovina is one among three national communities.

THE FALL OF YUGOSLAVIA

Faced with the refusal of Serbia and Montenegro to submit to the dictate on dismantling Yugoslavia into its constituent republics, the Western countries, through the UN Security Council, instituted a blockade and other sanctions against them. Thus, owing to their refusal of the projected new Balkan order, their entire population has been punished, and the West once again has fallen into a contradiction, this time with its own moral, political, and judicial culture, which decidedly rejects the concept of *collective* responsibility and guilt.

It is high time the "international community" seriously rethinks its policy of penalizing entire nations. If they still wish their repertoire to include the blockade and other sanctions, the United Nations should find the means to penalize the power holders, and not the entire populace. Nations should be integrated into an advanced world, not isolated. One of the best ways would be a direct link between Western "civil societies" and the "civil societies" of the penalized states: city to city, university to university, hospital to hospital, etc. Dialoguing and negotiating for reasons of "realpolitik" with the leadership of such states, the "international community" merely strengthens the belief of their populace that it as a whole (and not its power holders) represents the ultimate target. That stimulates political extremism and rallying around the state leaders. It turns out that *punitive triumphalism* of the West is totally counterproductive.

Utilizing the suffering of the populace of Serbia and Montenegro to blackmail the Serbs in Croatia and Bosnia and Herzegovina, the West wrongly assumes that the latter will sacrifice their interests, their self-determination, and even their elementary security in order to spare their compatriots in Serbia and Montenegro socioeconomic misfortune. How could it be expected that those who are at war and are consequently suffering incomparably more are expected to make extreme sacrifices for the sake of those who are not at war and are consequently suffering less?!

True, most recently the belief that all three warring groups in Bosnia and Herzegovina are to be blamed is gaining currency in the West, but now it is as a rule added that the Serbs are still the most to blame because they started the war and because they are stronger. But the Serbs ask themselves and others: if that is really believed, why then are sanctions not applied proportionally, but rather, instead, solely against them? How is it that Croatia has not been subjected to any sanctions, when it has even sent regular troops to fight in Bosnia and Herzegovina?

Serbs have overwhelmingly reached the conclusion that the West wishes to call into question their very identity as a nation and as a state, and they believe that they are supported in this conviction by a number of facts. The West does not want deliberately to specify the conditions for a lifting of the blockade and the other sanctions. It does not want even to lift those sanctions that affect the health, culture, science, and sports of the people in Serbia and Montenegro. Moreover, keeping Serbia and Montenegro in international isolation obviously helps the regime in power to conceal its own contribution to the socio-economic catastrophe. The blockade clearly impedes democratic and market reforms in our midst, while the West claims that such evolution constitutes its true intention and goal. Finally, Western mass media pay practically no attention (other than vengeful!) to the suffering of the people of Serbia and Montenegro.

1 February—15 March 1994

Postscript

More than two and a half years have passed since I wrote this chapter. I feel the need to add to the American edition a few thoughts on Western triumphalism, both in how it has emerged from the collapse of the USSR as well as its specific manifestations during the process of the disintegration of Yugoslavia.

* * *

To the reader I suggest that the following thoughts in the first part of this postscript be read together with the last section ("Between Triumph and Apocalypse") of the final chapter of the book.

Today, the opposition between *realpolitik* and *moralpolitik* in international relations is still talked about, without the recognition that "realpolitik" itself has become a form of "irrealpolitik," i.e. the politics of fatal self-delusion. The so-called realpolitik appears quite miserable if we know that the apocalyptic danger will stem increasingly less from wars between states, and more from technological failures or terrorist actions. The insight is humiliating indeed that technological contingentialism has grown so apocalyptic precisely during the century that invested so much utopian hope in techno-science, its laws and necessities. Let me add that, in my opinion, terrorist fanaticism is going to be a larger apocalyptic danger than the "clash" of civilizations (Samuel Huntington).

What would Max Weber's famous deliberations on "politics as a calling" look like if transposed to the apocalyptic key? How are we to survive as a genus if we do not replace the sort of politicians and statesmen we have had up to now with new-type visionaries and power holders, *humanists*, who would be guided by *social, demo-cratic, (con)federalist, and environmentalist mondialism?* We humans are doomed unless we find ways emotionally and practically to reconcile the opposition between ourselves as members of nation-state communities and citizens of the world, through the idea of *humanity as a community.*

Unfortunately, the West is continuously elated with the "realism" of its new-old world order, comparing it with Gorbachëv's naïveté, his "new thinking," and the expectation that he would encounter the same *humanistic globalism* at the other side, too. Can we hope for a Western Gorbachëv to appear, who would successfully resist mass egoism in order to help Eastern Europe and Russia as much as possible, not to mention the Third World? How could we expect that, when the whole "vision" of politicians and statesmen in the West as a rule extends to cover a couple of election years? Rich democratic-capitalist countries are incomparably more willing to dictate standards and ways of internal transformation to former communist countries than to commit any significant portion of their riches to help them. This is an attempt at social engineering from the outside, and at an extremely low cost. If things continue unfolding in this direction, neo-communist accusations are highly likely to arise against the West as a sort of *selfish empire* (as a belated "revenge" for the onetime Western attacks on the communist "evil empire").

In the West an ideology increasingly dominates that combines a triumphalist-absolutist self-evaluation about the "end of history" with a "postmodernist" nihilism and a vulgarized "pragmatism" when approaching the rest of the world.

It is a "pragmatism" that is characterized by basically changing the approach "from case to case." At that, in cases that are virtually identical, different, or even totally contrary, "principles" are employed that are tacitly or even explicitly justified by the interests of the state or group of states using them. For example: depending on whether the existence of a multinational state suits dominant circles in the West or not, it supports within that state either the *civic principle* ("one citizen—one vote"), or else the demand of *nationalities* for state self-determination.

Surprisingly, many intellectuals use the category "international community" unreservedly, though it is to a large extent a configuration of dominance that hides behind the term. Any genuine community ought to be characterized by equality and solidarity, instead of forcing and selfishness. When following closely this world power, including its obvious caprices and contradictions, intellectuals lose their political, intellectual, and moral autonomy and credibility.

Because there is currently no true counterweight to the power of the West, and especially to that of the US, the West's own *self-restraint* should be of utmost importance. How realistic is it to expect this? After all, as Karl Deutsch stated, "Power is the ability to afford not to learn." However, *such* power has, as a rule, historically lead to moral decadence. What is more important, it brings us all closer and closer to a self-inflicted apocalypse. Democratic competition for influence among individuals and elites unfortunately favors those who arrogantly impose Western views and interests onto the whole world rather than those who would be prepared for self-criticism, empathy, and cooperation on an equal footing with others. Instead of acting as a "check and balance" of sorts, the overwhelming majority of Western mass media "patriotically" support and encourage their leaders in this. Unfortunately, this is how a majority of Western intellectuals also behave. Their hasty "explanations" and the assessments of what is taking place on the territory of the former Yugoslavia bear witness to this approach. Peter Handke is correct, in my opinion, when he asserts that the West European intelligentsia has once more missed the opportunity to mature.

* * *

The International Commission on the Balkans, which was formed by the Carnegie Endowment for International Peace together with the Aspen Institute, met on 23 January 1996 with several university professors in Belgrade. I was asked by the Commission to be one of the introductory speakers at that occasion. What follows is the main part of my presentation:

> I begin with the assumption that you have no interest in any kind of stability in the Balkans besides that which is characterized by respect for human, civil, and national rights, justice, democracy, a modern market economy, and the inclusion of the Balkans into European integration. Otherwise, it would appear as if power *per se* (stability imposed by force) was identical to equality, justice, and progress. But it is also highly doubtful that such a stability could last.
>
> As you are well aware, the necessary formal condition for justice is impartiality. For this reason it is crucial to call not only for equal dialogue among Balkan peoples and their representatives but also for equal dialogue among these groups and the West. Impartiality, which I am confident you also favor, is surely not possible without essential adherence to principles. In other words, it should be said that the West takes human rights only as seriously as it is prepared to practice them at home as well. On this occasion I am thinking, above all, of the principle of self-determination of peoples and the rights of national minorities, say, in Spain, Canada, Great Britain, France, or Belgium. And even with the best of intentions it would be

impossible to say that, in the territory of the former Yugoslavia, the West has opted for impartial, consistent application of the principle of national self-determination and the rights of national minorities to territorial and political autonomy (even when it has been dealing with the Serbian minority in Croatia, who suffered terrible genocide there during World War II).

Based on shallow instead of in-depth Yugoslav political maps, the West has made several moves that have proved catastrophic. The following are some lessons to be learned from those mistakes.

1) The West rushed to recognize republican separatism in Yugoslavia instead of threatening every *fait accompli* policy with blockade and other sanctions. A conference should have been convened immediately under the auspices of the United Nations on Yugoslavia with the task of producing an acceptable procedure both for secession as well as for remaining in Yugoslavia through peaceful means.

2) The West was quick to accept the results of separatist referenda in the Yugoslav republics without demanding that a referendum of all citizens of Yugoslavia be held.

3) Further, the West interpreted the principle of nonviolence in Yugoslavia in such a way that it was for all practical purposes turned against the antiseparatist central government to the advantage of republican separatism. Contrary to international law, it was enough for one part of the country to decide "peacefully" and "democratically" on their secession for the West to accept it in practice as a *fait accompli* and threaten the central government not to use force. But we can see the selective and arbitrary way in which the principle of nonviolence is upheld as a blind eye is continuously turned toward a country like Turkey when it employs the most brutal methods on the Kurds to prevent their secession or even merely their attainment of political and territorial autonomy.

4) Why did the West not at least insist on the adoption of principles of dual citizenship for members of those national minorities that did not want to secede from Yugoslavia along with "their own republics"?

In this manner, with the explicit goal of preventing the creation of "Greater Serbia," the West has assisted in the *de facto* establishment of "Greater Croatia." Furthermore, the Serbs in the Krajina were forcefully prevented from remaining in Yugoslavia, and even from establishing only territorial-political autonomy in Croatia for themselves. In "exchange," Serbia is "in principle" left with the right to retain Kosovo within its state territory despite its being made up of over 80 percent Albanians. The end result of the campaign to prevent the formation of a "Greater Serbia," through the irony and cynicism of "history," will probably be the establishment of a "Lesser Serbia" and a "Greater Albania."

Let us hope that in Bosnia-Herzegovina it has now come not only to a temporary truce but also to a lasting peace. The pragmatic and functional (re)integration in the entire space of the former Yugoslavia should, therefore, be supported. Policy makers in Europe and the world should cease their reliance on negative, disciplinary treatment of actors in the former Yugoslavia and concentrate on policies that reward desired actions. Those Balkaners who propose that they be included in wider European integration must first exhibit a willingness toward (re)integration in their own neighborhoods. How can one region that is not prepared to reconnect, for example, its road, rail, air, and postal networks be capable of participating in higher forms of integration with the rest of Europe?

I end with the observation that the Serbian identity is also full of contradictions and that the better side of this identity should be relied upon. At this moment, the most important thing for your purposes and ours is that the Serbs are proud of their tradition of a democratic state and market economy existing in the first half of this century and of their having long since created one of the most multinational political communities (Serbia) in the Balkans. Anyone who seeks their support cannot overlook the fact that this is a people with an inflated sense of national dignity. There is increasing danger now that the West's manipulation of the ruling regime's weaknesses in

Serbia may degenerate into the denigration of the entire Serbian people.

Since the above talk afforded me no opportunity to convey some thoughts to the Commission about the Hague Tribunal for War Crimes in the Territory of the Former Yugoslavia, I shall now quote my open letter to *The United Nations: General Assembly, Security Council and General Secretary,* dated 20 July of this year and published in the Belgrade weekly, *Nedeljni Telegraf,* on 14 August 1996.

> Your decision to form an international criminal court *exclusively for certain countries* has evidently shown itself to be a complete legal and moral failure. I therefore kindly ask that you immediately disband such courts and institute a *World Criminal Court* in their place. It is only in this manner that it will be possible to demonstrate that the United Nations, and especially its dominant members (who in the form of an ultimatum demand that other countries cooperate with the existing criminal courts) respect the principles they are preaching.
>
> It would be of far-reaching importance also to open an immediate investigation into the *concealing* of reports by your own representatives in Bosnia-Herzegovina about war crimes committed by one side against their own population in order to pin the responsibility for them to the other side. Even your undersecretary, Yasushi Akashi, among others, has spoken publicly about this. Under whose jurisdiction and with whose knowledge were these reports concealed? It goes without saying that the concealment of such crimes is in itself a criminal act deserving of harsh punishment.

I wish to conclude this postscript with another general point expressed in the concluding passage of the letter to the United Nations quoted above:

> Finally, I suggest that you select a commission of the most respected and impartial world figures who would explore how the United Nations and its members, especially the

dominant ones, have reacted to the destruction of the Socialist Federal Republic of Yugoslavia. They should formulate some lessons for the future and make public their findings. The mistakes of the international community committed in my country continue to produce terrible repercussions. We should therefore ask ourselves what will become of humanity if similar mistakes are allowed to be made in some country with access to apocalyptic weapons of war.

October 1996

Five

Serbia under the International Blockade

How Dobrica Ćosić Became President of FR Yugoslavia

I will begin on a personal note, only in the capacity of speaking about Dobrica Ćosić. Early in 1992 I became increasingly convinced that a true catastrophe threatened our people and state, and I frequently discussed this with Ćosić. Along with some of his other friends, I tried to persuade him to become directly politically involved as soon as possible. Although a longtime leader among social critics and dissidents, even in the postcommunist period Ćosić did not relish involvement in official politics, especially those of a party character.

In the spring of 1992, when Serbia and Montenegro formed the Federal Republic of Yugoslavia and as soon as its Constitution was accepted, I began insisting that there was no one more suited for the Presidency than Ćosić. Not a formal and ceremonial President—but one who would strive to reconstruct the social and state edifice from the federal level down, since it could not be done from the level of constituent republics. At that time there was a precipitate increase among the already numerous friends, admirers, and bearers of

165

similar messages who passed through Ćosić's house. These also included dignitaries from the Serbian Orthodox Church. It is also noteworthy that Slobodan Milošević personally, with several collaborators and intellectuals from the Serbian Socialist Party leadership, importuned Ćosić to accept the presidential candidacy.

I closely observed Ćosić's resistance, his hesitation, and his last-minute acceptance of the candidacy. Crucial to my resolute insistence was a 25-year critical-dissident working relationship with Ćosić, during which time I came to know intimately his moral and political convictions and abilities. I was certain that if he accepted such an important state post, Ćosić would do it strictly from a sense of sacrificial duty, not from ambition and a thirst for power. During his Presidency it became clear that he tried to move the country in a beneficial direction, but he also wanted to expedite his return to literary work as soon as possible. While working with him, I became convinced that politics and morality do not necessarily have to fall into mutual contradictions, although they nearly always exist in a certain tension.

When Ćosić began presidential duties on 15 June 1992, his first act was to appoint me as a special adviser.

One must remember that the Federal Parliament that elected Ćosić was comprised almost exclusively of representatives from the Socialist Party of Serbia and the Democratic Party of Socialists in Montenegro.

The first meeting between Ćosić and Milošević had occurred only about two years previously. Since then Ćosić had spoken to him several times and sent him two or three written messages to communicate in such a compelling fashion his political analyses, evaluations, critiques, and suggestions. I hope that Ćosić will not delay long in releasing these messages and the corresponding diary notes, the sooner the better, since even after his removal, malicious characterizations of the nature of his relationship to Milošević continue to circulate.

Even in the unusual event that Milošević was insufficiently informed about Ćosić's views on the necessity of radical political changes, he certainly was in a position to learn about them in early

May 1992, when the two of us went to visit him. I had never met Milošević before. I had asked Ćosić to arrange our visit. The occasion was Ćosić's requested postponement of the elections scheduled for May of that year so that the opposition could participate. Ćosić and I had agreed that I was to do most of the talking, giving analyses and critiques of the Serbian Socialist Party and Milošević's policies, as well as suggestions for fundamental reforms. Milošević listened carefully, commenting briefly only once or twice. In the end Ćosić observed that those were our common opinions. As we left the office I told Ćosić that I was not certain of Milošević's reaction, or even if he took seriously our suggestion to postpone the elections. As is known, they were still held on the appointed day in May.

Shortly before Ćosić's election, the Socialist Party of Serbia chose as Prime Minister candidate Milan Panić, an American businessman with dual citizenship, born and raised in Belgrade. Ćosić did not know him personally, but he found the idea attractive, so he offered the mandate to Panić after waiting for a month and urging him to get permission from the United Nations Committee on Sanctions and the United States government (since Milan Panić is a United States citizen as well), so they could not eventually punish him for accepting such a position in a country under sanctions.

Divergent Intentions

Milan Panić's new government was comprised of capable ministers, even though it emerged from a compromise among Panić, Ćosić, Milošević, and Bulatović. I will cite only two examples of tension relating to its composition. Until the very last moment Panić opposed Vladislav Jovanović's appointment as foreign minister, considering him Milošević's man and a diplomat with whom the West was reluctant to deal. Soon Panić replaced this foreign minister, while Milošević continued to promote Jovanović, not only to the renewed post of Serbian foreign minister, but later, simultaneously as foreign minister in Kontić's federal government, lasting until the present—which demonstrates decisively that contrary to the Constitution of the Federal Republic of Yugoslavia, Milošević carries out the foreign policies of Yugoslavia through Jovanović despite being President of Serbia, and neither the President nor the Prime Minister of the Federal Republic of Yugoslavia.

To the consternation of many people, especially those in the governing party, the state apparatus, and the police and military, Panić himself retained the post of the minister of defense. These circles accepted this move only when assured that the defense minister had nothing to do with the military command, which was left to the President of the FR of Yugoslavia, and when they "realized" that with appropriate personnel and other measures if necessary, they could effectively control and block Panić.

In connection with Ćosić's election to the Presidency, two almost paradoxical scenes are instructive. In his inaugural address to the *just-elected and constituted Parliament that had elected him*, he stated that they could anticipate great political changes, and immediately thereafter that new elections would be held very soon, at the latest by the end of the year.

There was another unusual circumstance: almost immediately, Ćosić, in the spirit of his program, and wanting to open a democratic dialogue, invited representatives of the opposition for consultations, whose greater part announced to Ćosić that they refused to recognize the FR of Yugoslavia, its Constitution, its Parliament, and consequently him as President; they said that they had responded to his invitation for conversation only because he was a respected writer, an acquaintance, and for some a friend. At the same time they organized the "Vidovdan gathering" (at the end of June) with the explicit and immediate purpose of restoring the monarchy to Serbia.

Despite these circumstances, Ćosić calculated that democratic, evolutionary, and peaceful changes were quite possible in the new elections to be held shortly. He hoped the democratic parties of the political center would be significantly strengthened in this way, but, unfortunately, the December 1992 election results were disappointing: the extremes were strengthened and the cleavages in the center of the political spectrum were broadened. With the help of the ultranationalist and ultrademagogic Serbian Radical Party, the Socialist

Party of Serbia (with significantly fewer representatives than before) came to dominate the federal and Serbian governments. Slobodan Milošević defeated Milan Panić and was re-elected as President of Serbia.

After the December elections the socialists and radicals continued to attack Ćosić partly because he had not been *"party-neutral"* during his campaign. These same people, though, seemed not to mind that Milošević headed the ticket of the Socialist Party of Serbia and had been a candidate again and won as a *party* candidate during the campaign for the Serbian Presidency.

One can ask how Milan Panić had calculated. Was Ćosić's political program, examined and supported by Panić, a sufficient reason for his action, as well as a hoped-for favorable outcome in the elections to be held as soon as possible, a hope he shared with Ćosić? Did Panić, who did not know Milošević well when he arrived from the United States, really believe the latter was prepared to withdraw from politics if given sufficient guarantees? To this day Panić's close advisers remain convinced that Milošević had given such a promise.

Still more important is the question: what did Slobodan Milošević hope to achieve by ceding the most significant posts in the federal government to Ćosić and Panić? In my opinion, Milošević calculated primarily on using the two to weaken the political, diplomatic, economic, and media blockade and re-establish contact with the western world. And his other goal was to blunt the harsh domestic battles—significant at the time—and the democratic opposition's attacks on him and his regime. In addition, Milošević intended to cling to all the major instruments of power he had won earlier and, therefore, must have been confident that he was not undertaking a significant risk.

Foreign powers had evaluated the balance of power in the same way as Milošević, so they were skeptical of the chances of Ćosić and Panić. The politics of Ćosić counted on time, patience, tactfulness, compromise, reasonableness, and wisdom, as well as some luck, to say nothing of domestic and foreign democratic support.

Of course, one could not expect Ćosić to conduct politics with a moral asymmetry between means and ends. Opposition members who criticized him for "indecisiveness" anticipated and demanded precisely such an asymmetry, although they constantly hindered him, not even recognizing him as the head of state. Naturally, one can discuss Ćosić's "indecisiveness," but on the condition that one defines what it meant and how one would implement greater decisiveness in a situation where the real instruments of power were and still are in Milošević's hands.

During the election campaign Dobrica Ćosić spoke metaphorically of "ducking" (before the world), which elicited a sloganeering response from Slobodan Milošević: "We will not duck." By previous agreement with Ćosić, I responded to this statement by saying that every intelligent soldier ducks to avoid a foolhardy death and is not ashamed of it (in a polemical discussion with Borisav Jović, Milošević's closest collaborator, on Politika Television's program "Close Encounter," on 16 December 1992). I also referred to Ćosić's famous formula from the past, much calumniated for its militancy, about *Serbs being victors in war but losers in peace*, which touched an important syndrome in our national history and mentality.

By "ducking," Ćosić meant political compromise and making agreements with the world, and above all with the democratic West; this policy would characterize our government when part of it becomes stronger and the other part takes effect after the December 1992 elections. This government would present a more acceptable and trustworthy negotiating partner in this than would Slobodan Milošević and his regime.

In the previously mentioned debate, I suggested to Milošević's party, half in jest and half seriously, that their candidates not run because of conditions in the country—even given the improbable assumption that they bore no responsibility for that situation, but were themselves victimized by exceptionally adverse circumstances and misfortune. I began with the assumption that luck is also necessary in politics, so that consequently it would be propitious to give others, "luckier people," the opportunity to govern. I also argued that a transfer to the opposition would benefit the Socialist Party of Serbia, so that with internal regeneration and self-reformation, it would eventually be transformed into a modern social-democratic party so necessary for our conditions.

According to Ćosić, only a newly elected government acting as negotiator stood a good chance of defending the minimal national interests of the Serbs in the FR of Yugoslavia, as well as those Serbs across the Drina River, in the former Yugoslav republics of Croatia and Bosnia and Herzegovina, and *simultaneously* convince the decision-making powers to lift the political-economic blockade and recognize the FR of Yugoslavia. It is highly unlikely that the West would accept a regime in power in Serbia that it had openly attacked as neocommunist, to say nothing of accepting its political triumph based on its support for Serbs west of the Drina River.

Who was more realistic in the long term: Milošević, striving to buy time so that his "truth and justice" could triumph in the world, at the cost of ruining the people and state via the blockade and sanctions, or Ćosić, calculating on the correspondence of our state and national interests and representatives and the interests and representatives of the most powerful nations? *Clearly, the struggle between Ćosić and Milošević is not primarily a conflict between two personalities, one democratic and one authoritarian, but between divergent conceptions and strategies for leading our state.*

Slobodan Milošević and His Regime

Contrary to popular belief, Milošević "ducks" in the face of the foreign world whenever he thinks it politically expedient or when he has no choice. I will point out several familiar cases.

First: Milošević publicly attacked, and subsequently removed from his post, Milan Babić in the Serbian Republic of Krajina when the latter rejected elements of the Vance-Owen plan that Milošević considered acceptable.

Second: Along with the other delegation members at the London Conference in late August 1992, Milošević accepted all the key promises made by Panić, going even further by suggesting that we should open all our military units to foreign inspectors, not only our airports and our borders with Bosnia and Herzegovina. The majority of our delegation did not want to go that far.

Third: When the delegation of Bosnia and Herzegovina Serbs at the Geneva Conference first rejected the Vance-Owen proposal on constitutional principles for Bosnia and Herzegovina, Milošević pressured them greatly to change their position, which they eventually did.

Fourth: Milošević later did the same, during the discussion of the Vance-Owen proposal to divide Bosnia and Herzegovina into 10 provinces, which the West was trying to impose with the support of the Russian government. Milošević conducted himself as if the issue was choosing between good and evil, with no real dilemmas. In this way he repeatedly demonstrated the characteristics of a capable politician—the type who adamantly defends his position, but when it changes precipitously, argues that the new position is also perfectly reasonable, inviolable, and even fully contiguous with the preceding one.

The "international community" later discarded the Vance-Owen plan and permitted the confederal division of Bosnia and Herzegovina, thus demonstrating that the Bosnian Serbs had *calculated* more correctly the West's unwillingness to impose the plan at any cost than had Milošević, Ćosić, and Bulatović. It is still questionable, however, at the same time that the Bosnian Serbs *acted* better, if we evaluate their action from the broader, long-term Serbian perspective, since what followed was a major tightening of sanctions (already devastating) against the Federal Republic of Yugoslavia. True, with his conditional signing of the Vance-Owen plan for dividing Bosnia and Herzegovina into 10 provinces in Athens on 2 May 1993, Karadžić in all probability warded off air bombardment against the Serbs in Bosnia and Herzegovina, and perhaps even against the Federal Republic of Yugoslavia.

This is an appropriate moment to discuss the Western politicians' belief that Milošević has purposely deceived them on several occasions. However, it is my impression that he overestimates his power and influence when giving the West promises, rather than being intentionally deceptive. For example, he himself was rudely surprised when he failed to pressure the Serbian Republic into accepting the division of Bosnia and Herzegovina into 10 provinces. But it is also important to note: Milošević has immeasurably more influence on the leadership of the Republic of Serbian Krajina than on Karadžić, Krajišnik, and Koljević, but this influence too is not limitless, as is mistakenly believed in the West.

Milošević, indeed, occasionally let Ćosić make unpopular but necessary compromises, which were followed by a flood of criticism, some emanating from the group of Milošević's closest collaborators. A good illustration is provided in the agreement to withdraw our troops from Croatia in the area south of Dubrovnik, and to place the demilitarized Yugoslav Prevlaka border zone with Croatia under United Nations control (until a final solution is attained). Although Milošević had participated in the decision-making process that led to the signing of the agreement, only Ćosić was attacked for treason. The accusers, naturally, know or could have known that this was the maximum attainable when one considers that Croatia is internationally recognized within these borders, so that in the opposite case there existed the danger that we would be viewed as an aggressor and would be subjected to military attack ordered by the United Nations Security Council.

Slobodan Milošević and his people continue arrogantly to presume that they are the only true guarantors of national and state interests.

How did Milošević begin his ascent? In 1987 he precipitously emerged from the circle of second-rate Titoist functionaries. The occasion responsible for his rise was provided by the Albanian separatist rebellion in Kosovo and the ever-increasing separation of Vojvodina from Serbia. Milošević successfully brought Kosovo and Vojvodina under Serbian jurisdiction, thereby gaining tremendous popularity among Serbs.

However, during those years the Serbian people came to believe strongly that their interests and influence in Serbia and in Yugoslavia were also neglected in other ways. And when Yugoslavia began to disintegrate in the face of separatist attacks in the western republics, and when the Serbs offered armed resistance to the enforced status of being a national minority in the republics newly separated from Yugoslavia, the *national bloc* that supported Slobodan Milošević and his party gained in size and effectiveness.

The majority of the Serbs, not only the inhabitants of Serbia proper, stood behind *the state party of the Serbian homeland and its leader.* Certainly it is an exaggeration to accuse this party as a whole of (neo)communism, since most of its members never belonged to the Communist Party. Still, without question almost all of its top leadership is comprised of people who have backgrounds as Communist functionaries. Through them, Milošević controls cadres in the political arena and thus the power at all levels, a control that he completed after Ćosić's removal.

Due to family relationships and other connections and attachments of the Serbs on both sides of the Drina River, as well as the three-quarter million war refugees in Serbia and Montenegro from other parts of the former Yugoslavia, the psychological-political support for Milošević and his party during the elections spread beyond the "normal" circle of his supporters in Serbia. Besides this national bloc, Milošević and his party were supported by an enormous *social-economic bloc* that extended from the communist period to postcommunism. This is the block comprising the largest group of people living from the state: administration, military, police, economy, culture, retirement funds, etc. It is natural that these voters found in Milošević and his party, rather than in the anti-communist opposition, a guarantee against the dangers of privatization and capitalization.

A key question can be posed: what are the most important things that Milošević *could* have done, but either failed to do or addressed mistakenly?

It would have been much more acceptable, or at least much less objectionable, to the world if the Serbs, in those areas where they constituted the majority, had insisted *immediately* on their right to remain in one state, instead of fighting to retain the Socialist Federal Republic of Yugoslavia at all costs.

It is true that the commanders of the Yugoslav Army, in a short-sighted manner, too long insisted on maintaining the SFR of Yugoslavia, and even its Communist Party (obliquely transformed into the Leagues of Communists—A Movement for Yugoslavia) as an alleged factor in keeping together the Yugoslav state as well as its army. The leadership of the Yugoslav Army continued using communist symbols (such as the five-pointed red star), thus playing into the hands of the western separatists in Yugoslavia who successfully portrayed themselves as fighters for democracy (against communism), rather than destroyers of a unified state. Perhaps, additionally, the military leadership acted on the naïve assumption that the West would wink at its actions because of Titoism as a specific type of communism, which had been in league with that same West and had received decades of support.

Unfortunately, the Milošević team's ever more dominant influence on the Yugoslav Army was not used to bring about the rapid military withdrawal from the territory of those nations that at all costs wanted to leave the existing state. In general, under Milošević's leadership, Serbia lagged unconscionably in casting off the communist traditions, flags, and organizations, to say nothing of cadres.

What could such a Serbia expect, and where to place its hope, from foreign anticommunist arbiters amid our secessionist and anti-secessionist quarrels and wars?! Milošević and his people did not understand that the support for anti-Serbian nationalisms and other anti-Serbian measures by Serbian allies from the two world wars is not of itself an expression of anti-Serbian sentiments, but rather a means of destroying communism in Yugoslavia.

The regime in Serbia, perhaps unconsciously, appropriated Tito's self-confidence in relating to foreign factors, thus overlooking the disappearance of the bipolar structure of power between the two world blocs in which Titoism had flourished. For example: Milošević, like the head of some superpower, for a long time refused to give an audience to the American ambassador, Warren Zimmerman, in this way "chastising" him for meddling in Serbia's internal affairs. The ambassador's entire stay in Belgrade, more or less, was spent in such a tension. One would indeed be naïve to suppose that this was interpreted in Washington merely as a reaction to the ambassador's personality, and not to the country he represents.

As if such a "provocation" of the USA were not sufficient, Milošević and his regime shortsightedly and publicly rooted for the anti-Yeltsin opposition in Russia, even actively supporting it. The USA came to the conclusion (for Milošević a fateful one) that he not only continues his local Balkan resistance, but even tries to threaten their primary global interests. One need not waste words on the repercussions of such a political stance on the Russian government's position toward Milošević and his government.

Milošević was unable to liberate himself in a timely manner from the Titoist megalomania concerning Yugoslavia's world role. This pretentiousness is accompanied by a certain provincialism and autism in carrying out foreign policy—even in the period following the collapse of communism in Eastern Europe and the USSR and the impending disintegration of Yugoslavia, which means at the time when politics *in the long term* could not be successful at all without Western support and without a *global* perspective.

This significant shortcoming on Milošević's part was visible already at the moment when, with the return of Kosovo and Vojvodina to Serbian jurisdiction, the initial impetus of his ascent was exhausted; in other words, as soon as problems arose that transcended the local scene and flowed into the broader geopolitical and geostrategic current. Moreover, one can say that the short-term nature of Milošević's policies was already demonstrated in connection with Kosovo, because with the application of governmental repressive measures he put the problem on ice and left its resolution for the future.

Naturally Milošević's provincial self-confidence nurtured the Serbs' traditional reliance on arms in defending their cause, along with the costly neglect of nonviolent means and methods, as well as diplomatic skill and maneuvering. And the world certainly could not be favorably impressed with Milošević's undermining of Ćosić's demand to take energetic measures against the paramilitary groups that crossed the Drina River, participated in the war, and even plundered and committed war crimes.

And what can one say about the catastrophic failures of Milošević's regime in the dissemination of information abroad? How can a regime, which in domestic policy concentrates on controlling the classical instruments of state (including the dissemination of information) in foreign policy, rely primarily on the victory of its "truth and justice," which must somehow, of itself, become known to the world! He fatefully underestimated the influence of public opinion and the mass media in determining the foreign policy of democratic countries, due most of all to the influence, doubtlessly inherited, of the communist (lack of) understanding of Western capitalism.

Perhaps the citation of Milošević's mistakes should have begun, rather than ended, with the most decisive one. Instead of moving toward radical social-democratization and expanding the government's political base by forming coalitions with the most important democratic opposition parties and personalities, he attempted to maintain an ever stronger continuity with the previous "socialist" way of life and strengthen the *autocratic* nucleus of his government—it is true, in a *protodemocratic* formal-institutional framework.

By "showcasing" Panić and Ćosić, for a time Milošević attempted to show the Western world a more acceptable face, but simultaneously he prevented any significant sharing of power and governance. The results of the December 1992 elections and Panić's defeat Milošević interpreted triumphalistically, in keeping with his autism, especially toward the foreign world. Instead of opening itself to the democratic opposition, his regime began cooperating with the extreme rightist Serbian Radical Party.

Carried forward by this truimphalist syndrome, Milošević recently removed Ćosić, not taking into account even the appropriate constitutional procedures. However, this method stood in complete harmony with the unconstitutional reason behind the removal: Ćosić was really removed because of political disagreements with Milošević and his resistance to the latter's policies, and not because he "violated the Constitution," which in any event, by that same Constitution, could have been the only valid basis for replacing the President of the state. To make the matter even more ironic (to state it mildly), Milošević's supporters criticized Ćosić for lacking authorization to carry out foreign policy of Yugoslavia (acting as if they did not know that the FRY Constitution states that the President represents the country abroad), although after the dismissal of Ćosić, Milošević took this sphere completely into his own hands, even though he is Serbia's, not Yugoslavia's, President. He does not even take the new, nominal President of the FR of Yugoslavia, Zoran Lilić, with him to the Geneva talks.

The Democratic Opposition

Even before the opposition parties were allowed to form, Milošević had received support from the two large social blocs discussed in the preceding section. His substantial political astuteness accounts for this, and this is not due solely—as the opposition thinks—to his inheriting the cadres and legislative and general political control over state institutions: administration, the military, police, banks, enterprises, television, papers.

Milošević gains much strength from the democratic opposition's lack of unity, its programmatic disorientation, and its inefficiency. It has not presented a convincing political alternative for the majority of the people, nor a likely opposition presidential candidate. That the democratic opposition is more weak than Milošević is strong is shown in that a returnee from the United States, Milan Panić, had to become a candidate at the last moment in order for Milošević to be seriously challenged—and that in an election campaign where Panić had only a few days at his disposal.

Dobrica Ćosić was not only not supported, he was regularly attacked by the most influential segment of the opposition due to a certain jealousy, and somewhat because they underestimated the democratic potential of Ćosić due to the mistaken notion that Milošević's calculations ("bringing on Ćosić") coincided with Ćosić's real intentions. This objectively helped Milošević reduce Ćosić's position to one of authority without power and later to remove him from his presidential post.

Due to their monarchistic convictions or simply from political hopelessness, some members of the opposition tried to bypass Milošević by restoring the monarchy. But, in competition with Milošević, supported by two great segments of the population, what were the chances of a monarch raised abroad, at that time hardly knowing the Serbian language, to say nothing of insights into our political conditions and the ability to control them? Indeed, the monarchist opposition knew perfectly well that a restoration of the monarchy by democratic-constitutional means had no perspective, at least in the present, but they hoped to reach their goals through a short cut, a massive popular movement, never seriously asking themselves how this was to be attained concretely. A lack of fore-thought ("we shall see during the course of action") shown in their extra-parliamentary and street tactics of political battle generated much grief, not only to the opposition.

And to make the situation somewhat grotesque, powerless opposition leaders constantly threaten Milošević and his retinue with harsh punishment after their removal from office. However, they would do well to learn from their anticommunist but liberal colleagues in Eastern Europe about the importance of *nonvindictive* promises and guarantees in the peaceful transition from one system to another.

There were other reasons, apart from those mentioned above, why Ćosić was cautious, and distanced himself from most of the opposition parties. This applied especially to those in the opposition who had only recently separated themselves from communism, about 20 years after Ćosić had done so, and yet mistrusted him more than anyone else and boycotted his efforts because of his alleged procommunist sympathies.

According to Ćosić, the governing as well as the opposition "elite" lacked the required qualities that the people, the citizens, and the state really need. There were too many second- and third-rate people on both sides of the political fence. In a year of serving as President, Ćosić became convinced that we have few people capable of taking on important state and other political functions.

One of the most significant weaknesses in our political life emanates from the fact that people with a dissident past find it difficult to liberate themselves from the style of acting as a critical-intellectual group. Many parties have a more intellectual rather than political character. Becoming political leaders, intellectuals most often continue talking to each other, and not to the common voters. I am certain that Ćosić would not exclude himself from such an evaluation. And, if it is not pretentious and inappropriate, I would add that this applies to me as well.

For a long time the parties cast about in a search for political themes, preoccupying themselves with "elevated" politics, while vital politics offers itself to everyday life: poverty, hunger, shortages of medicine and treatment, superinflation, crime, paramilitary groups, the mafia. For example, the question of whether and to what degree Milošević's regime is a continuation of the previous communist one, does not concern the people, nor does it interest or motivate it. Such themes would be better left for scientific symposiums, academies of science, universities, and institutes.

The manner in which opposition leaders were recruited also poses a problem. Almost all of them come from the ranks of the humanist intelligentsia, which, certainly, has a specific view of society. There are not anywhere nearly enough leaders from circles of the economic, technical, and natural-science intelligentsia who by virtue of their training and work bring a different perspective.

To this point we have discussed Ćosić's relationship to the democratic opposition. Now it is appropriate to occupy ourselves with the opposition's relationship to Ćosić. For purposes of clarity, I will formulate the opposition's objections followed by Ćosić's possible responses—I say possible, because to this day Ćosić has not articulated them publicly. He has a very idiosyncratic conviction that *"one needs to respond less to criticism, and endure it more."*

O_1) When Ćosić accepted the Presidency last June, he saved Milošević and his regime, which the opposition claimed to have already "brought to its knees."

R_1) To begin with the least important fact: the opposition never leveled such a criticism at Panić. And now something much more important: because the United Nations Security Council sanctions against the Federal Republic of Yugoslavia, enacted only two weeks before Ćosić became President, had not yet taken effect, our economic situation and living standard in June 1992 were much better than on the eve of the December election, which Milošević won. Therefore, he was not "on his knees" at all even in December, to say nothing of June 1992 when Ćosić was elected. During the entire past year, the homogenization of Serbs has spread and deepened around Milošević due to the war in Bosnia and Herzegovina and because of the satanization of the Serbs in the Western media.

When the opposition reasons antithetically, it obviously has in mind its success in the mass protest demonstration that lasted for days, in the streets of Belgrade during the "Vidovdan gathering" at the end of June 1992. But here again it was misled, just as it was on 9 March 1991, by analogy to what was seen in Eastern Europe during the fall of communism. I refer to the opposition's reliance on the similarity between the peaceful implosion of those regimes and possible developments with us.

However, Yugoslav communism, and Milošević's regime whose decisive cadre is rooted in it, was not as weak as the opposition had presumed, neither in its manner of coming to power nor in conviction and self-assurance. For Milošević, during the "Vidovdan gatherings" it was most important to control his nerves (a lesson from the loss of tranquillity on 9 March 1991!) and wait for the masses in the streets and squares either to calm down or initiate the use of violence, and both sides knew the outcome in advance if violence were used to settle accounts.

O_2) It is true, Ćosić forced new elections in December 1992, but conditions were unequal, especially given the use of state television, which was practically in the hands of Milošević's people.

R_2) Television was not under federal jurisdiction at all, but under Serbian control. The opposition in Serbia (and certainly neither Ćosić nor Panić from their federal positions) could not eliminate Milošević's party control over state television. After all, since TV Serbia gave preference to Milošević over Ćosić, the head of state, no wonder that they treated the opposition the same. Ćosić's every attempt to make changes in state television was decisively blocked by Milošević and his people. In the final analysis, the opposition itself, after the "roundtable" organized by Ćosić and Panić, accepted the situation, including several other inequalities, deciding to participate in the December elections. Is Ćosić to blame for this as well?

O₃) Ćosić did not provide campaign support for the opposition parties, and did not want to run for the Serbian Presidency against Milošević, which then Panić had to do and, naturally, lose.

R₃) It is worth noting that the Socialist Party of Serbia accused Ćosić of the (opposite) sin of fully supporting the opposition. And the real truth is that he supported those parties that responded positively and explicitly to his state-political program.

The request also was not sufficiently convincing that Ćosić, as President of the FR of Yugoslavia and the supreme commander of the military, neglect these responsibilities to run for President of Serbia. Certainly to that part of the population (at least) sympathetic to Milošević, this would have looked like Ćosić's grabbing for a new position. And such action would not be in keeping with the generational differences between them, nor to Ćosić's personal political morality. Be that as it may, in light of the December election results it became clear that probably, had Ćosić moved from one position to the other, the new federal Parliament would have elected Milošević to the Presidency of the FRY.

Meanwhile, even in the absence of other important reasons to the contrary, the fateful fact remained that during the election campaign Ćosić precipitously had to undergo surgery. Ćosić's physical health made it impossible for him, after all, to realize his plan to travel intensively and carry on his election campaign within the country during the fall and winter of 1992. He is reluctant to talk about this, but it is my duty to do so, if only for the sake of historians.

O₄) Ćosić did not invalidate the elections, even though the campaign was conducted in unequal conditions and although there were other irregularities, even to the point of taking votes from the opposition by the Socialist Party of Serbia and the Serbian Radical Party.

R4) The critics must have known that according to the Constitution and the election law, the President of the FRY has nothing to do with the verification of election results, since it is the responsibility of the federal institutions—the Election Commission, the Court, and the Parliament. And what is one to say about the republican and local elections, which the federal President does not even schedule? In addition: opposition leaders who publicly questioned the regularity of the elections privately acknowledged that the irregularities and stealing were not so numerous as to have significantly altered the outcome.

O5) Ćosić did not resign after the December elections, although he had promised to do so if the results were unfavorable.

R5) The federal Parliament had rejected in advance Ćosić's request to change the Constitution so that he could *test* his mandate, although he was not subject to the new elections. The "socialist majority" roundly rejected his request, hoping to force him into resignation, which at the time was an easier and a more acceptable solution for it than removal. In addition, Panić's government needed to continue until a new government was elected, and Ćosić was responsible for trying to make it as good as possible or, at least, to be as little flawed as possible. There are written documents outlining the sharp conflict between Ćosić and Milošević regarding the Kontić government, as a result of which some projected ministerial nominees were rejected—one can hope that Ćosić will release them for publication. Ćosić's resignation would *then* have suited Milošević and his team because it would have enabled the following castle move: The most important post, the premiership, would be "taken" by Serbia, while the position of the head of state would be "left" to Montenegro.

Certainly, the question will be raised why Ćosić retained his position after the given reasons no longer applied. Here are two explanations. In the spring of 1993, the already serious threat of international military intervention increased, not only in Bosnia and Herzegovina but also in the FR of Yugoslavia. The departure of Ćosić, the "only remaining democratic option" in the state hierarchy, probably would have enhanced the likelihood of the West taking such action. One could not expect Ćosić to be more preoccupied with the narcissistic preservation of his own moral *image* (the Hegelian "beautiful soul") than with the people's interests.

Finally, some of our most distinguished people, as well as some foreign friends and officials, begged Ćosić not to induce still worse consequences by a "premature" withdrawal. Here I need only mention Patriarch Pavle of the Serbian Orthodox Church.

I would conclude this section with the following assertion: the opposition itself needs to acknowledge its considerably ambivalent attitude toward Ćosić—and the greater the ambivalence, the more they criticize him.

Let us clarify: while the opposition frequently hindered him, its members imperceptibly nursed exaggerated, almost charismatic *expectations* of Ćosić, but on the other hand, disappointed, they harshly *attacked* him. According to them, Ćosić was obligated somehow (?!) to reverse the structural as well as political constellation of forces in the country, thus doing everything that the combined opposition had not been able to achieve. We must add that the opposition did not treat Panić in this way.

The charismatic relationship is established when, without consideration and verification, it is postulated that someone *can* do everything ("unnatural" or "completely exceptional powers," in Weber's definition of charisma) that one *should* do. In discussing political actors, however, the rational question is not so much what they need to do, but whether the "should" is within the reach of their power and ability.

Instead of collecting themselves self-critically and uniting, opposition members most often reacted in frustration rising from their powerlessness to remove Milošević, and directed their dissatisfaction and even anger against Ćosić.

And what if the democratic opposition, incapable of suppressing their disunity, narcissism, and pretentiousness, missed the opportunity in Ćosić to uncover and foster those potential qualities and abilities which could have made him their key figure and successful alternative to Milošević? Even with the unconstitutional removal of Ćosić the democratic opposition did not want or did not know how to create a first-class political scandal to benefit themselves and the people.

The Balance Sheet of Ćosić's Presidency

Formulated conventionally, Ćosić's successes fall incomparably more in the realm of foreign rather than domestic politics. With the term "conventional," naturally, one is led to question the clear differentiation between these two spheres, at least in our case and for the present. Here are my illustrations and arguments:

It is obvious that literally the survival of our people and our state depends on relationships with the dominant powers. Because of their great interdependence, some alleged "domestic" issues, such as Kosovo, become in large part "foreign" policy issues as well.

Further: thanks to the premature international recognition of Croatia and Bosnia and Herzegovina as sovereign states, the Serbian and Montenegrin support for the Serbian side in the inter-national and inter-religious wars in the territories of the former Socialist Federal Republic of Yugoslavia (thus, in civil wars in one and the same state), immediately "took on" the character of punishable interference in the internal affairs of other countries.

Finally, with Ćosić's determination to hold general elections early, at the latest by the end of 1992, he achieved a complete foreign policy success in terms of legitimacy, security (how likely are democratic countries to intervene militarily against a country which is holding democratic elections?), image improvement, etc. The likelihood of any military attack on the FRY did not significantly increase even after the December elections produced negative results, since the Parliaments and assemblies at all three levels (federal, republic, and local) still became incomparably more pluralistic than before, with democratic-opposition groups whose numbers and influence could not be ignored. It is not impossible that precisely this fact will become enormously important when the social and economic collapse leads to restiveness among the population and makes imperative a radical political change.

Because our internal situation depended so much on relation-ships to the foreign world, and, to a degree, because he realized that he could do incomparably less to effect changes in the constellation of domestic political forces, Ćosić concentrated primarily on *communicating, educating, and negotiating* with that world, simultane-ously urging Premier Panić to do as much as possible in this direction.

In the year of Ćosić's Presidency the political-diplomatic and information-propaganda isolation of the FR of Yugoslavia was rather lessened. Even though our country was recognized by few among the world powers, Ćosić still visited the European Parliament, Italy, Greece, and Rumania, and one also could enumerate his participa-tion in and contributions to the London Conference and especially the Geneva talks.

In some important countries where we have lower-rank repre-sentatives (because we are not a recognized state) Ćosić acted "circuitously," sending our distinguished intellectuals as special em-issaries who felt at home there in terms of language, occupation, culture, and personal reputation.

He exerted great efforts in convincing the American administra-tion, whose views were most crucial in determining whether or not international military intervention would come, that it must be avoided at all cost and how much we wanted to normalize and de-velop relations, most of all, with the USA. The following statement which I issued on Ćosić's behalf did not pass unnoticed among American officials:

> It is obvious that the FR Yugoslavia must be concerned most of all with the United States of America. . . . If we do not find a solid connection (certainly, keeping our inde-pendence) between our national and state interests and the interests of the USA, no possible initiatives for the lifting of sanctions will be decisive, because the USA pos-sesses veto power. We do not see why a democratic and prosperous FR of Yugoslavia, acting peacefully and har-moniously in the Balkan peninsula, must be in collision with the strategic interests of the USA. Why would it be in

the USA's interests to carve up the FR of Yugoslavia as well, to say nothing of its destruction? (*Borba*, 28 April 1993).

Knowing that Milošević's politics catastrophically underestimated how much mass media and public opinion in general affected the attitude of democratic countries toward our state, Ćosić received foreign journalists, delegations, and distinguished individuals almost every day. Solely from his interviews with foreign newspapers and television and radio stations, one could compile a book of a thousand pages.

Ćosić viewed this unobtrusive "education" of foreign statesmen, politicians, diplomats, intellectuals, and journalists as a necessary prerequisite for our successful communication and development of understanding with the world. His central notion was the need to demonstrate the connection between the enlightened interests of the democratic countries and our real interests as a people and a state, instead of concentrating on the self-promotion of the Serbian "obvious truth and justice," as was the case with Milošević. Our inherited diplomatic and information services, with rare exceptions, did not approach the level of Ćosić's "conceptual work."

Ćosić activated and applied concepts and insights such as, above all: *dis-history, the ideologization and instrumentalization of civil rights, Serbian hubris, and the noncoordination of the domestic clock with the world clock.* The reader will be able to see the fruitfulness of this approach, especially as it relates to the three central *foreign-domestic* political problems: the war in Croatia and, especially, in Bosnia and Herzegovina, as well as the international sanctions against the FR of Yugoslavia.

Here Ćosić confronted quite a hopeless situation: the Western countries, Russia, and the UN Security Council had already characterized the wars on our territories as the consequences of foreign, Serbian-Montenegrin aggression, and this justified their using any means, from political-economic blockades to military attacks, to counter it.

Therefore Ćosić, already in his first interviews with Western reporters (in the second half of June 1992), launched into a redefinition of our war tragedy. Naturally, at the time his understanding of the situation in Bosnia and Herzegovina as an inter-national, interfaith, and civil war of Serbs, Muslims, and Croats met a brick wall of resistance; he saw it as a war in which all three sides committed many crimes and which could be stopped only by creating and recognizing a confederation of those three nations.

A year had to pass in order for the dominant world to accept this characterization, more or less, but unfortunately not drawing all the consequences therefrom. Certainly I do not want to exaggerate Ćosić's role here: the Western countries' unwillingness to sacrifice many soldiers in an effort to alter the military outcome was crucial; as was the fact that Muslims and Croats, until recently allies against the Serbs, turned their weapons against each other as they battled to draw borders between themselves as well.

If one seeks the real key to the West's lack of understanding about events in Croatia and Bosnia and Herzegovina (here we are not interested in a feigned misunderstanding which serves as a facade for naked interests), then Ćosić's idea of dis-history will be very instructive, since it is a phenomenon from which especially the developed world suffers. Namely, because of its drastic ignorance and misunderstanding about our history, the "international community" overlooked the fact that *underneath* the map of Tito's division of the SFRY into republics and autonomous provinces there lie other and deeper historical layers, faults, and potential borders. It became evident that this superior map was invisible to foreign politicians and their advisers, mainly lawyers (Badinter Commission!). They felt revulsion at the "archaic qualities" of our intellectuals who called their attention to such historical phenomena.

However, this was not a story about some dead past, but rather about the reality that one generation which experienced the "past" of World War II still lives. And naturally, we should also not forget their progeny, whose understandings, feelings, and struggles are powerfully affected by these traditions. What hints of the reality of present and potential relationships between the two peoples in

Croatia and the three in Bosnia and Herzegovina, could those feel who did not want to hear of World War II (to say nothing of earlier history), although they decided to act as arbiters, even to the point of imposing a solution?!

How can we understand any nation, to say nothing of anticipating its reaction in a *limit-situation* (in existentialist terminology), such as the tragic destruction of Yugoslavia, if we have not deeply probed its history: ethnogenesis, the feeling of continuity, the change of religion and church, mythology, partitions, migrations, state-building, victories and defeats in conflicts with other nations, the development of languages. . . . Inspired by Ćosić's idea of "dis-history," we could create the term *dis-nation*, as well as a whole family of similar derivatives.

Today it is trivial to assert that nations and their histories have erupted like volcanoes on our territory. The more this happened, the more relevant became Ćosić's critique of "dis-history" and anticipation, and now even a diagnosis, of the "eruption of residual national energies."

I speak self-critically as well: as a typical (in this respect) member of the *Yugoslav* Praxis group of philosophers and sociologists, *Yugoslav* both in composition and in orientation, it seemed to me until several years ago that Ćosić unduly emphasized the national problem and exaggerated his premonitions about the disintegration of Yugoslavia.

At the time communist officials harshly attacked Ćosić for his alleged archaic and provincial obsession with the national phenomenon. Since the collapse of the USSR, the SFRY, and Czechoslovakia, the most serious scholars in the world assert that there has arisen—and continues to gain strength—a *global* trend of multinational states fragmenting into nation-states. Is it Ćosić's critics or Ćosić who suffers from archaism and provincialism?

If one must mention here the harsher, in fact the harshest, attacks on him for alleged nationalism and chauvinism, then I will say that on various occasions Ćosić publicly challenged his accusers to point out a single sentence or act to prove their allegations, but no one accepted his "wager."

In trying to impose a unitarian-civil solution on Bosnia and Herzegovina—and that following Tudjman's fiasco with the Serbs in Croatia—the West obviously began with its *dis-historical and dis-national* matrix of "one citizen—one vote." It used the "*civil*" referendum of Muslims and Croats (which the Serbs boycotted because they had previously organized their *national* referendum) as an adequate legitimization for the separation and recognition of Bosnia and Herzegovina. By the way: the West did not seek a civil referendum of the population of the SFRY to find out whether they favored separation into independent national states, but rather, recognized the latter immediately. Ćosić has such things in mind, among others, when he criticizes the ideologization and instrumentalization of *civil* rights in international politics. Such an approach to Bosnia and Herzegovina, where the delicate balance of three national communities had been maintained with great difficulty, was an expression of pretentious irrelevance, but with tragic consequences.

All this is somewhat understandable in the case of the USA, given the nature of its formation as a state of immigrants, its territorial mixture of ethnic groups, and, in general, its "shallow" history. It was, however, cynically arrogant when coming from *national* states such as Germany, France, and Italy.

It is interesting that in this imposition of a unitary-civil state order in Bosnia and Herzegovina the West's liberal democratic "great story" found full support from the surviving domestic believers in the *actual* effectiveness of the communist-partisan "great story" of the Yugoslav "brotherhood and unity."

It is worth saying that with Ćosić and his advisers, Western politicians, diplomats, intellectuals, and journalists inquired about many things, but not about our national mentalities and the differences between them. I will add: the co-president of the Geneva conference, Vance, proved to be a rare exception, setting aside a considerable amount of time to listen to me talk about this subject.

Here, according to Ćosić, are some basic characteristics of Serbs that I tried to communicate to Vance: Due to an exaggerated sense of dignity and independence, frequently and tragically Serbs have not wanted to or have not known how to pull back from a disaster known as *hubris* (in the classical Greek tradition). They fall into it pretentiously and arrogantly defying fate, extending themselves beyond their available means, power, and limits—a defiance perhaps best expressed in Njegoš's dictum: "Let there be what cannot be!"

So then, what have been the prospects for success for those Western statesmen, politicians, and military men who, since the beginning of Yugoslavia's destruction, have been threatening the Serbs and even issuing ultimatums? If they had studied the behavior of Serbs in 1914, or 1941, or 1948, they would have known that they would get nothing from them by acting *in such a manner.* The same mistaken premise lies at the heart of the unjust, undifferentiated and collective sanctions against our country, for they serve only to homogenize Serbian resistance. Finally, by meddling directly and crudely in our election campaign, some official Western circles performed a disservice to Milan Panić and the opposition parties.

Ćosić would not be the person that he is, that is, critical of his own people as well, if he had not warned them about *hubris* as a temptation and a deathly danger. In this context it is beneficial to recall Ćosić's well-known metaphor about clocks: how much have Serbs suffered and died in history by refusing to align their political clock with the world clock!

Therefore he constantly calls to the attention of those Serbs using arms to defend their right to self-determination in Croatia and Bosnia and Herzegovina—and they are angry with him for this—that in the current international constellation it is unlikely that they can attain their ultimate goal: to join Serbia and the FR of Yugoslavia. According to Ćosić, in Bosnia and Herzegovina they should instead be satisfied to form some type of confederation with the Muslims and Croats, and in the former Yugoslav republic of Croatia be satisfied with the lengthy presence of UNPROFOR, postponement of a definitive solution through a referendum until a more appropriate time, and with as great a normalization of transportation, economic, and political relationships with the present-day Croatia as possible.

Speaking about the results of Ćosić's tenure, I must emphasize that with him, for the first time since its inception 75 years ago, Yugoslavia was led by an intellectual of exceptional caliber who attempted to make state policy inseparable from culture. How many leading foreign and domestic cultural figures engaged him in deep conversations and passed through Ćosić's office and home—and this continues after his removal from office!

By personal example as President, Ćosić attempted to put into practice a new moral, almost ascetic attitude and approach to state, political, and other public positions. Consequently he rejected the salary, residence, limousine, even coming to the Parliament building to take the oath of office in a taxi paid for by himself, and in the same way traveling home after removal and the transfer of responsibility. Such practice was not demagogic pettiness, but rather a calculated effort to establish a moral model, so necessary after Josip Broz's excessively extravagant lifestyle at state expense and even more necessary now during the enormous suffering of the people as a result of the war, sanctions, and a general social and economics collapse.

Despite this, and perhaps precisely because of it, Milošević's men could hardly wait for Ćosić's removal so that they could control (exceptional in the history of Yugoslavia, in its first, second, and third manifestations) the head of state's financial and other business matters to the smallest detail, obviously hoping to find a compromising detail. One can hope that the state organs will continue their "principled action" and "boldness," immediately carrying out financial and other inspections of Milošević's presidential office and making the costs public as they did with Ćosić.

It is a great pity that Ćosić did not want to use his position as head of state to inform the people decisively about his confrontation with Slobodan Milošević's regime and its policies. Why did he do this only after his removal? This *post festum* pronouncement had even less chance to reach the whole people via state television than it would have during Ćosić's Presidency. But an authority without power has no weapons at his disposal other than decisive and unambiguous statements to the public.

Ćosić gave only occasional hints to the public about political behind-the-scenes activities. And even this information reached only that part of the population which could follow the television stations not run by the state or the still smaller part which regularly read newspapers.

Here I will cite several conflicts, naturally not repeating information given in previous sections.

Milošević's SPS blocked numerous attempts by Ćosić to bring the republic constitutions and laws into conformity with the federal ones, not to mention his request to eliminate the ministries of foreign affairs and defense in the republics, or his request to eliminate the positions of Serbian and Montenegrin Presidents (what is one state to do with practically three heads of state!). The constitutional and legal deadlines for the republics to align their constitutions and laws with the federal ones have long since passed. And still, the leadership of one republic, Serbia, organized Ćosić's removal precisely because of alleged constitutional violations. It has turned out that Milošević is interested in the federal state only inasmuch as he can dominate it.

He and his collaborators also, wanted nothing to do with Ćosić's initiative to pass the Federal Constitutional Court, the Federal Supreme Court, the Federal Prosecutor's Office, as well as corresponding institutions in the republics, into the hands of the most competent and independent people, including those from the opposition parties.

The organs of the Serbian Ministry of Internal Affairs seized the building and its installations and took over the cadres of the federal police forces. Consequently, Ćosić publicly condemned the Serbian government for an attack on constitutional order.

Ćosić intervened to prevent the organized campaign disruption of Milošević's rival Milan Panić, carried out under the pretext of an insufficient registration period in Belgrade. Ćosić even had to suppress a threat to jail Panić after the election.

The state television of Serbia, even in its newscasts, is dominated by Milošević's ruling regime; Ćosić's attempts to eliminate such control were in vain. This television station systematically gave preference to Milošević, even over Ćosić—protests from the head of state's cabinet helped nothing, although this was a violation of state protocol, among other things.

Ćosić accused Milošević, more in state organs than publicly, of creating and equipping an excessively strong police force in Serbia (70,000 persons), as an armed force almost paralleling the FRY Army.

Last fall, based on the Ćosić-Tudjman agreement in Geneva, there was established an intergovernmental committee for normalizing relations between the FR Yugoslavia and Croatia. Milošević hindered this committee's work. On the other hand, on several occasions, especially after Ćosić's removal, he himself has met directly with Tudjman and conducted delicate political negotiations.

To wind up this list of instructive examples: Ćosić's intention of radically reorganizing the diplomatic and information-propaganda service was also squelched. According to this idea, the leading people in our diplomatic corps would be distinguished individuals who are not professional diplomats, but because of their reputations, knowledge, and connections in the respective countries would be more effective than professionals.

Neither could anything be done to change the philosophy of the information-propaganda services abroad. It was envisioned that the state organization of these services, which nobody trusts because of its official character, would be replaced by a *nongovernmental* cultural-information foundation, similar, say, to the British Council or the Goethe Institute.

Perhaps Ćosić's most serious failure in *educating and informing our people* was in connection with the international blockade and other sanctions against our country. It is true, he used every opportunity to do more than all our institutions put together to demonstrate to the world the injustice and counter-effectiveness of those measures. Even so, that the common people, hence the vast majority of the population, had no clue that there were no prospects for their revocation, nor even for lessening them, in the foreseeable future. The people saw even less how Milošević and his collaborators and propagandists were misleading them in this respect, and to a certain degree, even deceiving themselves.

People justifiably, but futilely, expected President Ćosić to demand of Milošević and his party publicly to tell them concretely and in a credible manner when and how they plan to effect at least a lessening of the blockade and sanctions. And if they were not in a position to do so, then they should resign and let others try to save the people and the country from social and economic collapse. Or, if they refused such actions, they would acutely demonstrate their selfishness and arrogance.

After all, last year (1992) Milošević had publicly stated that he would resign if he was a hindrance to the lifting of the blockade and sanctions. His supporters' mitigating assertion (otherwise correct) that the blockade and sanctions would not be eliminated based solely on Milošević's resignation makes no difference, since simply because one fact is not a *sufficient* (pre)condition for another does not mean that it is not one of the *necessary* conditions for it.

Neither is there sufficient justification for Ćosić not to make public several of his critical messages to Milošević in the three years following their initial meeting. One of the reasons for not making them public is Ćosić's strange conviction that morally he needed Milošević's consent. However, it is not clear that such an obligation exists, even when the issue is publication of Milošević's written responses, nor even Ćosić's diary entries on Milošević's reactions. Does Ćosić's extreme consideration in this instance not become a kind of moral masochism, especially since here one is dealing with a person who can in no way flatter himself with being considerate?

Let us recall Milošević's election campaign attack on Panić as a premier whose helmsmen were foreigners, and his somewhat milder insult of Ćosić, suggesting that only the future would show if he had a helmsman. In making these charges, Milošević hardly stopped to think that if they were true, he would emerge as inept and irresponsible since he had done everything possible to encourage both to accept the most important positions and responsibilities in the federal state.

I must conclude that to a certain degree Ćosić himself is responsible for continued circulation of misguided information about the "history" of his relationship to Milošević. While Ćosić maintains his principled silence, there are generated and disseminated the most fantastic and most malicious accusations. Those who engage in these activities, in the best case, can point to one or two of Ćosić's past moves. For example: it is true that at one time during the referendum in 1990, Ćosić publicly supported the new Serbian Constitution. He was motivated to do so because this Constitution codified the return of Kosovo and Vojvodina (practically separated autonomous provinces) to Serbian jurisdiction.

But, I would say, Ćosić at the time overlooked the Constitution's simultaneous legitimization of the exceptionally strong institution of the Serbian Presidency, which was known to have been devised for Milošević. When the federal Constitution was being written later, I must add, Milošević secured his own position by giving very limited power to the President of the FR of Yugoslavia who, after all, is not elected or removed by the people, but by the Parliament (under the decisive influence of Milošević's party).

But to return to the Serbian Constitution: it would surely have passed by referendum even if Ćosić had not lent it his moral and political authority, but for the people and for Ćosić it would have been better had he not de facto helped Milošević cement his autocratic power, with which he would soon strike President Ćosić as well. Here is still another irony of history: this happened to Ćosić, who wrote so much about how the outcome very often alienates itself from the intention of actors, especially political ones.

I hope that this has been an objective evaluation of Ćosić's Presidency. However, in life as in politics, an objective tally based on facts is often less important and influential than how people feel and experience and how they subjectively "enter" the results. Although they are catastrophically affected by the social and economic collapse, the masses will not remember that the sanctions were imposed before Ćosić became President; it is also of little importance to them that in the two months since Ćosić was removed we have gone from a downhill slide to a veritable plunge into an abyss; in these circumstances, who "cares" that during Ćosić's Presidency, in part due to his efforts, the danger of a military attack on our country was significantly lessened or that the picture of Serbs throughout the world became less negative.

With the calculation of a political balance sheet there exists, however, at least one more complication; it changes with the passage of time, not only because the evaluator changes, but also due to the appearance and accumulation of long-range consequences. What if in the light of events, say, in 1994–95, it is demonstrated that the statesman Ćosić of 1992–93 was more successful than it appeared in the initial short view?

What is the likelihood that those constantly irritated by his radical pessimistic sincerity, certainly best expressed in his public address on 6 January 1993, the Orthodox Christmas eve, are already now giving him the benefit of the doubt? They were surprised and even shocked by Ćosić's extremely unusual combination of pessimism and activism. They preferred listening to the ever-optimistic Milošević. How are they now reacting when, even in disaster, Milošević continues to promise the quick lifting of sanctions, renewed participation in the world community, economic renewal and development?

Ćosić's admirers ask themselves: Knowing that Milošević unquestionably holds all the decisive instruments of power, should Ćosić really have accepted the Presidency? Since I am among those who long and persistently had urged Ćosić to enter politics in this way, I certainly have no right to be "clever after the fact," even if I tried to do so. Besides, I firmly hold to my evaluation of Ćosić's achievements. One can only guess exactly how the situation would have developed were it not for the "experiment" with Ćosić (and Panić). Since I do not subscribe to the fantastic optimism of the type which says "the worse—the better," I cannot accept the assessment that Ćosić's work was not worth it and that it would have been better had he maintained a safe moral (?) distance while watching how everything goes to hell.

Ćosić himself (still in his official capacity, conversing with some foreign and domestic intellectuals), announced that the main mistake of "him and of his friends," he sees in the decision at the moment of institutionalizing political pluralism not to form a political party or movement. However, he overlooked the "extenuating circumstance" that at the time he was suffering from poor health resulting in three extremely risky operations in the next two years, with lengthy periods of recovery (he underwent a fourth operation during his Presidency).

At the end of this section there remains the question that dangles unanswered among friends and admirers of Ćosić: Did he, by entering the political arena "prematurely," irrevocably waste the chance to do more for the general good later? Certainly one can only speculate. For what it is worth, I have the feeling that the "story" of Ćosić's political role is not completely over. Therefore the final section of this text, which we now approach, will not be counted an epilogue, but a quasi-epilogue.

From Politics to Meta-Politics

Why did Milošević engineer the removal of Ćosić at the end of May 1993, rather than await his resignation, already planned for the anniversary of his election as President (June 15)? Would it not have better suited his purpose to have Ćosić remain with him to share responsibility for the impending collapse, even though he did not share power? These and similar questions are asked by many people, publicly and, even more so, privately. The outline of the following answer relies heavily on the knowledge of facts and events, and to a lesser degree on intuition.

With the constituting of the new federal Parliament in January 1993 the votes necessary for Ćosić's removal were assured, if and when Milošević decided on it: in the House of Citizens a majority (coalition of Socialists and Radicals) had been created by direct vote.

The only problem that could eventually arise would be in the House of Republics. But this problem was ameliorated by the election of several ultra-right radicals by the Montenegrin Parliament to their delegation in the House of Republics. Finally the stage was set when the socialist-radical voting machinery in the Serbian Parliament made it impossible for democratic opposition representatives to become part of the Serbian Parliament's delegation to that House. Such behavior expresses a typically undemocratic understanding of democracy, according to which decisions acquire a democratic character solely by virtue of a majority vote, even if some minority rights are violated in the process. Thus the democratic opposition in Serbia, otherwise represented in the House of Citizens in the federal Parliament, was unable to participate in shaping its House of Republics. We should not, however, forget why all this is important: to remove Ćosić, a majority in both Houses was necessary.

I must add that Momir Bulatović, the Montenegrin President, cooperated with Milošević in removing Ćosić—at least in that the representatives of his Democratic Socialist Party did not cast negative votes in the federal Parliament, which in the existing composition meant a de facto vote for Ćosić's removal. Indeed, from the very beginning of Ćosić's Presidency, Bulatović and some of his collaborators have been politically vexed by Ćosić's advocacy of eliminating significant *confederal* elements from the constitutional system of the FR of Yugoslavia.

Regarding the eventual "waiting" (two weeks) for Ćosić's resignation, in my opinion, Milošević thought he had more to gain by removal, especially since he must have known that Ćosić would turn to the people on the occasion of his withdrawal, informing them about those events and conflicts that as President he could not and did not wish to discuss. Now I am able to reveal that Ćosić's "Statement," given two days after his removal, was basically a text conceived earlier to address the public in connection with tendering an intended resignation.

The answer to the other question posed at the beginning of this section certainly becomes self-evident, since Ćosić did not intend to remain in the office of President beyond June 15.

This, then, is my interpretative reconstruction of Milošević's decision to remove Ćosić, which I see as one, albeit a key, element in Milošević's political course:

Despite Milošević's great ability to deny unpleasant reality, around the middle of May 1993 he at last saw that objective indicators pointed to an impending "free fall" of our economy and society. At about the same time he arrived at the conclusion that his strong advocacy of the Vance-Owen plan to divide Bosnia and Herzegovina into 10 provinces had cost him some support among his followers, and in return, besides a temporary improvement of his image, he had gained nothing abroad. Moreover, Milošević knew that there would be no lifting of the blockade and sanctions, made even harsher in April 1993—but he also knew that because of that, we were sliding into the abyss.

The fear of all this awakened in Milošević a fear of Ćosić. Already on several occasions Ćosić had harshly criticized the existence of a vast police force in Serbia. Milošević also began with the assumption that if and when chaos and disaster struck, the supreme commander of the Yugoslav Army could obtain decisive influence. He also feared Ćosić's influence on the choice of many generals soon to be retired. Formed in Tito's Communist Party, and remembering how Tito settled accounts with Ranković, Milošević was to proclaim his move against Ćosić a preventive measure to thwart his alleged intention to organize a military coup.

Milošević, then, decided to take complete control of *all* instruments of power and might, even those more potential than real. Thus, in his way of thinking, in advance he would definitively eliminate Ćosić's democratic alternative in the existing state hierarchy, which was additionally important at the moment when he and his regime were approaching the greatest possible danger. Thus the world, to say nothing of our people, would have to communicate and deal only with Milošević. It was definitively demonstrated that Milošević would not and did not know how to cooperate as an equal with anyone (not even with a Ćosić), but governs only with inviolable personal power.

However, monopolizing decision-making, influence and communication has the "tangential" effect of taking the full burden of responsibility on one's own shoulders. The question is only how great a price one must pay for it.

I have the impression that Milošević and his collaborators were still surprised, shocked and panicked by the speed and depth of the social and economic disaster that has been spreading with the power of natural catastrophe. As a university-trained person, Milošević is aware that only the feeling of powerlessness to take any serious actions is worse than the objective indicators of failure—and for now this feeling is irrepressibly passing from the regime to the entire population.

So before Milošević's eyes the *social-economic bloc* that had until recently supported him was collapsing—the reader can return to the third section. The realistic question is no longer how to regain that support eventually, but rather how to prevent that bloc from being transformed into one radically challenging Milošević and his regime.

However, misfortunes never come singly: the *national bloc* as well is rapidly dissipating due to approaching peace and a confederal political solution in Bosnia and Herzegovina. Because the Serbian national problem, initially focused on guaranteeing the survival and interests of the Serbs beyond the Drina River, is quickly transformed into concern for the survival and interests of Serbs in Serbia—threatened by a blockade, sanctions, and social and economic collapse—there hangs over Milošević the Damoclean sword of the transformation of that national bloc into a national bloc turned against him and his government.

Because of this geopolitical transfer of Serbian imperilment, the greatest moral-political dilemma can no longer be articulated in this way: *national-patriotic perseverance with Milošević at all costs or the betrayal of Serbian-ness.* The national and moral veneer for Milošević's regime has worn thin; it had been nurtured, in part, by the analogy to Serbian deontology in 1914 and 1941 ("Better the grave than to be a slave," and "Better war than a pact with Hitler"). And it has also been nurtured by the Serbian mythology of "God's people," which has been used as a powerful moral-political and even military tool for Serbs on the other side of the Drina River.

Besides, the Serbs, who are not only proud but also critical of their national tradition, are aware that in reality it often oscillates between two extremes: warrior-capitulator, hubris-slavery, dissident-Titoist. . . .

After all: "We are not a suicidal people," as President Dobrica Ćosić stated on different occasions. Because this is true, it is not surprising that beneath the dilemma described above, the following irrepressibly intrudes and shows itself: *saving the people and the state or saving Milošević's regime.* In the future as well Serbs will be proud of their historic sacrifices for the right cause and for the good side of humanity, but I do not believe that anyone can lead them so far that they literally sacrifice their survival.

Initially Milošević's regime experienced political success, but became entangled in aporias which have now developed into antinomies (A). I will present for the reader's perusal "only" nine such unavoidable and self-destructive contradictions:

A_1) In order to survive, Milošević's regime must effect a greater leveling—but simultaneously they will inalterably offend the most powerful and privileged groups, and most dangerously, their own supporters in the military, police, administration, economic, education, cultural, and medical . . . apparatus, who will also compete among themselves for ever scarcer resources. Still, if it avoids such a leveling process, the regime will not be in a position to stave off social revolt. Until recently, critics of the regime had warned about a social distribution of suffering and increasing social differentiation, but today poverty threatens to engulf as much as 90 percent of the population, so that the category "social differentiation" practically loses all meaning.

A_2) If the regime wants to halt the unheard-of superinflation that threatens to make all monetary transactions meaningless and impossible in the near future and bring about a total barter system (what will the poor city population barter?), then it will be forced to give up "maintaining" much of the population by printing money, and the people will rise up against it. The current panicky contrivances of the regime call to mind the image of a Chinese juggler who balances plates on reeds so that they turn, and at the very last moment succeeds in spinning the plates that have almost fallen. And so on, but not ad infinitum, because even in the circus this occurs only with an extremely limited number of plates.

A_3) In order to survive, the higher organs of government, and ultimately Milošević himself, will be forced to blame the collapse on their lower organs and cadres, first the local, then the higher ones—but these organs and cadres will increasingly resist the top echelons and their tactics. Thus, in a regime that needs unity more than ever, a deeper fissure will appear, until finally the top will remain narrow, naked and without support.

A4) In efforts to remove the foreign blockade and sanctions, Milošević's regime will be forced to make enormous concessions—and if it goes too far, its own supporters will topple him.

A5) The only parties that might support it at that moment will be some "opposition" ones, but only temporarily and for tactical reasons, so that they can remove it from power at the opportune time.

A6) If by some miracle the regime survives all these attacks from without and from within its own ranks—in spite of all the concessions to foreign powers it is prepared to make—it will have no guarantee that with the continuation of the blockade and sanctions it will not turn out to be totally used as an instrument, led about and humiliated by the West.

A7) The regime has at its disposal "war-communist" measures (a command-distributive statist economy, obligatory purchase and obligatory selling, repression in the noneconomic spheres as well, etc.). Only, to the degree this is done, it will "prove" even more the Western characterization (self-fulfilling) of its communist nature, causing the West to further increase pressure on it.

A8) If Milošević's regime seeks support from the anti-Yeltsin opposition in Russia, it will completely alienate Yeltsin's government, to say nothing of the West which would view such a policy as meddling in its global interests.

A9) As hope dims for some kind of *modus vivendi* with the decisive powers—then nothing remains for the regime but (self) deception in the hope that the surrounding countries, driven by the cost to themselves, will disobey the blockade and sanctions against the FRY. But if, miraculously, our neighbors would be so bold, then not even we would benefit greatly, because probably they themselves would be hit by the decisive powers.

At the end of these analyses, evaluations, and forecasts, it remains for us again to personify the entire problem, although one should not "charismatically" exaggerate Milošević's role and participation in comparison to other factors, circumstances, and agents. What has Milošević done to himself and what has happened to him—so that after a virtually triumphant beginning he winds up with a losing end move?

It was so glorious: landing with a helicopter from the "heavens" before a million Serbs massed at Kosovo Polje, the ovations of the immense crowds at the gathering at Usce in Belgrade; the workers, as if bewitched, follow his charismatic call—"And now, back to work!" . . . At that time, he most needed an honorable, sincere, and critical relationship with his collaborators, except that he did not seek it, and neither did they dare offer it to him. So the feeling of self-confidence, power, and strength grew to a fantastic degree in Milošević.

Personal *hubris* has pushed him relentlessly in this direction, but it began to produce ever more (self)destructive consequences when it lost the synchrony with the national *hubris*. At the edge of the abyss, our people stand horrified and stop.

To remind the reader (see the previous section): *hubris* is a pretentious and arrogant taunting of fate by overreaching one's own means, power, and limits. It is true, even some politicians more capable, self-critical, adaptable, cooperative, and more fortunate than Milošević would experience enormous difficulties with the heritage of an ossified and extravagant, debt-ridden Titoism, with the dissolution of Yugoslavia and its common market and economic territory, civil wars, to say nothing of the torments with a strict international blockade and sanctions.

If Broz's charisma was a model for Milošević, then he lacks in only one "minor detail"; in the meantime the bipolar structure of power has disappeared and, with it, the possibility of steering a middle course between two superpowers. Indeed, even Broz's charisma collapsed in less than 10 years after his death, primarily due to the fall of Yugocommunism as a social and state system—but still it had lasted for several decades. But Milošević's charisma, if this is not too strong a term, will not endure much longer than several years after it was generated in 1987 with the cry at Kosovo Polje: "No one dare beat the people!"

I conclude the writing of this text at a time when politics in the ordinary sense of the word obviously becomes less relevant, since our people find themselves at the very edge of the abyss. All signs indicate that the central place until recently occupied by politics will be taken by meta-politics: a practical concern for the *survival* of a people, society, and state as the *question above all questions*. Naturally, survival is the necessary prerequisite to make possible a meaningful engagement in politics as well.

Given these conditions, it is no surprise that people rapidly lose interest in political parties, their tensions and fights; or that the public reacted rather indifferently to the scandal of Ćosić's removal. Finally, it is no surprise that the public, not even the intellectual part, is no longer moved by discussions concerning the transition from postcommunism to democracy and from the statist to a private market economy.

Not only is the democratic-market evolution of our postcommunism completely and literally blocked, but there also exists the threat that with it an entire people, society, and state will fall. During this time the West, not considering the nature and cost of the consequences, tightens the noose as much as possible; in so doing it acts irresponsibly, as was the case with prematurely recognizing the breakaway parts of the former Yugoslavia.

For these reasons, we absolutely need a "party" of parties, a movement of movements having only one program: the survival of our people, society, and state. In this context I want to mention the church (as well), although I am not a believer: it avoids politics as much as possible, but as a meta-political institution it must sound the alarm and gather the people together. And if it is correct, as many people have said, that Ćosić neither wanted to be nor knew how to be a politician, perhaps it is equally true that only now his "story" as a meta-politician is beginning.

1–15 August 1993

* * *

Postscripts (I–IV): The Serbs under the Blockade of Serbia

One year after the December elections of 1992 new elections for the Parliament of Serbia were held. What was the reason for holding these premature elections?

At the end of May 1993 representatives of the Slobodan Milošević and Vojislav Šešelj parties in the federal Parliament of Yugoslavia (Serbia and Montenegro) removed from office the President of Yugoslavia, Dobrica Ćosić, who was elected a year earlier. This success encouraged Šešelj to put greater pressure on Milošević and his party; his immediate objective was to bring about some fundamental changes in the personnel of the general staff of the Yugoslav Army and the federal government which, like the government of the Republic of Serbia, depended on the tacit Parliamentary support of the Šešelj party.

An open and very sharp clash between Milošević and Šešelj occurred in September 1993 when the latter tried to topple the government of Serbia made up exclusively of Milošević's socialists. To prevent Šešelj from overturning the government, Milošević, as President of Serbia, disbanded the Parliament and announced that new elections would be held on 19 December 1993. He wanted to free himself from the Parliamentary dependence on Šešelj, who was only compromising him in the West, and also to win a majority in order to form a stable government and again demonstrate (particularly to the West) the legitimacy of his rule. The elections produced the following results:

Of the total of 250 seats in the Parliament of Serbia, the *Socialist Party of Serbia* (SPS), led by Milošević, received 123 seats—which means that it is 3 seats short to form a one-party government.

The *Serbian Renewal Movement* (SPO) of Vuk Drašković and several smaller parties of the center, jointly known as *Democratic Movement of Serbia* (DEPOS), received 45 seats.

The ultranationalistic *Serbian Radical Party* (SRS) of Vojislav Šešelj received 39 seats, which is half the seats it had prior to this election.

The Democratic Party (DS), led by Zoran Djindjić, won 29 seats.

The Democratic Party of Serbia (DSS), led by Vojislav Koštunica, won 7 seats.

The Democratic Alliance of Vojvodina Hungarians (DZVM), led by Anton Agošton, won 5 seats.

Finally, *two small Albanian parties* not disposed toward separation won 2 seats. (As before, all other Albanian political parties and groups boycotted the elections.)

Once again, many small parties and groups took part in the elections, so that the electorate was again faced with tens of lists. There was a special interest in the results of two such parties: *The Party of Serbian Unity* (SSJ) led by Željko Ražnjatović, and *The League of Communists—Movement for Yugoslavia* (SK-PJ), a candidate of which was also Mirjana Marković, the wife of Slobodan Milošević. The former (SSJ), together with Šešelj's party, forms the ultranationalist part of the political spectrum, while the latter (SK-PJ) represents the communist part of the spectrum. Although Ražnjatović invested a lot of money into a well organized mass campaign, he accomplished nothing: he failed to win even a single seat, thus loosing even his own seat he had until then. Parenthetically, the catastrophic defeat of Ražnjatović spoiled Milošević's calculations to acquire in Ražnjatović an obedient supporter since he could no longer count on Šešelj for cooperation in Parliament. As well, SK-PJ did not get a single seat—not even Mirjana Marković was elected.

Thanks to the electoral system used in Serbia—all parties which receive less than five percent of the votes cast gain no seats—Milošević's party won big. Another factor that made his victory possible was that most of the Albanians refused to participate in the elections and so enabled a very small number of voters in Kosovo to secure 21 seats for the party of Milošević.

Thus, with some 36 percent of votes received, the SPS obtained almost one-half of the total number of seats. Considering that only 62 percent of registered voters actually voted, as well as that practically all Milošević's supporters had again voted, there is a great disparity between the number of the SPS representatives elected and the support this party received from the people—even if we do not count the hundreds of thousands of Albanians who did not take part in the elections, but would have certainly voted against Milošević's party. In short, only 22.3 percent or slightly more than one-fifth of the total number of voters in Serbia voted for the SPS.

The SPS fared relatively badly in the electoral district of Belgrade. It won only 16 seats, while the opposition won the remaining seats: DEPOS—11, DS—8, SRS—7, and DSS—4. Nor was the SPS party much more successful in other important cities.

Milošević's party is still massively supported by state employees, peasants, and those who work in cities but live in nearby villages, so that the social-economic disaster caused by the international blockade does not nearly affect them as much as those city dwellers with no relatives in villages to help them.

We cannot understand the support SPS enjoys if we do not take into account also the concern of Serbs in Serbia for the Serbs west of the Drina River because their struggle for self-determination and statehood has not been brought to an end. Thus the SPS profited in this election also because the electorate in Serbia is in a certain sense (psychological-political-moral) "greater" than the formal one. A goodly part of Serbs also thinks that the SPS in power is the best guarantee that there shall be no eventual yielding to the separatist movement of Albanians in Kosovo and the international circles that support it.

Because they had burned themselves badly in the previous elections by disregarding the national-patriotic factor, this time the democratic opposition parties did their best to prevent Milošević and Šešelj from monopolizing the issue. The first to move in that direction was Koštunica a few months ago, and just prior to election also Vuk Drašković. Even Djindjić's election platform was subjected to corresponding changes, although his DS party in this respect had made smaller mistakes than the parties of the other two. We have to take these facts into consideration if we want to understand why the democratic opposition fared this time better than in the previous election and why Milošević's party managed to win over only one-half of the voters who turned their backs on Šešelj.

It is to be hoped that Western democratic circles will also learn the lesson from the (otherwise trivial) fact that our elections are won and lost in Serbia, and not in the United States, Great Britain, France, and particularly not in Germany. A policy that favors *anational* democrats rather than *national* democrats in Serbia has no chance of success. One must also pay strict attention to the Serbian mentality and its forceful feeling for national independence and national dignity. A policy that ignores this feeling helps only the *nationalistic-authoritarian* parties and leaders in Serbia.

The protagonists of such a policy will continue to wonder why the devastating sanctions do not produce the desired political changes. It is high time for the democratic West to replace its policy of blockade with an imaginative and constructive support of those circles in Serbia who are engaged not only in bringing about democratic and market changes but also in the preservation of national interests, sovereignty, and dignity. This is certainly in the interest of the democratic West, considering among other things that Serbia, that is to say, the Federal Republic of Yugoslavia, is still the strongest state on the territory of the former Yugoslavia, that its territory is crossed by the most important European waterway transversal (Rhein-Main-Danube), and that its road and railroad network ties western and northern Europe directly with the Near East.

At a time of justified concern in the West about the results of recent elections in Russia, it is worth noting that the electorate in Serbia has shown greater political maturity—Serbian "Zhirinovskis" (Šešelj and Ražnjatović) did not fare well, although the economic situation in Serbia is worse than in Russia.

Milošević may try to form a coalition government with the democratic opposition without making any substantive concessions. If they turn him down, he may try to form a minority government and then blame the opposition for its instability. Nor can one exclude the possibility that Milošević may try again to form a government to be headed by a prominent Serb from abroad. In any case, he faces one additional problem: due to the new composition of the Serbian Parliament, the composition of the House of the Republics in the federal Parliament will likewise be changed. It is a big question, however, whether this federal Parliament will be able to function or whether new elections for it will soon have to be scheduled.

Be that as it may, the democratic opposition now has the first opportunity to exact significant concessions, such as fundamental personnel changes in the state television now fully controlled by Milošević and a change in the election law that favors Milošević's party. These two changes could have the decisive role at the next elections. I already speak of the next elections because one can anticipate with considerable certainty a long period of political instability with frequent elections.

15 January 1994.

* * *

In mid-March 1994 there prevails in Serbia a deceptive monetary and postelectoral political stabilization. The national currency is consolidated temporarily and the hitherto empty shelves in the food stores and shops are filled with a variety of goods. The leading economists consider that this stabilization can last only about half a year at best but they are apparently not sufficiently counting on the positive results of the upcoming harvest.

And yet the creator of the monetary reform, Dragoslav Avramović, himself declared at the outset that ultimate success depends on whether the international economic blockade would be relaxed somewhat and whether international financial aid would be forthcoming. To judge by everything, this will not occur, at least not in the near future. In any case, one must distinguish between the chances for mere survival from realistic prospects for the rehabilitation and development of our economy. This will certainly not be possible as long as the blockade persists.

Even though it is temporary, this breathing spell is more than welcome to Slobodan Milošević's regime in saving itself from the social and political consequences of a real monetary and economic chaos like the one at the end of last year and at the beginning of this year.

In the midst of this chaos, Parliamentary elections were held in Serbia. As his Socialist Party did not succeed in winning a majority in

the Parliament of Serbia, Milošević was compelled to launch the idea
of forming a "government of national unity." But, encouraged by the
monetary stabilization as well as by Russia's engagement in matters
concerning the former Yugoslavia, he quickly decided he had no
need to make any significant concessions to the democratic opposition. In this way, he again manifested his inclination not to undertake anything that has to be done till the very last moment and even
after it.

The government of Serbia is now formed, but its premier and
principal ministers are formally or informally members and supporters of Milošević's Socialist Party, with the addition of several ministers from the circles of the League of Communists—Movement for
Yugoslavia on which Milošević's wife exerts a decisive influence,
and with a small democratic window-dressing by a handful of
members of the party called the "New Democracy," which was until
recently in opposition to the Socialist Party.

As a rule, the democratic opposition does not take part in the
government and did not vote for it. This also holds true for the
Serbian Radical Party, an extremely authoritarian, ultranationalist,
and extremely demagogic party led by Vojislav Šešelj. Although it
was considerably strengthened in numbers after the December elections last year, the democratic opposition is still disunited and mutually hostile. It is also somewhat confused by the momentary
monetary and political consolidation of the ruling regime. In a word,
it is incapable of being seen by the population as a realistic alternative to the Milošević regime. The intellectuals at the head of the opposition do not realize that they must give the electorate prior evidence of their cadre preparedness for it to assume power in all fields
and at all levels.

So long as the war lasts in Bosnia and Herzegovina, and as long
as there is no prospect in view for settling the problem of the Serbs
in the Serbian Republic Krajina as well, it is difficult to see how an
opposition with a patriotic and democratic platform (not to mention
an anational and antinational opposition) can seriously challenge
Milošević and his regime.

Of course, it does not follow that Milošević has real prospects of extricating himself from the basic antinomy in which he has found himself during the last two years. This means that in the *long term* he can hardly retain power if the international economic and political blockade persists and the West insists on it, so that the Serbs across the Drina River might, via Milošević, be cajoled or compelled to make huge territorial and political concessions. But if Milošević attempts to "sell" those Serbs, he will face the danger of experiencing the fate of a traitor of the nation and as such be toppled from power. It would indeed be an ultimate historical irony if the West managed to remove Milošević as a "Serbian traitor" when it has not succeed in doing so with the accusation of him being a "Serbian nationalist."

However it may be, we can safely forecast renewed coolness and even more acute relations between Milošević and the Serbs across the Drina, as was the case in May and June of last year. Milošević is now doing his utmost with the help of Milan Martić, President of the Serbian Republic Krajina (whom he imposed on the Krajina with much effort) to install Borislav Mikelić as the premier, and to prevent the election of the disobedient Milan Babić who, it appears, has the support of the Parliamentary majority.

As is his custom, Milošević is working simultaneously on several different political looms. It is in this light that one must view the current visit of his wife to Russia. In addition to a personal affirmation, her purpose is to investigate all the possibilities for cooperation with the Russian communist and nationalist circles, these being the rare foreign supporters of her husband's regime. Milošević is fully aware that the present official Russian support of the Serbian cause on the other side of the Drina River is fairly limited and conditional, as well as that Yeltsin is "interested" in his retaining power just as much as Milošević has been "interested" in Yeltsin's political survival.

15 March 1994

* * *

Since mid-March 1994, when the previous analysis was made, some important changes have taken place and should be understood and evaluated.

The major change is the widespread concern for the future of Avramović's program of monetary and economic stabilization. Even the largest banks have no liquidity, among other reasons because the large enterprises (usually state-owned or "socially" owned) are incapable of repaying the huge domestic loans they took a few months ago. For this reason, there are no funds that can be used to purchase the coming plentiful harvest at the guaranteed prices.

The population can no longer buy for dinars convertible foreign currency in the banks, which is resulting in the unofficial devaluation of the domestic currency on the black market. True, Avramović's program was drawn up on the assumption that soon the sanctions against our country would be reduced, but now it is increasingly clear that the likelihood of this happening is very slim. The tactics of Milošević's regime in such circumstances are for the Avramović measures to be kept alive as long as possible and to postpone massive lay-offs of workers to whom the state and "social" enterprises pay some semblance of wages although they are practically not producing anything. From time to time Milošević also fans the hope of the population that the sanctions will be lifted in the near future.

In the relations between the political parties the most important change is the definitive clash between Šešelj and Milošević. Šešelj has launched a huge verbal offensive, going so far as to publicly attack Milošević as the "biggest criminal in Europe." Employing the sharpest language, he also insults Milošević's wife, whose political and intellectual ambitions have in the meantime assumed international dimensions (travels to Russia and Bulgaria, which are covered dutifully by the Serbian state TV on prime time newscasts). In passing, let me say that her fingers are felt more and more also in cadre policies, even in our diplomatic service.

Several opposition-democratic Parliamentary parties have finally begun cooperating in the preparation of legislative initiatives, the most far-reaching ones dealing with the democratization of the state

TV management, changes in the electoral system, and more rapid privatization of the economy. The greatest weakness of the opposition remains its inability to bring forth from amongst its ranks a personality who could, in the eyes of the electorate and ordinary people be a convincing personal rival to Milošević. It is, in fact, a general impression that the Socialist Party of Serbia without Milošević would have incomparably less strength and would even disintegrate. On the other hand, the personal ambitions and jealousies of the party leaders in the democratic opposition make it impossible to find such a candidate among eminent personages outside of their own ranks. The same mistake is also being made by the democratic circles in the West, which would otherwise like to support progressive changes in Serbia and its reintegration into the international community. In this context, it must be reiterated that in competition with Milošević there are no prospects at all for the anationally and even less for the antinationally oriented personalities and political parties, but exclusively for those of a national-democratic provenance.

The recent criticism by Z. Djindjić (president of the Democratic Party) of the Federal state, and his demand for changes in the Constitution of the FR Yugoslavia for the purpose of eliminating the confederal elements in it, created a great stir, particularly in Montenegro. Djindjić is certainly correct in his assessment that Milošević does not want a strong federal state before he can centralize it under his own formal leadership and, pending that, that he will be satisfied with ruling it de facto as President of Serbia. Let me mention two of the most important objections to Djindjić's initiative. First: accent in his criticism should not have been placed on Montenegro, that is, on its leadership, when everyone knows that the biggest problem stems from Milošević and his regime in Serbia. And second: the time for raising this issue was badly chosen, since the fate of the Serbs west of the Drina is now being decided.

In this context, perhaps the most significant news during the past three months has been the quite open rift between Milošević and Karadžić's leadership in Bosnia and Herzegovina (the Serbian Republic). It is the general conviction (in official Western quarters as well) that Milošević is much more disposed to relent than Karadžić, because above all else he wants to perpetuate his rule and because he believes he can do so if the sanctions are lifted in exchange for decisive pressure on the Serbs across the Drina and for their agreement to large territorial and other political concessions. In any event, in the national sense as well, Milošević will soon be revealed for what he actually is and will no longer be able to make use of rumors to the effect that his compromise in April–May 1993 (the Vance-Owen plan) was only a clever ruse to trick the West.

15 June 1994

* * *

A large majority of Serbs believed up to August 1994 that Slobodan Milošević was an unrelenting fighter for the "unification of all Serbian lands." Even after he blockaded the Serbian Republic and indirectly also the Serbian Republic Krajina, many people sought consolation in the story of this being "another brilliant Milošević trick" for the purpose of protecting Serbian interests.

But the West itself has studiously observed Milošević, concluding that it was dealing with a political opportunist rather than an unrelenting protector of Serbian interests. Although in June–July 1992 he withdrew his promise (made to Milan Panić) that he would resign, the West decided to continue betting on Milošević's interest to stay in power at all cost. After all, it was already at the "Conference on Former Yugoslavia" at the end of August 1992 in London that those present became convinced of his readiness to make concessions, even much more so than some other members of the Yugoslav delegation. The West, however, has been mistaken, but only on one count: it has decided that Milošević wields sufficient power to force the leadership of the Serbian Republic to accede to the plan of the so-called Contact Group for Bosnia and Herzegovina.

We have seen that Milošević himself overestimated his strength and that in his anger he lost all sense of decorum in his campaign against the Karadžić leadership. However, all his accusations are now boomeranging because, without expressing any important reservations in public, he had long supported that leadership. This also holds true for Milošević's criticism according to which a minority of Serbs (those living in the Serbian Republic) has no right to adopt decisions that can strike a catastrophic blow at all Serbs. That, of course is true, but the truth also is that Milošević did not have the right to make a crucial about-face regarding national policy in a dictatorial way, especially as he is the President of a constituent republic and not of the Federal Republic of Yugoslavia as a whole.

How can Milošević now respond to the accusation that the policy of "We shall not bow down to foreigners," with which he won several elections, is implicitly reversed into "We shall kneel before the foreigners"? After all, his sanctions against the western Serbs are more merciless than the international sanctions against the Federal Republic of Yugoslavia. By blockading the western Serbs, Milošević has lost any *principled* ground for the rejection of blockades of whole nations, including his own.

I do not believe that Milošević decided on this measure in a deliberative way. It would seem that it was a rather panicky move: the West threatened even harsher sanctions and so he renounced the western Serbs in pure fright. He has received very little in return: a pilot lessening of those sanctions, which has more of a symbolic and psychological nature rather than any substantive benefits for the prospects of Milošević's regime retaining power—and all this has included the humiliating presence of the international monitors along the Drina River. Those people who are looking for the decisive reason for Milošević's rift with the Serbs in Bosnia and Herzegovina in an ideological disagreement, are mistaken. The fact that the Serbian Orthodox faithful, the monarchists, and adherents of radical privatization prevail amongst those Serbs would not in itself necessarily bring about a changed balance of forces at Milošević's expense, if there were to ensue a state unification of Serbia with them. This, of course, under the assumption that he would continue with his role of a relentless leader of all Serbs.

On the contrary, Milošević has become embroiled in new aporia and antinomies:

He had enjoyed great political benefits from his support of the western Serbs and now he has become, in a sense, a greater and not lesser prisoner of their destiny. If the western Serbs were to begin losing the war, Milošević would be exposed to increasing pressure from the ranks of his own Party, the army, and the police to assist them. However, if he assists them, the West would resort to even stricter sanctions. On the other hand, if those Serbs maintain the military *status quo*, the West will probably meet them half way, and then they would prevail in their conflict with Milošević.

The Serbs in the Federal Republic of Yugoslavia have stoically borne the international sanctions in order to help their brethren in hardship. But the question may be posed: is there a sense in further suffering of the Serbs in FR Yugoslavia after Milošević has imposed his sanctions on their brethren?! Despite Milošević's optimistic pronouncements, it is more and more obvious that there are no real prospects for the sanctions to be lifted in the near future, especially now that the Republican Party is in control of the US Congress. And in order to obtain any further easing of the sanctions, Milošević will be required to recognize both the borders of Bosnia and Herzegovina and Croatia. If he refuses, then he will no longer be useful to the West; if he agrees, the question will be asked why in the first place did he support the Serbs across the Drina in their war for state and territorial self-determination. Furthermore, even if there were to be a complete lifting of the sanctions in *less important fields*, this would not significantly improve the chances for survival of Milošević's regime. On the contrary, it would only serve to divert the victims of *such* sanctions from any further rallying around Milošević.

The West keeps open a list of preconditions for lifting the sanctions in order to force the regime to allow equal access of the democratic opposition to the state controlled mass media, to introduce changes in the organization and monitoring of the elections, and perhaps even to call new elections under strict international control.

Among the unremovable contradictions, Milošević is faced with yet another: the more he relies on Russia, the more merciless will be the West toward him. Yet, it is also certain that it is not in Yeltsin's interest to jeopardize his relations with the West and that his attitude toward Milošević is no less instrumental than Milošević's is toward him.

Some vital re-alignments within the political scene have taken place in the Federal Republic of Yugoslavia. One part of the democratic opposition has sharply disassociated itself from Milošević's new course and thereby considerably improved its chances in future elections. Another part offers Milošević its support but only on certain conditions and without relinquishing its ultimate goal to remove him from power. An even greater danger for Milošević is the growing rift between him and the Serbian Orthodox Church, which in times of national peril wields enormous influence on the Serbs.

Milošević has placed himself in an absurd position: he has abandoned the struggle for unification with the Serbs from across the Drina, while within Serbia itself he is keeping *by force* just as many separatistically oriented Albanians. If he accedes to their secessionist demands or even only grants them genuine autonomy in Kosovo, he will be confronted with an open conflict with the Serbs living in that region and other Serbs who support them. In that case, Milošević's political circle would be closed exactly where it began. What if the Serbs of Kosovo set out once again to Belgrade, this time demonstrating *against* Milošević? What if such an "antibureaucratic revolution" is joined by columns of Serbs from the Serbian Republic and the Serbian Republic Krajina? Would the police and the army resort to force to put down such an anti-Milošević movement, even after Milošević's 1987 declaration that "no one will dare beat the people?"

15 November 1994

Six

The Pseudomorphosis of
Communism in Serbia

Pseudomorphosis

Postcommunism is a mix of communism, precommunism, capitalism, nationalism, authoritarianism, and democracy. With regard to the extent of their break with communism, we can arrange postcommunist countries along a continuum. The transformation from communism to postcommunism in Serbia has three basic specific characteristics:

1) Yugo-communism both disintegrated and pulled the Yugoslav state down with it. The Milošević regime has been trying to survive in a highly unfavorable international environment and, having failed to integrate those territories in Croatia and Bosnia-Herzegovina where Serbs live, to keep under its control at least Serbia.

2) This regime has so far survived international isolation, sanctions, hyper-recession, hyper-unemployment, hyper-impoverishment.

3) In contrast to other former communist countries, communism in Serbia did not implode, rather it *transformed itself into postcom-*

219

munism. I call this *pseudomorphosis.* The expression actually stems from mineralogy and means the appearance of certain crystals *in the form of* other crystals. Oswald Spengler was the first to apply this term to social phenomena. In using it here, I want to suggest that communism in Serbia, for deceptive purposes, adopted a *democratic form.*

The initial institutional step in this self-"transformation" was accomplished in 1990 through the merging of the League of Communists of Serbia and its mass "transmission belt," the Socialist League of Working People of Serbia, into the Socialist Party of Serbia (SPS).

Upon allowing the multiparty system, Milošević's authoritarianism temporarily transformed itself into an authoritarianism in *proto-democratic form* (1991–92), but this form quickly began to change into a *democratic facade.* A similar type of regime is called "demokratura" ("nomenklatura" and "diktatura" disguised as "democracy").

By showcasing Dobrica Ćosić as President and Milan Panić as Prime Minister of the Federal Republic of Yugoslavia (FRY) in mid-1992, however, Milošević weakened his control considerably by placing that proto-democratic form in their hands. Rather than allowing their offices to be mere decorations for Milošević's self-rule, Ćosić and Panić tried to give their positions democratic substance and an anti-Milošević direction. Only after subsequently ousting both Ćosić and Panić was Milošević fully able to re-establish his autocracy.

Today, Milošević rules through a formally half-presidential regime, but it is in practice completely presidential. Moreover, he rules together with his wife, Mirjana Marković, who has united approximately 20 openly communist and procommunist groups in the Yugoslav United Left (JUL). It is now the case that the present constitutional President of the FRY and the Parliament and government of the FRY are virtually the personal "transmission belts" of Slobodan Milošević, although he is still formally only the President of Serbia.

More than four years after the adoption of the Federal Constitution, the Constitution of Serbia (and to a lesser extent of Montenegro) has not been adjusted to it. The President of Serbia, in violation of the Federal Constitution, retains even the power to introduce a state of emergency and lead the country into war. Milošević also conducts key negotiations and signs agreements with foreign countries even though these powers fall under the jurisdiction of the Federal Government. The subordinate position of the Federal Government has become so customary that it does not even consider it necessary to hand down a purely formal decision, albeit an unconstitutional one, to so empower Milošević.

It goes without saying that as long as Milošević autocratically controls the federal state, there can only exist a *pseudo*federation. It is true that the Montenegrin ruling regime is itself also at least partially responsible for this continuing situation. With its support more than three years ago, Dobrica Ćosić, political opponent of Milošević, was removed from the office of the Federal President. And recently the Montenegrin regime played a still more active role in Milošević's ousting of Dragoslav Avramović, Governor of the Yugoslav National Bank. A side note: the public mistakenly believes that Milošević turned against Avramović because he was ready to make concessions to the International Monetary Fund and the World Bank. Actually, what motivated Milošević was his desire to retain a personal monopoly on making all concessions to the West and thus getting all of the subsequent credit.

Milošević and his wife understood early on that communist "continuity and succession" must as well be provided for in the leading television, radio, and newspaper media existing in "postcommunism." It is in this way that they have made the opposition "invisible," "inaudible," and "unreadable" to a great part of the population. In addition to the SPS, the Yugoslav United Left (JUL) is so ever-present in the management and programs of the state-controlled mass-media that the uninformed might think it has a large number of representatives in Serbia's Parliament, even though it has not a single one. Consequently, it is not only the SPS but the JUL as well that are actually much more "equal" than either of the Parliamentary opposition parties.

Slobodan Milošević, his wife, and their propaganda apparatus do not even attempt to create any kind of systematic and lasting ideology, rather they are constantly improvising, borrowing from the left and right, and offering *ad hoc* explanations, justifications, excuses, and attacks.

With regard to ideological rationalization, a most symptomatic reversal has occurred. Erstwhile communists used to discount "bourgeois democracy" as merely *formal* and simultaneously proclaimed their own dictatorship as being a *substantively* democratic form of government. It is worthwhile to remember that Milovan Djilas, during the beginning of his falling-out with Tito, published in 1953 an essay, "The Form and Content," in which he maintained that the bourgeois democratic form had a substantive capacity and importance. It is exactly because Tito knew this very well that he never allowed this form to reappear. Unlike Tito, Slobodan Milošević decided to revive democratic forms for cryptocommunist purposes in the new international environment. He makes use of numerous inherited institutional and structural advantages (e.g. control of the state administration, police, military, courts, finances, information and communications systems, schools and universities, health services, pension funds, trade unions, cultural institutions, etc.), while he defines democracy as a merely formal procedure comprised of multiparty elections and the universal right to vote. In keeping with this stance, Mirjana Marković declares "equal rights" to be the highest value for the Left, even though the true Left has always called attention to the discrepancy between "equal rights" and "equal possibilities" for their usage. On the other hand, the opposition parties, even when radically anti-Marxist, still use the substantive view of equality and democracy in order to attack the ruling regime.

One of the Milošević-Marković regime's favorite slogans, aimed primarily at the West, is that there exists in Serbia "complete equality of all forms of ownership: state, social, and private." In actuality, the regime favors and props up "state" and "social" companies through all possible means. Under such conditions, however, one can adequately speak only of *pseudo-state* and *pseudo-social ownership*. The regime's terminology hides its monopolistic structural control over economy. This control spreads itself out also into the process of privatization. If capitalism must emerge, then let the regime's cadres be the ones to create and use it. They are carrying out a *political (statist) and criminal accumulation of private capital.* Among very influential members and leaders of the JUL, those that especially stand out are the communist capitalists. Not even Milovan Djilas or any other previous critic of the "class degeneration of communism" foresaw that the "new class" would transform itself in quite this way.

Let me here remind the reader that Milošević precipitously emerged from the circle of second-rate Titoist functionaries in 1987. During his populist phase, which lasted several years, he relied primarily upon two blocks: the *Serbian-national* and the *socio-economic* (sufficiently described and analyzed in the previous chapter). However, both these blocks have in the meantime eroded.

Milošević was unable to come to the March 1996 SPS Congress with convincing positive results. Instead he announced a program, "Serbia of the year 2000—a Step Toward the New Century." Skipping over the extreme difficulties of the present and upcoming years, and acting as if his program describes a secure future for Serbia, Milošević's Congress adopted a list of nice wishes (for example, the "prediction" that its GNP will double by the year 2000!) irrespective of the available domestic capacities and a very unfavorable international environment. This was a demonstration of an autistic utopia designed as a blend of "socialist realism" and information age technology. In order to make evident that the ruling party is just one of his "transmission belts"—and certainly less important than the police and military—Milošević made sure that the Congress lasted only one day and that there was absolutely no discussion, not even of a purely formal sort. The basic message of the Congress was that there existed no realistic alternative to Milošević's policies. This stopped just short of conveying the explicit conclusion that Milošević must therefore retain power for life!

If we use only available statistics on incomes, it is completely incomprehensible how the population survives through so much scarcity. In the search for an explanation we must first turn to the peasantry, who produce sufficient amounts of food not only for the people's needs but for export as well. Among other reasons, Titoism was, to a certain degree, economically viable because as early as the mid-50s it left private farmers alone to work the land without much interference. Yugoslavs have been fed up by those whom the communist ideology considered a remnant of an outmoded mode of production. Among them are a large number of "polutani," as the communist called them, who are situated one foot in the agricultural sector and the other in the city and industry (so called farmer-industrial workers). It was precisely this dual status, the fact that they retained sufficient property and income in the village, that opened the possibility for the industry in Serbia to reduce the huge excess work force without major social unrest. Milošević's regime, however, did not use this historic opportunity because it did not want to lose an important part of the electorate, those to whom it has continued to pay out pitiful wages for working very little or not coming to work at all. In spite of that, today both "polutani" and pure farmers are not satisfied. The policy of shifting the social costs of the incompetence of the regime and its international isolation toward private farmers is becoming less and less feasible.

In an attempt to satisfy, and at the same time deceive, the West, the possibilities for a great deal of privatization have been declared, but the decisions on this are left to the "state" and "social" companies themselves, which actually means to the regime cadres. Would Milošević and his wife actually be prepared to see the privatization process through if they concluded that it would give them the chance to be finally accepted by the West? And why not, particularly if the main implementers and beneficiaries of privatization are their own followers? This response, however, is complicated by a second look. Namely, with true privatization institutionally, politically, and legally guaranteed, Milošević-Marković's cadres would make themselves independent, especially if they concluded that external conditions for the survival of the regime were negligible. (Would the fear of possible re-examination and revision of privatization be enough to keep them loyal to the regime?) Moreover, radical privatization would *eo ipso* finish off the system of state (re)distribution on which rests the very survival of the regime, especially under international isolation.

Radical and Unscrupulous Opportunism

Dominant circles in the West had long considered Milošević to be a *radical and unscrupulous nationalist*. I have repeatedly and publicly contested this, convinced that he is, on the contrary, a *radical and unscrupulous opportunist* who has instrumentalized the Serbian question. In contrast to the Serbs led by Milošević, a former Titoist functionary, there exists Alija Izetbegović at the head of the Bosnian Muslims who was imprisoned under Tito for his nationalism. (The general phenomenon of nationalists-former prisoners in postcommunist politics deserves separate consideration.) Similarly, the President of Croatia, Franjo Tudjman, former communist general, also suffered under Tito because of his conversion from communism to nationalism. Here it is worthwhile also to mention the generational difference between these two and Slobodan Milošević. Unlike them, Milošević did not experience the Second World War and the domestic civil wars within it, and therefore did not pass war test.

Still, there is no reason to doubt that Milošević himself at first really believed that he was a fighter "without fault or fear" for all things Serbian. The problem is, however, that humans are, as a rule, not fully conscious of their own priorities before situations ("temptations") force them to make a clear choice (*prioritization*) between their proclaimed values and interests. When he finally found out that he *had* to choose between staying in power and supporting the struggle of Serbs in Croatia and Bosnia-Herzegovina, Milošević revealed to himself, all Serbs, and Western governments, the *real* Milošević.

This insight led to the extortionist "Holbrooking" of Milošević to introduce the blockade to the Serbs west of the Drina and Danube, accept the Croatian military liquidation of the Serbian Republic Krajina (SRK) and the expulsion of its Serbian population, and finally to the signing of the Dayton Agreement. The rest is Milošević's *rationalization* and *ideologization*, including his recent lecture to the

Serbs west of the Drina and Danube that they should constantly re-member the "generosity" and "solidarity" manifested toward them by Serbia.

However, those Serbs became far more dependent on Milošević than was dictated by the domestic and international conditions. It does no good for them to accuse only him now for their plight, in-stead of critically re-examining themselves and their leadership. The tragedy of the Serbs is also the consequence of big mistakes of their national policies and of their instrumentalization by Milošević. After all, those Serbs gave mass support to Milošević when his police used force against the opposition on 9 March 1991 in Belgrade as well as in all later political conflicts and elections. Further, how did they not notice that Milošević never visited even one refugee camp, one refugee family, not even one person wounded or disabled in the war! Serbian refugees from Croatia and Bosnia-Herzegovina were previously granted the right to vote in the FRY because they had supported Milošević, while currently their efforts to gain FRY citizenship, and consequently the right to vote, are being frustrated be-cause they are now against him. It is only belatedly that these refugees, as well as the Serbs who have stayed west of the Drina and Danube, have concluded that nothing good will ever befall them while Milošević's regime is still in power.

Neither Slobodan Milošević nor the leaders of the Serbian Republic Krajina (SRK) ever honestly explained to the Serbs that with the present international power configuration there was no real possibility for them to retain such a degree of politico-territorial separation which would incapacitate Croatia's functioning. They relinquished all chances of supporting pragmatic moves that would complicate the job of warmongering circles in Croatia and in the "international community." On top of this, internal conflicts among the leaders of the SRK were constantly facilitating and exacerbating their manipulation and domination by Milošević.

The liquidation of the SRK and the ethnic cleansing of Serbs from those long-standing settlements is to a great degree the result of the political and military support of international factors for the Croatian government. In his triumphalism, the President of Croatia,

Franjo Tudjman, has gone so far as to intend to move the remains of Ustashas and bury them in Jasenovac, in order to "set a historical injustice right" and bring about "civil reconciliation." To whom in the world would it occur to torture innocent Serbian, Jewish, and Gypsy victims of the Ustasha genocide by mingling them with their executioners, thus turning paradise into hell! It would be a radically nihilist underground dystopia (Jasenovac).

I do not believe it is possible to justify the position of some arrogant intellectuals in Serbia who have characterized as "manipulative necrophilia" the removal of the bones of Serbs from the karst caves (where the Ustashas threw the still-living bodies) and the Orthodox burial of the same half a century later on the eve of the civil war in SFR Yugoslavia. Cultured atheists, not to mention believers, cannot be so insensitive toward innocent victims. Finally, not a single descendent of those victims could agree with such intellectuals.

As far as the Serbs in Bosnia-Herzegovina are concerned, it should be pointed out that their leadership was provincially convinced that it could dictate a considerably more favorable outcome (than that given later on in Dayton) leaning on its war control of about 70 percent of the territory of Bosnia-Herzegovina. They were not sufficiently acquainted with the West which, out of its own internal-political and strategic reasons, was unwilling to recognize a larger territory (more than 49 percent) for the Serbs than that for the other two national groups taken jointly. Were the leadership of the Serbian Republic (SR) ready, timely and voluntarily, to cede (while not under NATO bombs) considerable territory for peace, it probably would have had the chance to continue directly negotiating with the West, but instead it was forced to surrender its fate into the hands of Milošević, who instrumentalized it, along with the territories and the Serbs living there. The impression one is left with is that the leadership of the SR squandered a lot of time in the vain expectation of political changes in Russia which would presumably be favorable to them.

Those Serbs would have left a much better impression on the world had they also showed much more war restraint and sorrow about the *fratricidal* character of the war. It was literally fratricide, not only because of the common South-Slavic origin of all three sides but also because the Serbs were fighting against a great number of descendants of the Serbs themselves (i.e. those converted to Islam and Catholicism). Instead of suggesting and practicing a convincing legal alternative, the Serbs had underestimated the strength and influence of the International War Crimes Tribunal for the Former Yugoslavia. But is it not in the interests, not even the historic interests, of the Serbs that the *real* perpetrators of such crimes on their side as well be punished?

And, as if the aforementioned mistakes in foreign and military policy were not enough, the SR leadership stubbornly imposed Pale, and not the large city of Banja Luka, as the capital, thereby alienating many Serb-Krajishniks. Furthermore, that leadership has continued the national sectarianism that reduces the body of Serbs to Christianity (and for that matter only Orthodoxy) and excludes Serbs of an Islamic religious background. Finally, this leadership has even attempted a narrow-minded recognition of only the ekavian (Eastern variant) dialect and Cyrillic script for the Serbian language excluding the ijekavian (Western variant) dialect and Latin letters.

In trying to complete this review and assessment of the results of Serbian, and particularly Milošević's nationality policies, I must return to the Serbian-Albanian conflict. This is even more relevant today because the debate has again flared up in Serbia with the speech of Aleksandar Despić, President of the Serbian Academy of Sciences and Arts, at their 1996 Annual Assembly—a speech in which one of two rational possibilities was designated as the political division of the Kosovo territory.

In this context it is important to keep in mind the following statement of Adem Demaci, the undisputed hero of Albanian separatism, who reminded the West of an otherwise "forgotten" fact. I quote from the daily, *Nasa Borba* (Belgrade, 13 March 1996):

> President of the Kosovo Council for Human Rights and Freedoms Adem Demaci stated that "the Albanians deserve greatest credit" for the disintegration of Yugoslavia. At the meeting on the occasion of the fifteenth anniversary of student demonstrations in Pristina, Demaci esti-

mated that events in 1981 were "the continuation of the
Albanian national movement from the Second World War"
and that they represented "national rebelliousness from
the heart of the nation."

Demaci is actually correct. The 1981 Albanian national movement in Kosovo, with massive and fairly violent demonstrations for
"Kosovo—Republic," was the first to question the so-called Brioni
Constitution of the Socialist FRY, adopted in 1974. And while we are
already on the subject of the sequence of events leading up to the
destruction of the state order established by this Constitution, we
must also be reminded that the Albanians immediately received
massive and open support for their demonstrations from Slovenia
and, somewhat later, from Croatia.

Does Demaci sufficiently take into account the Serbian reaction
when he proudly stresses the continuity of present Albanian separatism flowing from "the Second World War"? Demaci, doubtless,
knows that this euphemistic formulation cannot mask the reality of
the Italian Fascist, and later on the German Nazi, occupation of that
part of the Yugoslav state, massive Albanian collaboration with the
occupiers, as well as the expulsion of tens of thousands of Serbs.
The Serbian people also remember that this was not the first attempt
with the support of foreign soldiers to unite the Albanians to the
detriment of the Serbian people. There is great similarity between
Demaci's position and Tudjman's characterization of the Ustasha
(Nazi) Independent State of Croatia, which existed from 1941–45, as
(not only a criminal establishment, but also) an expression of the
historical aspirations of the Croatian people to create their own
state.

The Serbs let go their unique chance radically to *universalize* the
right of national self-determination at the beginning of the disintegration of Yugoslavia. Instead they continued insisting on the distinction between "constituent nations" and "national minorities." On
the contrary, it should have been proclaimed to the entire world that
the Serbs were not asking anything more for their co-nationals in

Bosnia-Herzegovina and Croatia than what they were prepared to grant Albanians in Kosovo.

The Serbs need to consider seriously the question of what is being hidden behind the "principled" stance of the West that Serbia has the right to retain all of Kosovo (as an autonomous province), which is over 80 percent Albanians. How can Serbia do so when it is obvious that what the Albanians want and seek is complete independence? What kind of future does the outside world intend for the Serbs if they have to continue using force to keep in such a large national minority? Some influential circles in the West tacitly even expect this of Serbia because, according to their calculations, to do otherwise would lead to the disintegration of Macedonia as well. As if the Serbs, that small nation, are more obligated to look after others than after themselves!

It seems to me that the Serbian initiators of the division of Kosovo will have to make their position as carefully nuanced as possible if they want to gain support from their own people. I would imagine they will explain that they have in mind a multiphase process over some years in which the degree of autonomy of the Albanian part of Kosovo would increase if some conditions are met. The level of autonomy would have to stay in proportion to the repayment of enormous funds that all of Serbia has invested in the development of Kosovo; dependent on evidence that the Albanian majority respects human, civil, and national rights as well as churches and other cultural monuments of all minority groups in this territory; parallel with the realization of state self-determination for the Serbs west of the Drina; and finally also under condition of an international guarantee for long-term demilitarization of that part of Kosovo after it becomes independent.

The problem is, without doubt, extremely difficult, but talks and negotiations need to get started in earnest. Albanians will not attend such talks without the participation of the West (read: their arbitrage), but also because they think that direct, unmediated contact with the Serb side would constitute a practical recognition of Serbian authority. Serbs, again, take a completely contrary stance. I will now repeat a suggestion that I aired (among other places) at the conference, "The European Balkan Wars: Lessons for the International Community," which the Ministry of Foreign Affairs of Great Britain organized in the Wilton Park House from 23–27 May 1994. Would it not be possible for the Albanian side to restate publicly that its ultimate goal is secession and that consent to participate in talks would not, under any circumstances, mean the recognition of Serbian jurisdiction; and for the Serbian side to emphasize that the only possibility that can be considered is the autonomy of Kosovo within Serbia and that the negotiations would *de facto* mean the recognition of Serbia's jurisdiction; and then for both sides to begin direct talks and negotiations? To be sure, in the first phase they would concentrate on the everyday life problems of the population. This would without doubt be a return to the initiative of the federal government of Dobrica Ćosić and Milan Panić launched in the fall of 1992. At that time three ministers of the federal government, Momčilo Grubać, Tibor Varadi and Ivan Ivić, tried to negotiate with the Albanians. Milan Panić even visited Kosovo and held talks with the Albanian separatist leadership. Unfortunately, the Albanian side rejected all of their offers.

Until recently, the Serbs in Kosovo swore by Slobodan Milošević, but now they openly claim that he is prepared to betray them as well. Recently they sent him a petition with over 40,000 signatures asking him to visit them. When they did not receive a reply, the local leaders held a meeting in the monastery of Gračanica on 22 June 1996. They pointed out that Milošević's ascent to the very pinnacle of power was initiated precisely in Kosovo on 24 April 1987, when he declared in front of television cameras to the battered Serbs, "No one has the right to beat you!" The group also recalled that Milošević's position in the leadership was sealed by a million of Serbs gathered at Gazimestan on 28 June 1989, to commemorate the 600th anniversary of the Battle of Kosovo.

As for the Albanians, they are still convinced that it is much better for them to count on the West's blackmailing Milošević than to help (through their participation in elections) the Serbian democratic opposition to come to power since it could not be blackmailed. Why are Western governments putting no real pressure on the Albanian side to vote in Serbian elections?

From Arrogant to Capitulatory Improvisations

Milošević's relationship with the West ranged from arrogant, through rush and panic, to capitulatory improvisations. The beginning of this process is best symbolized by Milošević's refusal to grant an audience to the American ambassador, Warren Zimmerman, and the end by complete retreat in and after Dayton. Now the charge against Milan Panić (and "nearly" also to Dobrica Ćosić) that there was someone directing Panić's actions from Washington is backfiring like a boomerang into Milošević's face.

I would like now to remind the reader of some of Milošević's actions only in his haughty phase, since the memories of his later phases are fresher:

He tried to save the League of Communists of Yugoslavia (LCY) while also establishing personal control over it when the Slovenian and Croatian delegates left the LCY at the last LCY Congress held in Belgrade on 20–22 January 1990. He also supported the so-called Party of Generals, the "League of Communists—Movement for Yugoslavia," founded on 19 November 1990 in Belgrade. Massive demonstrations against the regime held in Belgrade on 9 March 1991 were put down with police repression and army tanks.

Milošević's people did not hide their sympathy for the coup leaders against Gorbachëv in August 1991 in the Soviet Union.

Milošević just did not learn the lessons for foreign policy in time, not with the failure of the coup, nor from the fall of Gorbachëv and the rise of Yeltsin, nor even with the fall of communism in the USSR and of the USSR itself. Even until recently, he actively hoped to find in Russia (as well as in China) an effective counterbalance (something akin to Tito's "see-saw") to the United States and other democratic capitalist countries.

Many are quite impressed with the skill with which Milošević took and held onto power without it being noticed that he is essentially a provincial politician. To his dismay, it has been proved that the outside world bears absolutely no resemblance to the Eighth Meeting of the Central Committee of the League of Communists of Serbia in 1987, at which he attained the highest post in Serbia.

In his international policy he began with specific "nonaligned" steps, but it slipped his mind that Tito could afford "nonalignment," not because of his alleged genius but because of the balance of power between the two superpowers. In the present-day international power relations, however, the most successful foreign policy would consist of a change in the social system in Serbia.

However, even if Milošević were to make systemic changes now, it would still be hopelessly late because he has gained such a bad reputation in the US (and in the West in general) that no administration there would dare, even if it wanted to, definitively to accept him. His regime has no prospects for the future *primarily* for these reasons, and not because of the incompetence of his (diplomatic and) propaganda offices which recently have been "complemented" by a hired British PR firm.

Slobodan Milošević and his wife are intensifying the effort toward an international gathering of "the left" and thereby provoking the West even more. Of course, he realizes that the West is following all of this intently.

Their relationship is, naturally, one of *mutual utilization*; that of Milošević by the West as well as Milošević's use of the West. He still has not lost hope that, through maneuvering and stalling, he will in the end win over the "West" finally to accept him for good.

True, at the same time Milošević is preparing himself for the opposite scenario as well. I have described such an idea in a public statement, part of which I repeat here:

> The fundamental reason for the state's takeover of NTV Studio B is Milošević's intention to establish a monopoly on the mass media now while he still has the support of the West. Since this support is purely instrumental and therefore temporary, Milošević is making every effort to prevent any serious challenge to his power once the West eventually turns against him again (*Nasa Borba*, Belgrade, 20 February 1996).

At that point he would be left with the only option of trying again with demagogic politics: "Serbia will not bow down to anyone!"

Milošević's regime is becoming more and more *self*-destructive. With his support for the policies of the "international community" against the Bosnian Serbs, he is practically creating the precedent for his own political elimination, if and when the West decides to use it. I am referring to obligations for creating equal opportunity for all participants in political contests, including access to the mass media; decisions made by the West concerning which parties and individuals are allowed to take part in elections and under what conditions; making voting possible for domestic citizens while residing permanently or temporarily in other countries; the international ban on undesirable leaders from holding public office and forcing them to withdraw from public life altogether; moral blackmail of those leaders, calling for them to step down voluntarily or threaten the further survival of the people and the state, etc.

The mass media of the regime, the only ones that reach the entire population of Serbia, systematically conceal unfavorable news from the country and disturbing reports from the outside world. This is done not only with the goal of manipulating the people but also because Milošević's aides know that he is, as has been the case for some time, psychologically incapable of fully facing reality. He has long since practically stopped communicating with the public, ceased explaining or justifying anything whatsoever, and has turned to relying exclusively on the argument of power.

According to Machiavelli, a ruler is supposed to combine the qualities of a lion and a fox. Why did so many Serbian intellectuals, even those with sufficient experience, believe for some years that Milošević truly was such a leader? Why did it take them so long to realize that the outside world was actually only dealing with a fox (and a frightened one at that)?

After all, Milošević was not even a reform communist but a conservative, career Titoist. Besides this, until the fall of 1987, he was noted for his strong opposition to "Serb nationalism" rather than a defender of Serb interests. It would have been difficult for him to reach the political peak of Serbia had his mentor Ivan Stambolić and the group of old communists in the background not made such a poor case for the Serbian question, and this restricted exclusively to Serbia (i.e., Kosovo and Vojvodina). They did not even notice that the main question in *Serbia* had become the *Serbian* question! In this way Milošević was given the chance to use it to arrive at the very top of power. Their attempts to place historical responsibility for Milošević's rise on others are in vain.

True, instead of being wary, if not actively opposed to Milošević, a majority of the Serbian people—and what is even worse, also of the intelligentsia—supported Milošević's institutionalization and legalization in Serbia's new (1990) Constitution of his formally semi-autocratic, but in practice completely autocratic, rule. And all this with the illusion that democratization can be postponed until there is a resolution of the Serbian question. A nation's elite should never take such a stance toward any politician, not even to one who has given sufficient proof of a democratic inclination, much less to one who has not.

Why is Milošević quite perplexed with what he is facing now, since he was "daring" enough personally to monopolize all decision-making (and therefore also bear full responsibility) about no more and no less than the size of the country, citizenship and borders, war and peace, emergency and nonemergency situations, relations with the outside world, and even for the trans-generational consequences of such policies?!

Lessons for the Democratic Opposition

For quite some time now it has been recognized that the force of Milošević's regime, as time moves on, springs more and more from the weakness of the democratic opposition. It would therefore be exceptionally important for the opposition to draw some lessons from its previous cardinal mistakes.

A good portion of the democratic opposition is attempting with great tardiness to complement its civic-oriented platform with a national one. How could they have overlooked that they were fighting for "civil society" and "civil democracy" in the country in which one nation (Serbs) forms nearly two-thirds of the population. Would any party, for example, in France, be able to hope for success if it did not present itself in the name of French interests? In Serbia, as both the Serbian and the civic state, if they want to be not only democratic but also successful, political parties must watch out for both *citizenism* (my term) as well as *nationalism*. This is also an important condition for attracting the support of democratically oriented Serbs in diaspora throughout the world.

As is well known, a characteristic tenet of the civic position is exemplified by the principle, "one citizen—one vote." Contrary to this, the national position stems from the collective rights of national groupings. Depending on the degree of radicalism, they span from minority rights, through various forms of political and territorial autonomy, and finally to separate statehood. Citizenism is the ideology and practice of domination of a nation (or coalition of nations) under the pretext of democracy understood simply as the "rule of the majority." It is wrong to believe that in a multinational state like the FR Yugoslavia, purely civic-oriented parties occupy the political center. In reality they occupy one end of the spectrum while the opposite is taken up by the national parties. Both the civic and the national standpoints pass over to the unacceptable extremes when they are deformed into citizenism and nationalism. It is only those who combine both of these principles that represent the true political center in a multinational country. So that I am not misunderstood, I must stress that any kind of coalition of civic-national and national-civic parties with nationalistic, much less with radical nationalistic parties, should be out of the question.

Those parties that insist only on the civic principle in state organization are in no position to support consistently the *collective* rights of nationalities and national minorities, not to mention the separatist pretensions of the overwhelming majority of Albanians in Kosovo. Because they supported citizenism (unitarism) in the secessionist Croatia and Bosnia-Herzegovina, such parties would now have to insist, if they wanted to be consistent, that the Albanians accept a purely civic (unitary) arrangement in Serbia!

We have been witness to a great many quarrels but not to many productive discussions between national and a-national democrats. In this regard we should ask ourselves why it is so difficult for so many Serbs, especially intellectuals, to acknowledge to themselves that the end of Yugoslavia is not an exception or mystery of history? Moreover, we should ask ourselves why many Serbs cannot reconcile themselves with the fact that the other peoples in Yugoslavia really did want to separate and form their own national states, and that the Serbs as a people were not able to dissuade them from this in any sort of democratic way. What is even worse, some Serbs blame their nation for the separatism of other nations in the former Yugoslavia. In this way they show their (inverted) national megalomania and hubris. In an arrogant settling of accounts with other Serbs over the causes and blame for the destruction of Yugoslavia, some Serbian intellectuals have been caught by a completely emotional and conceptual confusion.

A part of the opposition has been rhetorically resurrecting the old politico-ideological struggle of the "Chetniks" against "Partisans" during World War II, probably in the belief that its anticommunist credentials will thus be strengthened in the West. However, the generation that actually participated in that conflict is already dead or grown quite old. In addition, there is very little interest in the West in our conflicts from over half a century ago.

Primitive vengeful anticommunism causes enormous damage to the democratic opposition, if for no other reason than that a large majority of voters rightly do not see their whole lives under communism as a political and moral failure and complicity. For this reason a sharp difference should be made in criticism between powerful, privileged, and corrupt cadres of the regime on one hand, and the mass of adherents and voters on the other. The latter should be made aware that, even after a change in the regime, they would keep their jobs and positions—even more so, because many members of and voters for the SPS honestly, though mistakenly, believed that SPS was a substitute for social democracy and at the same time a major guarantor of Serb rights and interests. Nevertheless, further cooperation with those in power is not any longer humanly understandable, keeping in mind the national catastrophe they have brought about and the fact that there is now no serious risk in deserting them.

The democratic opposition needs to mobilize as many respected people as possible, but such people are often not members of parties. After all, neither do parties in the West rely only on their own cadres. The opposition must offer a concrete platform and people capable of running the country. That is why they should immediately form common committees for state administration, military, police, social welfare, culture, education, etc., drawn not only from their own members but also from unaffiliated people who are respected, knowledgeable, and experienced in those institutions and activities.

This would be one way to overcome the negative influence left from *antipolitics* as a dissident attitude that was formed under Titoism and post-Titoism. Disgusted with the communist politics, many intellectuals did not want to take part in the political competition for power even when political pluralism was institutionalized. Possibly the best illustration of this is the group of intellectuals that founded the Democratic Movement of Serbia—half-way between antipolitics and party engagement—who eventually withdrew, disappointed, back into antipolitics. With extremely widespread (anti)political reservations among the most respected intelligentsia, some second-rate intellectuals as well took advantage of the chance to take over important positions in party politics. The bad relations among the leaderships and parties of the democratic opposition have added fuel to the antipolitical disposition among intelligentsia and the public in general.

The democratic opposition must constantly stress that a democratic, pluralistic state, private property, and a market economy are not striven for because this is what the West demands, but because these are conditions that our people were already enjoying in the first half of this century and that we have no future without relying on this tradition. It should also be constantly stated that the opposition treats their contacts with the democratic-capitalist West as communication among equals, as with the representatives of the

Allied countries in the two World Wars, who hold a special place in the hearts and minds of the Serbian people. There should be not the slightest hesitation over the public disagreement with Western governments when their policies are unacceptable and not in accordance with democratic and humanistic traditions.

In an interview given to the weekly *Nedeljni Telegraf* (Belgrade, 14 August 1966) I said:

> Successfully to oppose Slobodan Milošević, and not only his party, the opposition needs leaders who will unite them. Unfortunately it cannot find such leaders among its own ranks, and because of its narcissism does nothing to find any outside. It is now letting slip an excellent opportunity with Dragoslav Avramović. Why would it not offer him the opportunity to form a shadow government of experts? In the case of Avramović, a good part of the opposition is continuing to adhere to its assessment that he "got what he deserved since he saved Slobodan Milošević's regime!" But that radicalism of "the worse, the better" type overlooks the great suffering of the people and even seeks to instrumentalize it. Avramović is no doubt much more popular than these critics among exactly those people who were hardest hit by the inflation and accompanying economic chaos almost three years ago. Moreover, Avramović would easily be able to counter with the assertion that the democratic opposition, by participating in the elections and in the Parliament, has objectively "served" the regime as a democratic facade. In addition, he could also invite them to imagine that the "experiment" with Ćosić and Panić and with himself later on, had not ever happened, and then honestly ask themselves if they would have been in those times capable of pushing Milošević's regime out.
>
> If they are not capable of uniting themselves against the ruling regime, our democratic parties will have to bear an enormous burden of political and moral responsibility. Should our people have to turn to mass demonstrations not only against the government but against the opposition as well?! But then perhaps some dictatorial regime would disperse both of these sides and manage to find a

modus vivendi with the West, to which democracy is often less important than capitalism and integration into its political and military strategy.

Fortunately, the main democratic opposition parties were able to create, at the beginning of September 1996, an election coalition under the name "Together" headed by Avramović. Although he resigned several days later, the parties have stayed together. Milošević beat them at the 3 November 1996 elections for the Federal Parliament but they defeated him badly in the municipal elections (all major cities in Serbia have fallen into their hands). However, Milošević has annulled their victory and thereby provoked mass demonstrations all over Serbia. They are not only continuing but growing in strength at the moment when I am finishing this manuscript. It seems to me that this historic movement is spelling the beginning of the end of the Milošević regime.

True, there is widespread fear of violence, collapse, and chaos. Many people still doubt that this "refolution" can be realized peacefully. They believe that even though Milošević did not come to power through violence but at a Meeting of the Central Committee of the LCS, he would most likely, because of his fears, defend himself with violence. Besides, too many people are still confused and paralyzed by the impression created by the state mass media in Serbia that the West has not only made a temporary deal with Slobodan Milošević but that it has definitively accepted him. I have always denied this. There is every indication now that Milošević has exhausted his usefulness to the West and that he is about to be discarded.

October–November 1996

Part Three

What Has Happened to Communism and Marxism?

Seven

Why Did Communist Statism Collapse?

The Nature of the System

For the past three decades I have been building up a theory of communist statism, defining it as a society in which a group (the statist class) exercises the monopolistic structural control over the *state* and *through it* over (whence the term "statism") other fields of social life—with the purported intention of laying the foundations for a classless and stateless society.

When in the early 60s I started giving serious thought to this problem, I immediately entertained doubts as to the justification of Marx's generalizations concerning his economic paradigm for the understanding of history. I then arrived at the conclusion that in the history of humankind there have been various primary sources of power. In capitalism, economy is indeed the principal source of power; whereas in some other societies, not only before capitalism but even parallel with it, this role is played by politics, that is, by the state.

Communists were not propelled to the position of rulers by economic power based on the development of production forces but rather by force and violence in the circumstances prevalent during the two world wars. Before assuming power, the communist revolutionaries were, economically speaking, nonentities. Communist statism belongs to the species of socio-*political* formations and capitalism to that of socio-*economic* ones.

The trend toward the establishment of statist systems has a long history not only in Europe but also in Asia, Africa, and Latin America. To my mind "statism" is a much more comprehensive concept than "the statist mode of production" (as Henry Lefebvre termed and researched it long after I did). Naturally, I am primarily interested in the communist type of statism in view of its specific character, which stems from the organization of the people who created it, from the way in which they did it and from the ideology they applied in justifying it, etc.

For my definition to accommodate noncommunist types of statism, it has to take into account goals other than the proclaimed communist intentions. A general definition of statism would then run as follows: statism is a society in which a group (the statist class) exercises the monopolistic structural control over the *state* and *through it* over the other fields of social life—with the purported intention of . . . .

As can be seen, in my opinion, "statism" is a much stronger notion than "state interventionism." There has been a good deal of that kind of interventionism in capitalism as well. However, in capitalism, especially if it is democratic, the bourgeoisie is not capable of attaining monopolistic structural control over the state and thereby over the other fields of social life.

In my foregoing book (III–7) I described and analyzed the structural room for reform of communist statism and criticized the overextended and pretentious theory of "communist totalitarianism." I set the top limit of communist statism as being *total, hyper-centralized, and detailed* structural control and its bottom limit as being *selective-strategic control*. I called the former statism *totalitarian* and the latter a *liberalized* one. Unless we apply this distinction, we shall not be able to understand the progressive changes *within* the system of some communist countries and especially in the Socialist Federal

Republic of Yugoslavia (the SFRY), in Poland, and in Hungary, which occurred much before the collapse of that system.

In order adequately to differentiate among the possibilities and modes of communist statism, I also spoke of *statism with a human face* and of *statism with an inhuman face*. I emphasized that from the humanist standpoint the difference between liberalized statism and democratic capitalism was incomparably smaller than the difference between liberalized statism and Stalinist statism.

I also pointed out that the humanization and liberalization of communist statism depends also greatly on the contingent historical factors, including great leaders such as Gorbachëv.

Finally, I underlined that even liberal statism was still far from a genuinely democratic state. Of course, when I suggested that the only possibility was a liberalized but not democratic statism, I did not wish to exclude the possibility of the democratization of some groups, organizations and institutions within the frame of statism, but only the ability to set up a real democratic state while at the same time preserving a statist system. The existence of such a state would presume the total elimination of monopolistic structural control over it and would thus no longer represent a statist system as I define it.

It should be acknowledged that totalitarian theory revealed the *economic* delusion proffered by a large section of leftists who have done their utmost to narrow down our basic choice to the dilemma: socialism or capitalism. In doing that, they removed from our view the dilemma: democracy or totalitarianism, and coupled with this the significant structural similarities between the Stalinist and Nazi regimes, the leftist and rightist totalitarianism.

Unfortunately, because it was applied to *all* the stages and forms of communism, totalitarian theory could not allow and still less explain the possibility and reality of its becoming liberalized. And even less, that communist statism with a human face could be the culmination of such a liberalization. However, such an overextended theory of totalitarianism became totally impotent only when the peaceful implosion of communist statism in Eastern Europe and in the USSR occurred.

In my view, the theoreticians of totalitarianism were guilty of pretentiousness when they wanted to encompass, along with Stalinism, the pre-Stalinist and post-Stalinist situations. The point is that "totalitarian control" cannot be graduated, that is to say, partial. And control by the statist class was really not total before the triumph of Stalinism in the intra-Bolshevik conflicts (not even during the "war communism," let alone during the "NEP" period). This control gradually decreased after Stalin's death and during the de-Stalinization phase in the USSR and in Eastern Europe.

To my mind, Maoism, Pol-Potism, and Kim-Il-Sungism are also obvious examples of totalitarian megamonopoly.

The conceptual strategy which in a single *extreme* attribute such as "totalitarianism" embraces pretty different stages and phenomena, is untenable. Does not the absurd question of how total is a specific "totalitarianism" indicate that this category is too rigid to cover adequately 70 years of the existence of communist statism, let alone to explain successfully its changes and variations?

On the opposite ideological side, a similar weakness has been manifested by the communist critics according to whom democratic and dictatorial capitalism are only formally different and not substantively so.

One would expect the experience and feeling of people who lived in communist statism to count for something in the assessment of the depth and significance of its changes over time and from country to country. I do not believe that those people who lived through the ordeal of Stalin's tyranny and then experienced the "perestroika" can agree with the opinion that under Gorbachëv the "totalitarian essence" of the system remained untouched. And what are we to say about Poland under Gierek, Hungary under Kadar and the SFR Yugoslavia under Tito? May a theory be so arrogant as to belittle the above-mentioned and other differences, some of which meant the difference between life and death for a huge number of people?

Let me make it quite clear: I do not criticize the formula of totalitarianism primarily for not leaving room for the implosion of communism and even less so for not foreseeing this implosion (I myself did not foresee it). I mainly find fault with that theory because it excluded the possibility of vital inner-systemic transformations.

Had the critics and dissidents in the 60s, 70s, and 80s deeply believed in the unchanged, totalitarian diagnosis of communism—they would have fallen into the darkest despair or have undertaken actions judged beforehand as hopeless or even suicidal. Incapable of harmonizing their rhetoric with the post-totalitarian reality and their own survival and actions in it, some of them continue retrospectively to speak about their struggle and suffering under "totalitarianism." After finally surrendering without firing a single shot, that kind of communism must have represented a very poor and strange sort of "totalitarianism" indeed!

The reader will now forgive me for a small excursion into literature. There is hardly an educated person who is not acquainted with a negative utopia such, for instance, as Orwell's *1984*. Only five years had elapsed since that fictional year in which, according to Orwell, totalitarianism was to triumph, when we experienced the implosion of communism in Eastern Europe, and two years later in the USSR. How is it that no one had a presentiment that a nearly positive utopia of 1989–1991 would happen! It may be that the experiences of our century of world wars, Nazism, Stalinism, genocide, life in the shadow of a nuclear apocalypse, and the like, were so distopian that even the people with the liveliest imaginations thought only of negative utopias. After all, what looked like a positive utopia has rapidly degenerated into the distopias of terrible civil wars on national and religious grounds on the territory of the former SFR Yugoslavia and the former USSR.

Beside the thesis on the unchangeable "totalitarian essence" of the communist *system* from its inception to its disintegration, its implosion also refutes the precept of the "iron-clad" totalitarian logic of Marxist-Leninist *ideology.* Could it be that two opposing "iron-logics," the totalitarian and the anti-totalitarian, were active in Marxism-Leninism? How is one to explain the conversion of many convinced communists into noncommunists, some of them even into anticommunists? How are we to tally the totalitarian thesis with the fact that the alleged "iron Stalinist logic" of Marxism-Leninism

proved to be even weaker than Gorbachëv's, since for the Stalinization of Marxism-Leninism it was necessary to carry out super-terrori-
zation, whereas Gorbachëv introduced subversive changes in it
without any violence?

Some adherents of the formula of totalitarianism even asserted
that the way to Stalin and Stalinism was *inevitably predetermined*
not only in Lenin and Leninism but in Marx and Marxism as well.
Obviously, it is no longer worthwhile to discuss this seriously and
therefore I do not intend to repeat my counter-arguments as
brought out in my previous book (III–3).

Just as the defenders of the totalitarian diagnosis, I, too, was astonished by the rapidity and depth of the changes in communist
countries. But my reasons for this were different. I had thought that
a longer period of liberalization would elapse between the erstwhile situation and the end of the system, because I judged that the
statist class would succeed in consolidating its selective-strategic
domination.

At any rate, even the Polish "Solidarity" at first only endeavored
to achieve some dimensions of an independent "civil society" without believing that it could eliminate the communist domination of
the state—consequently its strategists and theoreticians proclaimed a
"self-limiting revolution" and a "new evolutionism."

Which structural weaknesses are we to adduce if we want to
understand why the statist class did not succeed in consolidating at
least a selective-strategic domination?

Structural Weaknesses

The negative dialectic of communist statism was operative since its
inception but was not sufficiently visible until recently. And then the
internal tensions and contradictions, both latent and actual, became
so acute that they brought about results that led to totally opposite
consequences from those intended by the architects of that system.

Various classes, groups, and generations exerted tremendous
pressure on the holders of power. Usually there were mass as well
as nonviolent movements, which showed to what degree the popu-

lation in the communist countries had matured politically after having learned the lesson from earlier attempts to overthrow the ruling class by violent means.

In East Germany the population used an ingenious form of peaceful pressure and protest. This is how Berthold Brecht once ironically characterized totalitarianism: when the government's polices are bad—then it should replace its people with another. Under the considerably weakened post-totalitarian regime in East Germany, the people "voted with their feet" by fleeing from their country in increasing numbers.

Here are some key structural weaknesses of the statist class and the statist system:

1) In the communist countries, pressures from below expanded and deepened the existing divisions in the ruling class. That class comprised various groups: the politocracy, the technocracy, the functionaries of the administrative, military, police, and propaganda apparatuses, etc.

In accordance with the theory of totalitarianism, all these groups had to have the identical basic interests and to react in identical ways to pressures and crises. But in reality, a considerable section of the technocracy was more or less interested in economic reforms that would lead to decentralization and even to the partial independence of enterprises as well as to a market competitiveness among them. Generally speaking: within the ruling class there were various reformist and anti-reformist coalitions as well as coalitions between its groups and parts of the population.

2) The nucleus of the statist class consisted of *professional* politicians, functionaries, and administrators who through their careers were firmly linked to the "nomenklatura" system. This was long one of the principal factors making for the homogeneity of the ruling class.

However, when several years ago their self-co-optation began yielding its place to free elections, the professional politicians, functionaries, and administrators, in order to save their careers, began quickly leaving the communist party, joining the new parties, and even forming their own. How else can one explain the fact that some of these people began heading nationalist-separatist movements and parties, transforming themselves from a *"proletarian avant-garde"* into *"nationalistic avant-garde"*?

3) Although it was branched in the nationalities-territorial sense, the ruling class and party in the multinational communist states long operated as "democratic centralistic" entities. At that time they successfully controlled nationalities discord both in their own ranks and among the masses. But as soon as this class and party began breaking up along *nationalities-territorial lines*, this *in itself* called into question the integrity of these countries. As this involved the *state class* and the *state party* (that is, a *class state* and a *party state*) their disintegration was automatically transmitted to the state from them and back to them.

In contrast to the statist system, the capitalist state is not nearly so sensitive or vulnerable to a multinational composition and to inter-nationalities conflicts in bourgeois quarters because the bourgeoisie is a *non-state, economic class of a "civil society."*

4) Because there was no *market* or a *civil society as a trans-nationalities basis for the preservation of state integrity*, and the integrative force of the central authority increasingly weakened, the political pluralization assumed predominantly nationalities-territorial and even separatist forms and proportions in the USSR, the SFR Yugoslavia, and in the Czechoslovak Federal Republic. In all these three countries, the collapse of the former social system proceeded parallel with the disintegration of the state system.

I would like to recall some historical moments. The Bolsheviks exploited nationalities-separatist tendencies in order to topple the Czarist system and then also to terminate the temporary democratic regime in Russia in 1917. And when they gained power, they shattered with fire and sword the aspirations for separation from Russia and for the formation of independent national states. But in the long run, this did not prevent the disintegration of the state because, among other things, the Bolsheviks destroyed the small existing market and small "civil society" inherited from prerevolutionary Russia.

Stalinism eliminated the market and the "civil society" also in Eastern Europe after World War II.

The Soviet military intervention in Czechoslovakia in 1968 broke the communist reformist efforts that had tried to revive a market-oriented economy and some other aspects of a "civil society."

In the SFR Yugoslavia, with the deliberate forcing of "nationalities-republics' economy and statehood" during the 70s and 80s, the beginnings of a unified Yugoslav market and unified Yugoslav "civil society," set up during the 60s, were repressed.

Gorbachëv encouraged large-scale political liberalization in the USSR but in the absence of a market and a "civil society" as trans-nationalities factors of integration; he thereby opened the door mainly to nationalities-separatist organizations and actions, which he undoubtedly did not desire.

Naturally, and in capitalism as well, state unity considerably depends on the existence or nonexistence of the separate territorial concentration of nationalities. Along with territory, there is usually also the aspiration of national communities for political autonomy and later also for independent national states.

In the USA, the unified market and "civil society" successfully curb the tendency toward the territorialization of nationalities. The question, however, is: Will these factors in the future as well be sufficiently powerful to break up the growing territorial concentration of, say, the Latin American population in the south of the USA?

It is well known what consequences for Canada's integrity are to be found in the concentration of the French-speaking population in Quebec. When such a state as Canada, with a fully developed market, "civil society," capitalism, democracy, education, communications, integration in the world market, and openness to the world, finds it very hard to withstand ethnic disintegration—then it is no wonder that all the three above-mentioned communist federations fell apart.

5) The statist class enjoyed the following important but also deceptive advantage in comparison with the bourgeoisie: as it itself comprised the leadership of the state apparatus, this class did not, like the bourgeoisie, have to wage a struggle to influence the state

apparatus. It transpired however, that this was its great structural weakness: when it loses its hold on the state, then *as a class* it automatically loses it in other areas as well. The statist class is not capable of dominating society if it does not directly rule the state, while the capitalist class can dominate even though it does not rule the state. In my terminology, as stated in the previous book, the statists represent the ruling class and the capitalists only the dominant class.

The statist class *as a class* has nowhere to retire to from politics because the source of its entire power is in the monopolistic structural control over the state. The first structural line of defense of this system is also its last. The capitalist structure of power is incomparably more flexible. The capitalist defense is distributed in depth while the statist is shallow. The capitalists need not be personally represented in state institutions; with their economic power and, of late, with an ever-increasing globalized world market, they can set up effective barriers to anticapitalist politicians, functionaries, and administrators if these were to jeopardize the system.

In the final analysis, the bourgeoisie will defend itself by withdrawing its capital and taking it abroad. In contrast, the statist class as a class cannot find salvation abroad because it does not represent the class of the owners of the means of production. True, for the same reasons, *as a class* it cannot be punished by means of a so-called "expropriation of the expropriators."

6) I have written sufficiently (in book III–4) about how the statist power is structurally transparent while the capitalist power is structurally concealed. This is not true, a reader might protest, because capitalism allows for democratic public opinion and independent social science, whereas in communism everything relating to the state is held a secret. But, I did not deny *this*; I only asserted that the people in a statist country can very easily identify the group and institutions that rule the state and society. This, of course, does not mean that the people also know of concrete relations between the power-holders and the ways in which they function.

In capitalism domination over the state is indeed concealed, as the primary source of power does not reside in politics but in the background, in the economy. In contrast to this, political monopoly of power in all spheres constantly strikes the eye in statism. In capitalism, it is necessary first to penetrate through the legal-political sphere of equality to arrive at the crypto-inequality and crypto-dimension of domination. In communist statism, on the other hand, everyone knows that political rule is the main source of power and they also know where it is concentrated.

The *structural combination of the transparency and centralization of power* in statism, in contrast to its concealment and dispersion in capitalism, finally proved to be very vulnerable. The visible concentration of power formerly allowed for the mass mobilization and control over the population and, of late, it transformed itself into the *single target* of all criticisms, pressures, and attacks.

And in this context, here is one more specific feature of communist statism in the SFR Yugoslavia. After Tito's death, the statist class ruled in a completely decentralized manner, to such an extent that its Yugoslav center attempted to function on the principle of consensus among the representatives of all the federal units. That fragmentation of the ruling class brought in its wake a similar fragmentation among the critics, the dissidents, and the opposition. However, as soon as the general attack on the system began in the early 90s, that advantage turned into a weakness: the fragmented, mutually conflicting, and paralyzed ruling class suddenly found itself left to its own devices in each of the Yugoslav republics. Moreover, the statists in one republic did their best to ease matters for the non-communist and anticommunist opposition in the other republics.

7) The statist *class* as a rule grew out of, and acted within, the framework of the communist *party*. This made the following benefits available to it:

By means of the communist party, the statist class organized, mobilized, and controlled a significant section of the population. For example: 450,000 members of the "nomenklatura" stood at the head of about 17 million members of the Communist Party of the Soviet Union. The ruling communist parties usually constituted between five and 10 percent of the population.

The Party organization made it possible for the statists to conceal their class character. Due to the focus on the communist *party*, as well as on the mass redistribution of goods and services based on "state-social ownership," even many sharp critics of communism avoided describing its ruling group as a ruling *class*.

In the ramified system of "transmission belts" of the statist class, the communist party was the *central* "transmission belt." The ideologists of this class stressed that all the other organizations and institutions represented the "transmission belts" of the communist party, but parallel with this, they concealed the fact that the communist party occupied the same instrumental position vis-à-vis the statist class (namely, that "party within the party").

However, from the very outset there was a latent tension between the statist class and the communist party. The ruling class was organized and concealed in the form and image of the communist party, and this eventually became its structural headache once the party base, or more precisely one part of it, began alienating itself from the class-party hierarchy and freeing itself from its control.

It goes without saying that the communist party was much less homogeneous than the statist class. And since the communist parties were practically the only legal and legitimate political parties in the communist countries, it is quite logical that they should have become the first legal and legitimate framework for political fragmentation and pluralization. Whenever grave social crises occurred, the ruling communist parties exhibited the tendency to disintegrate. Several years ago they did disintegrate in Eastern Europe and in the USSR. Numerous new parties were even born out of them as from a matrix.

The Victorious "Capitalist Encirclement"

The global market economy dominated by capitalism, exerted a considerable structural pressure on the communist statism in Eastern Europe and in the USSR, compelling it to adapt itself to the world level of technological and economic progress.

E. Gellner rightly pointed to the spread of successful historical systems by way of conscious imitation. I quote:

> . . . once a new and visibly more powerful order is in exis-
> tence, it can be, and commonly is, consciously and delib-
> erately emulated. Those who emulate it may also end up
> with more than they intended and bargained for, but that
> is another story (*Plough, Sword and the Book*, University
> of Chicago Press, 1988, p. 20).

Naturally, the demonstration of the superiority of democratic capitalism over communist statism would not have been possible without the relevant information. But the West had already made the initial significant steps toward the creation of an international information and communications network under its preponderate influence, while communism created with its mass educational system an intelligentsia that broadly diffused information on the superiority of the democratic capitalist system. True, it is much easier to prevent the diffusion of information in the non-European communist countries, making this one of the reasons why communism in those countries is still ruling.

It may not be amiss at this point to recall the relevant historical context. The Bolsheviks spent much time trying to devise the ways and means within the Marxist concept for creating prospects for a "proletarian revolution" in Russia. As is well known, they tried to find a solution for this in the formula of a "permanent revolution," which they expected would first shatter Russia as the "weakest link" of world capitalism and imperialism. But even at that time they hoped a proletarian revolution would rapidly break out in the developed capitalist lands as well, which would in turn have a salutary effect on their own revolution in underdeveloped Czarist Russia.

When this did not happen, the Bolsheviks had recourse to the formula of "socialism in one single country" and endeavored to "reach and overtake" the most advanced capitalist countries by forced development in their own. Throughout that period they were in fear of "capitalist encirclement," but it never occurred to them that their system also in the future would remain inferior in the technological and economic fields.

Being aware of their inferiority, the Bolsheviks tried to insulate the USSR as much as possible from capitalist influences. During the "war communism" the internal market was even suspended in Russia. And when this caused economic collapse, Lenin decided to rehabilitate small private economic undertakings and a part of the market (NEP).

With his large-scale terrorism, Stalin eliminated the "NEP" and introduced superwar communism with a total antimarket "command economy." Following World War II, he launched the "theory" of the existence of two world markets, the capitalist and the socialist, in the attempt to compensate for the inferiority of the latter.

For a while it seemed that this autarchic communism had a future because it enabled accelerated economic development. Nonetheless, results continued to decline the more it became necessary to shift to an intensive, and more recently to a postindustrial, information system of development. Being a specific mix of premodernism (antimarket, antilegalism, and antidemocracy) and of modernism (industrialization, urbanization, mass education) communist statism had no adequate response to the postmodernist challenge.

Due to the permanent militarization of politics, the economy and other areas, the USSR had to allocate for military purposes a percentage of its national income incomparably larger than that of the USA or other capitalist countries. It may well be said that the social order in the USSR as well as in the whole of Eastern Europe from the beginning to its collapse was characterized by "war communism," which for the sake of military requirements squandered the best skills, most financial resources, the best developed technology, and the most advanced organization of work.

The ruling class must have experienced a real shock at the knowledge that the USSR lagged behind in many fields of civilian production, even behind a group of until recently underdeveloped countries in Asia.

Only one year after assuming the position of Secretary General, Gorbachëv at a meeting of the Central Committee of the Communist Party of the Soviet Union in May 1986, defined the problem in the following words: "We are encircled not by invincible armies but by superior economies" (quoted in the book by Duško Doder and Louise Branson, *Gorbachev: Heretic in Kremlin*, London: Penguin,

1990, p. 207). From this he drew the conclusion that there was only one single world market and that the communist countries had to integrate themselves into it. Subsequently, he began realizing that this was not possible if the statist economy failed to transform itself into a market economy.

Before Gorbachëv, the Soviet leadership had been accustomed to deluding the world about the development of the USSR to such an extent that it itself began believing that Potemkin-like picture. This was a specific amalgam of *self-vaunting* and *inferior communism*. Various ideological tales were invented to conceal an inferiority that was envious of the capitalist economy and "bourgeois democracy." I described and analyzed this "sour grapes" ideology in my previous books.

The inferiority of the Bolsheviks was already manifested in their obsession with "reaching and overtaking" the USA and other capitalist countries. The history of communism in power is replete with the efforts to make a mysterious "great leap forward."

The long-standing underestimating and aggressive Soviet rhetoric vis-à-vis the USA was a sign of weakness rather then strength. This is why I was astonished by the hysterical reaction in the USA to Khrushchëv's declaration: "We will survive you" as being an alleged threat meaning "We will bury you" (which in fact was an inaccurate simultaneous translation). The so-called Cuban crisis should rather have been understood as a thoughtless step by Khrushchëv's leadership in the "struggle for the recognition" of the USSR as a power equal in strength and rights with the USA and not as a measure to attain strategic superiority. Khrushchëv reckoned mistakenly that the USA in possessing nuclear rockets in Turkey would tolerate the introduction of similar rockets into Cuba.

The Decadence of Ideology

I understand ideology (III–4) as a set of ideas that social groups use *at the expense of truth*, to justify their own actions and to discredit those of their rivals, opponents, and enemies. With this definition I am, of course, postulating only the original and primary function of ideology. The examples of its derivative or secondary function would be: motivation or de-motivation, integration or disintegration, stabilization or destabilization.

An important role among potentially ideological ideas is played by ideals. This role is so important that we need a special concept for this dimension and phase of ideology. I have therefore coined the term *ideal-logy* (III–4). Before becoming reality, liberalism and democracy were ideal-logies. Communism likewise stepped onto the historical stage as an ideal-logy.

This initial, ideal-logical phase of communism I have called *socialist realism* by extending the application of this Soviet expression from the normative ideology of literature, art, and culture to the whole of ideology (III–6). In this phase, officials spoke of their policy as "the dictatorship of the proletariat in the transition period to communism." They justified all their omissions, mistakes, problems and crises as "inevitable" and "understandable" on the road to a communist future. Ultimately it was only important for their policy allegedly to *tend* to move in that direction.

That ideal-logy was markedly utopian. The communist party intelligentsia played the major role in its development and justification. But this utopia was nonetheless unable to withstand the ravages of time. The last major attempt to revive the communist utopia among the ruling communists in Europe[1] was made by Khrushchëv in the third Program of the Communist Party of the Soviet Union in 1961, in which he proclaimed that in the next 20 years the USSR would "reach and overtake" the USA and pass from the socialism of scarcity and the distribution according to work done, to a communism of abundance and distribution according to needs.

The end of ideal-logy of "socialist realism" is linked to the Soviet military intervention in Czechoslovakia in 1968. It became necessary to respond to the reformist project (termed "Socialism with a human face") of the communists in that country with more than only a military occupation. To this end, the term "real socialism" was ap-

---

1. Renewed utopian energy, combined with totalitarian terror, was used by Mao in the so-called Cultural Revolution, which I described in detail in Book II.

plied: contrary to the alleged fantasies of the communist reformers relating to some kind of different socialism, practice showed, as they alleged, that the only possible socialism was that which already existed in the USSR and in other of the Warsaw Pact countries.

"Real socialism" represents the second basic phase in the history of official communist ideology. Since it was imposed by military means, this answer to the program of "Socialism with a human face" was cynical. Critics of that ideology have also pointed to its tautology: a reality was being legitimized by being a reality. A third criticism of this ideology was that it was conservative: a status quo was proclaimed the supreme criterion.

I have written (in III–6) that the transition from "socialist realism" to "real socialism" was at the same time a transition from ideal-logy to real-logy. *Real-logy* is my term for the ideological phase in which justification is sought primarily in reality (of course, in the "reality" as purported to be seen by that ideological group) rather than in ideals.

In the real-logical phase of bourgeois ideology (so-called democratic elitism) something of democratic ideals is realized. Contrary to this, the communist ideal of a classless and stateless society had nothing in common with the reality of "real socialism."

It goes without saying that between the two mentioned communist ideological phases, there was no clear-cut boundary. People were still expected in "real socialism" to use the language of "socialist realism" at the proper times or at least to tolerate it tacitly. But they were no longer required to prove that they believed in its veracity. The communist authoritarians were satisfied with the control they exercised over the *public discourse*, whereas the previous communist totalitarians tried to control even the *beliefs* of people.

The official Soviet ideology, undoubtedly, could not be satisfied with the USSR being only one of the countries of "real socialism," so it declared the USSR as being the only land of "developed socialism." Thus, there was an international ("internationalistic"!) hierarchy of "real socialisms" headed by the USSR as the compulsory model for all the other socialist countries.

Had there been free discussion in the USSR at that time, the illogicalities of that ideology would immediately have come to the fore. If, for instance, the USSR had already entered the stadium of "developed socialism," how was it that in line with its own Marxist-Leninist design it had not yet passed into a classless and stateless order? Naturally, the ruling class had no wish to move in that direction. By the way, at the first Congress of the Soviet Communist Party held under the leadership of Gorbachëv, his report still utilized the formula of "Further development and perfection of developed socialism in the USSR." And here is another immanent ideological difficulty: if the USSR was a model of developed socialism, how was it that it still had to reach the developmental level of the USA?!

However, the main blow to ideologies is not struck by logic but by social practice. As soon as the future as a prime ideological prop ceded its place to the existing situation, the official policy had willy-nilly encouraged the people to judge it by the results achieved. The ruling class could no longer expect forgiveness by invoking the communist future.

Communist reality did indeed seem more and more unacceptable, especially in comparison with the rich and democratic capitalist West. In the literature, this has adequately been called the "comparative crisis" of communism. As the eastern part of the German people kept comparing their life with that of the other part in West Germany, it was natural that communism there should have been the first to collapse.

Gorbachëv rose to the top of the Soviet Communist Party at exactly the time that the "comparative crisis" became acute. His answer to this was the "*perestroika of socialism*" This was the third phase of the official communist ideology.

But in the second half of 1989, Gorbachëv radicalized his position to such an extent that we can freely speak of a *post-perestroika*. He did not call it that partly because he was not aware of such a high degree of radicalization and partly also because he did not want to alienate the dangerous communist conservatives. One can assume that he did know about the tendency of social groups to reject as truth anything new until it could be integrated within the body of hitherto truths with minimal shocks and maximum continuity (William James). After all, "perestroika" would not have become an effective ideology ("distorted consciousness") had it not concealed even from its own protagonists the degree of the radicality of social changes.

Taking as our starting point the attitude toward *social reality*, we have so far brought out the three stages of the official communist ideology: "socialist realism," "real socialism," and "perestroika of socialism." Of course it is possible to describe its path differently. We could, for instance, on the basis of the attitude to *truth* again differentiate three phases. Like other ideologies, communist ideology also originated as an amalgam of truths and falsehoods—which phase I termed (III-6) *distorted consciousness*. The next phase consisted of a *false consciousness*—which was thoroughly permeated by falsehoods but still there were enough communists who failed to see this. The final phase of ideological decadence was the *mendacious consciousness*. In the previous phase there had also been lies, but the communist ideology was at that time characterized more by self-delusion than by deliberate deception.

The expressions "distorted consciousness" and "false consciousness" I have borrowed directly from Marx. For him, however, they are synonymous, while for me they are designations of various ideological phases. I must add that Marx would not have spoken of "mendacious consciousness" in connection with ideology as he would have considered this as being an outdated approach of enlightenment. But for me likewise the "mendacious consciousness" does not belong to the nucleus of ideological phenomenon but only to its final, completely decadent phase.

The case with the "mendacious consciousness" cautions us that significant social conceptions from earlier times, such as the enlightenment, should rarely be proclaimed fully anachronistic. Their ideas can often be useful even today on condition that we free them from pretentious universality and give them limited meanings and functions.

Gorbachëv's "glasnost" policy worked against "distorted," "false," and especially "mendacious" consciousness. He offered the people an opportunity to speak publicly about the true nature of "real socialism" and to compare it with democratic capitalism as well as to fight for social changes.

The Loss of Legitimacy

I call the initial phase of communism "authoritarian-egalitarian." In my view (II–part 2) it had the following main characteristics: 1) centralized organization; 2) violence as the main means of gaining power and effecting radical changes; 3) collectivism; 4) egalitarianism; and 5) asceticism.

This phase came about mainly during the two world wars and in the civil wars. This *"war communism"* was functionally and morally well-suited to underdeveloped and undemocratic societies. Such conditions prompted the communists to be highly organized, disciplined, and self-sacrificing. For instance, in the 1920s the Bolsheviks prided themselves on their "revolutionary Sparta," which was intended to combine the virtues of soldiers and workers.

Many scholars compared this *initial communism* with early Christianity and even ranked it among forms of religiosity. However, in it the divine role was assumed by a perfect Future to which lives, their own and those of others, were sacrificed. To be sure, those erstwhile communists harbored no illusions about how they themselves would live to see a classless and stateless society, but they nevertheless believed that in some spiritual and moral way they would participate in it. This lent them some similarity with the Christian faith—except that in contrast to Christianity, this initial communism had no real metaphysical-transcendent mainstay, so it could not be successfully transmitted to several future generations.

When the communists rose to power they quickly lost the feeling of community with the people and among themselves. I purposely combined two incompatible concepts in the ideal-type category of *authoritarian-egalitarian* communism, in order to suggest how from the very outset it was undermined by fundamental con-traditions. That is to say that the rigid and violent hierarchy (the first two components) was not a fertile soil for the care and preservation of collectivism, egalitarianism, and asceticism (the remaining three components). It was only a question of time when those who were politically "more equal" than the other communists and people would begin creating material privileges as well, for themselves, their families, relatives, friends, and adherents. In so doing they tried to conceal the privileges as much as possible while excluding the critics from their ranks as "demagogues" and "petty bourgeois levelers."

The communist rulers who, in societies where great shortages prevailed, satisfied their own interests, became more and more hypocritical in requiring others to sacrifice "subjective" interests for the sake of "common," "objective," "historical" interests. Of course, the greater the abyss between their words and deeds, the more those rulers took to lying, moralizing, and preaching in the name of collectivism, egalitarianism, and asceticism.

From a quasi-religion, communism transformed itself into ideological and political kitsch as well. However, I shall leave discussing the general topic of kitsch as an imposed spiritual *uravnilovka* and the special topic of socialist kitsch degradation of communist symbols, heroes, and martyrs, for another occasion. Here I shall only use as an illustration the novel *Mother* by Maxim Gorky, which served as an official model of "socialist realism." The privileged rulers kept pointing to the fictional personages in this novel as models of self-sacrifice to the naïve and impoverished Komsomol members.

There is not a single serious researcher who has not emphasized the communist successes in industrialization and urbanization as major factors of their legitimacy. It seemed to many at that time that the USSR would rapidly "reach and overtake" even the USA. With their launching of the Sputnik the communist rulers began exploiting the impression of their predominance in the technological and scientific revolution, for the purpose of legitimizing their monopoly power. But they soon lost the race with the USA in sending an expedition to the Moon. It became evident that the *communist dictatorship over needs* (phrase coined by A. Heller and F. Feher) in the scientific and technological field as well were incurably inferior to the *capitalist democracies that were meeting needs.*

It is in *social*-dictatorship that one must look for the most persistent source of the legitimacy of communism. Many people have written about the tacit "agreement" whereby the citizenry were given, in exchange for toleration of the rulers' monopoly, lifetime employment, free health services and social protection, free schooling, cheap housing, highly subsidized culture. However, with the decline in the communist ability to keep step with the scientific, technological, and economic aspects of the West, the level of state guarantees for a living standard relatively decreased. And so in this area as well, the lagging behind of communism vis-à-vis the *social-democratic* capitalist countries and the *social-Christianized* ones, became more and more a thorn in the side of the people.

Because of their role during the second world war, the communists had a kind of patriotic legitimacy in the USSR and in the SFR Yugoslavia, and to a certain extent also in Albania.

True, the link between Soviet legitimacy and the mass cult of wartime victims became fairly loosened when the people learned also from official places that it was precisely through Stalin's fault and the fault of Stalinism that the USSR was unprepared for Hitler's attack.

All Soviet leaders prior to Gorbachëv believed that it was the Soviet victory in World War II that gave them every right to rule Eastern Europe. Zdenek Mlynar describes in this way how Brezhnev lectured Dubchek and the other confined Czechoslovakian leaders in August 1968:

> Then Brezhnev explained to Dubchek that the end result of all this was Moscow's realization that the Dubchek leadership could not be depended upon. . . . Because, at this stage, matters of the utmost importance were involved: the results of the Second World War.
>
> Brezhnev spoke at length about the sacrifices of the Soviet Union in the Second World War: the soldiers fallen in battle, the civilians slaughtered, the enormous material losses, the hardship suffered by the Soviet people. At such

a cost, the Soviet Union had gained security, and the guarantee of that security was the postwar division of Europe and, specifically, the fact that Czechoslovakia was linked with the Soviet Union, "forever." According to Brezhnev, this was a logical and justifiable result of the fact that thousands of Soviet soldiers sacrificed their lives for Czechoslovak freedom as well and Czechs and Slovaks should therefore honor their graves, not defile them. Our western borders were not only our own borders, but the common borders of the "socialist camp." The Soviet polit-buro had no right to allow the results of that war to be jeopardized, for it had no right to dishonor the sacrifices of the Soviet people (Zdenek Mlynar, *Nightfrost in Prague*, Karz Publishers, New York, 1980, p. 239).

Another powerful source of legitimacy was the pride of the Soviet people (of the Russians incomparably more than of the others) of the USSR becoming a superpower.

Titoism enjoyed the longest and the strongest legitimacy by dint of its avant-garde role in the liberation of the country from the occupying forces, as well as in the recreation of Yugoslavia in 1945 and also in establishing and preserving its independence from Stalin.

The Albanian communists also legitimized themselves by using the liberation struggle during the second world war.

However, in the USSR, in the SFR Yugoslavia, and in Albania, the patriotic merits of the communists relatively soon became the mere past in the eyes of the new generations, although they did see this past as worthy of their respect but not of their agreement to the continuation of communist rule without democratic testing and a democratic mandate.

Today it is more than clear that the assertions of the then authorities in the USSR, in the SFR Yugoslavia, and in the Czechoslovak Federal Republic that they had resolved the nationality issue were simply propaganda and at best naïve self-delusion. In all the three communist federations mentioned, there smoldered accusations, sometimes even openly expressed by the other nationalities, relating to the alleged domination of the Russians, the Serbs, and the Czechs, as well as the counter-accusations by the latter about the separatist ingratitude of those nationalities. We now know that the religious differences and animosities played a considerably deeper role in the nationalities identification and nationalities conflicts than could be supposed under the influence of the official atheist ideology. Political jokes can in this case also be very indicative. Here is a relevant one: "I know he is a communist and as such an atheist, but I just wonder whether he is an Orthodox, a Roman Catholic, or a Muslim atheist."

Contrary to the USSR, the SFR Yugoslavia, and Albania, patriotism in the East European countries was a powerful factor affecting the *nonlegitimacy* of the rulers who were imposed and supported from the outside, particularly in the Roman Catholic and Protestant countries that identified the USSR with Orthodox Russia.

At the end of 1981 in Poland, General Jaruzelski tried tacitly to legitimize the state of emergency and other repressive measures against the Solidarity movement as a "lesser evil" in comparison with a possible Soviet military intervention. We do not know how convincing this was to the Poles. But we do assuredly know that this kind of justification came to naught as soon as Gorbachëv altered Soviet policy regarding the Warsaw Pact countries. In any event, if that "lesser evil" enjoyed any legitimacy at all, then it certainly was minimal, in fact, practically bordering on the lack of legitimacy.

Ceaucescu also successfully manipulated the Romanians' patriotic fear of the USSR but it is questionable whether even when facing the firing squad he realized that the phenomenon called Gorbachëv was responsible for his downfall.

We have come to the end of the section on the legitimacy and nonlegitimacy of communism. It should perhaps have been recalled at the outset that when communism ruled it never enjoyed the most crucial and the most enduring legitimacy that stems from democracy in the modern world. Democratic capitalism successfully exerted pressure on East European and Soviet communism among other ways also in the name of human and civil rights, which that communism had committed itself to in signing the Helsinki Charter in 1975. Judging by these circumstances, one of the explanations for the continuation of communism as the ruling power in other parts of the world must be sought in the fact that there is an absence of an *immanently* grounded foreign pressure on it.

The communist rulers in Eastern Europe and in the USSR, by the end of the 80s, had already lost their self-confidence. "Only" a catalyst or driving force rising from their ranks was lacking to have the communist system overthrown.

The Gorbachëv Factor

Zdenek Mlynar, Gorbachëv's friend during their studies at Moscow University and well-known communist reformer during Dubchek's "Prague Spring" in 1968, was asked a question by a newsman immediately after Gorbachëv was elected Secretary General of the Soviet Party. In answer to the question, Mlynar said: "As everyone else at that time, Gorbachëv was also a Stalinist. For someone to become a genuine reformist communist he had to be a true Stalinist (*L'Unità*, Rome, 9 April 1985)."

This was accurate enough but it is also true that the notion of a "true Stalinist" can be very deceptive. Gorbachëv both was and was not a "true Stalinist." He was that—if the *idealistic Stalinism* of his youth as well meets that criterion: just as the masses of Komsomol, Gorbachëv was charismatically "enamored" of Stalin, although he really knew very little about him. But it is much more important to know that Gorbachëv did not participate in the *criminal* aspect of Stalin's policies without which there could be no true, *real Stalinism*. I long ago introduced this distinction between the idealistic and realistic Stalinists, which I have further elaborated in the first chapter of this book.

It was precisely because he had committed no criminal acts that Gorbachëv dared to initiate the "glasnost" policy. The *struggle for a true history* became a powerful weapon of the communist reformers who had a clean past, in Eastern Europe, even before the advent of Gorbachëv in the USSR. It would not have been plausible to expect communist leaders with criminal records to support the idea of a true history of communism and even less to step down peacefully from their positions of power, which Gorbachëv subsequently did.

In the beginning, he was frequently compared with Khrushchëv. Nevertheless, despite Khrushchëv's anti-Stalinist merits, we must not forget that as a long-standing member of Stalin's Politburo he was a participant in the organization and implementation of mass state terrorism. Three years after Stalin's death, a decision was adopted under his leadership for the Soviet army to stifle the Hungarian revolution, and later, to execute Nagy and his closest collaborators. It was also during Khrushchëv's rule that the Berlin Wall was erected.

Mlynar confided to me in the summer of 1985 that Gorbachëv could become one of the greatest and perhaps most pleasant surprise of this century. This helped me immediately to assess Gorbachëv's potentials with more optimism than was felt by many others, even by the participants in a conference on this subject held in September 1985 in Washington, D.C. and organized by the Stanley Foundation (already mentioned in this book).

George Kennan, the well-known American historian and diplomat, admitted at the time the communist regimes fell in Eastern Europe in 1989 that there was no satisfactory explanation for the Gorbachëv phenomenon, and he metaphorically called it a "miracle." Still, one must clearly distinguish what is comprehensible about Gorbachëv from what even today is still an enigma.

He certainly was not the first idealist-Stalinist to develop into an anti-Stalinist and communist reformer. A good many such reformers, critics, and dissidents much before Gorbachëv stepped onto the historical stage from among the circle of idealistic Stalinists.

Nevertheless, it is not easy to understand how a man with such radical potentials could emerge to stand at the head of Soviet and international communism. It is even more difficult to explain how he managed in a mere six years to traverse the road from a moderate to a radical reformer and then to be the liquidator of communism. It will long remain unexplained how in that space of time Gorbachëv succeeded in remaining at the peak of the communist nomenklatura and then finally bringing about its demise.

True, in his climb to the top, Gorbachëv had a good deal of luck. In this climb he was helped by "unexpected events that often play a decisive role," as he himself stated. He had been a party functionary in a part of the country where the top leaders often spent their holidays. Naturally, had the conservative members of Brezhnev's Politburo who noticed him there, sensed that he was a potential reformer of communism, they certainly would not have elected him to the Central Committee of the Soviet Communist Party. It was something else about him that attracted the attention of the Soviet leadership: his intelligence, education, eloquence, decisiveness.

Gorbachëv's biography as a functionary sheds an interesting light on the topic of politics as a profession and mission. In order to survive and advance in the deeply conservative Soviet hierarchy, Gorbachëv acted as a *homo duplex* who conceals his real face, even a little from himself. He revealed his own and his society's reformist potential only gradually. He subordinated moral purity to the policy of concealment and compromise in order to win and consolidate his power, as a crucial prerequisite for social change. It is still necessary, however, to establish how he advanced so swiftly at a certain moment, reaching the very top of the party and state position and yet preserving elementary personal honesty and a progressive political orientation. His was a big gamble with history that could easily have ended in trivial hypocrisy, so characteristic of opportunists and career-seekers in politics.

Once Gorbachëv attained the highest political peak, however, it became easier to understand how he managed to consolidate and increase his authority. He had under his control the Secretariat of the Central Committee of the Soviet Communist Party, which prepared the meetings of the Politburo and proposed the cadre changes. From experience he knew that in this system "cadres are of decisive importance" (Stalin's maxim). With Khrushchëv's fall constantly before his eyes, Gorbachëv did not want to engage in any political adventures but rather prepared every decision in line with the relevant cadre changes and ensured it by enlisting the support of the majority in the changed Politburo and Central Committee. As Secretary General, he had the privilege of speaking with anyone about anything without the risk of being accused of "factionalism." This was his big advantage when assessing the intentions of other political actors as well as the relative strengths of the political forces.

Gorbachëv's source of power also resided in the traditional prestige of the position of Secretary General of the Party, in the eyes of the communists. At one time, Gorbachëv was also assisted by the fact that the conservatives were more inclined than the reformers and reactionaries to submit to the Party's considerations and discipline. When the great *historical mover* that Gorbachëv was, gained control over "their Party," the communist conservatives were at a loss as to what they should do and how to confront him in an organized way and with an eventual alternative leader, all the while complaining that they felt they were flying in an airplane that he had hijacked. This image precisely expressed their confusion, astonishment, and paralysis.

But it must be admitted that all I have mentioned so far explains Gorbachëv's survival at the head of the Soviet Communist Party and of the USSR only in the phase of its intra-systemic changes. Milan Kundera explained what happened in Czechoslovakia in the spring of 1968, in the following words:

> And suddenly these young, intelligent radicals had the strange feeling of having sent something into the world, a deed of their own making, which had taken on a life of its own, lost all resemblance to the original idea, and totally ignored the originators of the idea. So those young, intelligent radicals started shouting to their deed, calling back, scolding it, chasing it, hunting it down. If I were to write a novel about that generation of talented radical thinkers, I would call it *Stalking a Lost Deed*. . . .
>
> Historical events usually imitate one another without much talent, but in Czechoslovakia, as I see it, history staged an unprecedented experiment. Instead of the standard pattern of one group of people (a class, a nation) rising up against another, all the people (an entire generation) revolted against their own youth (*Book of Laughter and Forgetfulness*, Penguin Books, London, 1981, pp. 8–14).

However, what happened under Gorbachëv and his associates in Eastern Europe in the fall of 1989 and two years later in the USSR, was no longer "stalking a lost deed" so as to *de-alienate* it but rather to *liquidate* it.

Who could have assumed that a potential liquidator of communism was "concealed" in the conservative hierarchy of the Soviet Communist Party, not to speak of such a one becoming its leader? It was no small wonder that at the 1990 congress of the Soviet Party and after having "lost" Eastern Europe, Gorbachëv would succeed not only in retaining his position but even in radically changing the composition of the Party's Central Committee in his favor (of the 412 members only 59 of the previous members remained).

Had someone in the summer of 1989 contended that Gorbachëv would soon quietly accept the (self)negation of communism in Eastern Europe and even the unification of the two Germanies, he would certainly not have been considered serious. Frankly speaking, I, too, believed that the Soviet leadership would go on linking the geo-strategic interests of the USSR with some domination of the communist parties in the Warsaw Pact countries.

I shall here repeat my interpretation (published a long time ago) of what Gorbachëv then did. Approximately in the summer of 1989, he decided to cease allowing the political developments in Eastern Europe from running their own course. Realizing that his structural "perestroika" (in contrast to "glasnost") had reached an impasse and that he was dangerously threatened by the communist conservatives, Gorbachëv decided to do his utmost to confront them with an Eastern Europe that would also be in the hands of reformist communists, in case the conservatives tried to overthrow him. Incidentally, the communist conservatives were rightly more pessimistic than Gorbachëv in assessing the real chances for the consolidation of the system in Eastern Europe, if his radical reforms were allowed.

While visiting Eastern Germany in 1989 (to take part in its 40th anniversary celebration!) Gorbachëv cautioned Honecker that "life itself will punish those who delay the changes." Soon afterwards Honecker was toppled from power. It was enough for Gorbachëv to indicate that the USSR would no longer use force to salvage communist conservatism, for the communist rulers to begin collapsing throughout Eastern Europe. It is difficult to find a better example in history of *nondoing* that had the effect of decisive *doing*.

Of course, I thereby do not mean to suggest that Gorbachëv hoped for, let alone intended to bring about, the *downfall* of communism in Eastern Europe. It is more likely that he wanted to *reform it radically* so that the final result would be some kind of division of power between the communists and the noncommunists but still with communist domination. This would have been somehow the way events began to evolve in Poland in the first half of 1989. Gorbachëv's *decisive* role is to be found in his acceptance even of the ultimate unintended consequences of the anticommunist avalanche.

People are inclined to read back necessity into important historical phenomena and events. In order to avoid a *retroactive deterministic fallacy* (when something very important happens in history many people seem to think that it *had* to happen), it is best for us to make thought experiments. Therefore, let us imagine, for instance, that Chernyenko did not die so soon and that he consolidated the composition of the Politburo and the Party's Central Committee in line with his conservatism and choices, in a word, that Gorbachëv had not come up to head the USSR. This could easily have occurred since what happened was the result of a biological chance event. Would the USSR under such leadership have allowed the East European countries to set out on their own roads? The West could not have stopped a Chernyenko from intervening just as it could not hinder Khrushchëv in Hungary in 1956 or Brezhnev in Czechoslovakia in 1968. After all, even after Chernyenko's death it was by a happy circumstance, and a bit through manipulation, that a very narrow majority was scraped up in the Politburo for Gorbachëv's election to the post of Secretary General.

Let me make it quite clear: I do not contend that the communist system in Eastern Europe and in the USSR had the prospect of a long and bright future, but only that it did not have to collapse so rapidly and so ingloriously. Moreover, the economic situation in the USSR was better under Brezhnev, Andropov, and Chernyenko than under

Gorbachëv. A control test also speaks in favor of my thesis: although they are poorer, communism still prevails in some countries.

Even Gorbachëv himself at one time reached the conclusion that he should not exaggerate in tempting political fate. Were not the communist conservatives already sufficiently alarmed by the downfall of communism in Eastern Europe and the withdrawal of Soviet forces from Afghanistan, not to mention the unification of Germany, as Gorbachëv's "deathly sin"? The disintegration of the pseudo-federalism and redistribution of power had already begun in the USSR in favor of the constituent republics, which had opened their floodgates even to nationalism and separatism. Political pluralism was also being born. And as if all this were not enough, the liberal and democratic forces demanded that Gorbachëv should enable the rapid transition to a private and market economy, and this without paying a big social price. Nevertheless, if we are to isolate one danger for Gorbachëv from this merciless list, then it would undoubtedly be the collapse of the USSR as a state. Because he was a communist internationalist, Gorbachëv was totally unprepared for the separatist torrent.

Gorbachëv possessed a sufficient force to defend the state and social system, but he did not want to use it. Thus, for a second time, a decisive role was played by his *nondoing*, which was now even more fateful than that in Eastern Europe. The West would certainly not have been able to stop him had he acted differently, just as it was incapable of preventing Deng from preserving the communist political authoritarianism in China.

Gorbachëv's enormous power prompted the coup leaders in August 1991 to try to overthrow him in order to save the state and social order. But it was precisely that power that also fatally confused and paralyzed them. The action by the coup leaders only helped to accelerate the downfall of that system.

Prior to the coup, the liberal-democratic forces, domestic and foreign, exerted tremendous pressures on Gorbachëv to make him decide to transform the whole system. But he was willing to undertake further changes only to the extent that they should not alienate the conservatives with whom he surrounded himself more and more. It is well known that in a stalemate situation, the political game is usually lost by those who are the first to lose their nerve and the first to undertake radical moves. This was exactly what the organizers of the coup did. Of course, such moves fail if they are not carried out swiftly and ruthlessly. However, the organizers were not out-and-out brutal Stalinists but post-Stalinist conservatives without the guts to go from the demonstration of force to its massive and harsh application. I believe that the memory of Ceaucescu's end also contributed to their indecision.

The organizers of the coup also turned out to be great dilettantes, a typical feature of the Soviet apparatus that had been fairly widespread during the previous years. Let us recall the catastrophe in Chernobyl and the early official reactions to it. Being veritable political dilettantes, the putschists made a gross mistake in relying on Gorbachёv's lesser popularity at home than abroad. Still, this did not mean that they were more acceptable then he was. The coup leaders did not know how to exploit sufficiently the following eventual pretext publicly: As it is a question of a superpower possessing apocalyptic means, if the USSR disintegrates, a catastrophic danger will threaten the whole of humankind. They were, however, second- and third-rate communist apparatchiks unequal in terms of propaganda as well as to the tasks they had set themselves.

The President of the Russian Federation, Yeltsin, with his enterprising courage, played a *decisive* anti-putschist role. In doing so he invoked the Constitution under which the President of the USSR could be recalled only by the Congress of People's Deputies. All this, of course, would not have helped had Russia not had a decisive role in the USSR. How did the coup leaders envision seizing power into their own hands and consolidating it without thwarting Yeltsin and his associates?!

Nevertheless, however significant it may have been, Yeltsin's role became a "parasite" of the primary role that Gorbachёv had already played. In speaking of Gorbachёv I would not like the reader to gain the impression that I have made a *charismatic fallacy* so as to avoid a *deterministic fallacy*. Let us recall Weber's definition:

> The term "charisma" will be applied to a certain quality of
> an individual personality by virtue of which he is set apart
> from men and treated as endowed with supernatural, su-
> perhuman, or at least specifically exceptional powers or
> qualities. These are such as are not accessible to the ordi-
> nary person, but are regarded as of divine origin or as ex-
> emplary, and on the basis of them the individual con-
> cerned is treated as a leader (Max Weber, *The Theory of
> Social and Economic Organization*, The Free Press, New
> York, 1947, p. 358).

As I am not characterizing Gorbachëv in charismatic terms (and
even less in divine terms), I have first analyzed the structural-
systemic (internal and international), ideological, and legitimation
reasons for the fall of communist statism. It was only after all these
objective (pre)conditions accumulated that a Gorbachëv could, with
his doing and nondoing, play a decisive role. Only a *multicausal
explanation can be accepted, ranging from the structural-systemic
weaknesses of communism to the chance constellation of factors,
one of which was the appearance and role of Gorbachëv.*

Why was communism so fatefully dependent upon the action or
inaction of its leader? I have hinted at an answer to this question in
the section entitled "Structural Weaknesses" by pointing to the *vul-
nerability of the centralized and transparent political power as the
primary source and primary defense of the whole power of the ruling class.* Let us now apply this explicitly to Gorbachëv. It is a rule
that the careful guardians of such a system reach the top position.
But what if an *exception* occurs and this *power falls into the hands
of a radical reformer filled with humanist scruples?* The communist
statist system is much more easily exposed than a democratic-
capitalistic one to the mercies of such contingencies as ambition,
traits, viewpoints and the decisions of its leaders. After all, this vast
dependence of the social and state system on a leader was also typical of precommunist Russia. Thus, for example, the abdication of the
Czar in 1917 spurred the revolutionary avalanche that wiped out the
previous system.

Up to now, we have been discussing how Gorbachëv could rise in the Soviet hierarchy, reach its peak, and carry out vital changes. I prognosticate that in the future critical focus will increasingly be centered on his international *moralpolitik* in a world in which *realpolitik* dominates. What did Gorbachëv's USSR receive in return from the West for withdrawing the Soviet army from Eastern Europe, making possible the unification of Germany and the disbandment of the Warsaw bloc? Let us assume that Gorbachëv, in referring to the results of World War II and the Soviet strategic interests, had agreed only to a number of years of gradual unification of the two Germanies and conditioning it on the permanent presence of the Soviet army in the eastern part, as well as requiring huge financial compensation. Would such an offer have been rejected at the time when the re-unification of Germany seemed a pure utopia? It is certain that West Germany would not have been able to annex East Germany without Gorbachëv's concurrence.

It seems that Gorbachëv and his associates wanted *at all costs* to prove that the democratic humanist principles were more important to them than a policy of manipulation, maneuvering, hesitation, haggling. Perhaps the most radical aspect of Gorbachëv's "new thinking" was his giving explicit priority to *universal* human values over the class and other particular interests and values. One has still to investigate how great was the *humanist* Marxist (self)education of Gorbachëv and his associates and supporters. One question in passing: was the indecision of the coup leaders partly the result of the collective sense of guilt felt by the ruling class because of the unparalleled suffering imposed on their own people over seven decades? This, of course, would not explain their previous passive and even resigned observation of the collapse of communism *in Eastern Europe*.

It is evident that Western ruling quarters were themselves completely amazed by what they were "given" by Gorbachëv while giving him practically nothing in return. What would contemporary history be like had Gorbachëv acted differently?

Political activity should be evaluated primarily according to success or failure. In this context, for example, M. Merleau-Ponty wrote:

"We have never said that any policy which succeeds is good. We have said that in order to be good a policy must succeed" (*Humanism and Terror*, Boston: Beacon Press, 1969, p. xxxiv). Here is a good illustration of that point: "Metternich has succeeded by 1825 and failed by 1914; and writers disagree whether he had succeeded or failed by 1914" (Stanley Hoffman ed., *Contemporary Theory in International Relations*, Englewood Cliffs: Prentice-Hall, 1960, p. 36).

Gorbachëv is an exceptional historical leader. Such leaders as a rule give rise to enormous consequences as well, which they are unable to control or direct. As Max Weber says:

> The ancient Christians, too, knew very well that this world is ruled by demons, and that he who meddles with politics, who in other words makes use of the instruments of power and violence, concludes a pact with the infernal power. They knew too that for such a man's actions it is *not* the case that from good only good, from bad only bad can come, but that often the opposite holds true (*Politics as a Vocation*, quoted from W. G. Runciman ed., *Max Weber: Selection in Translation*, Cambridge: Cambridge University Press, 1978, p. 220).

The "ultimate" judgment about Gorbachëv will depend on whether the disintegration of the USSR will lead to democracy or to even worse dictatorship, to peace or wars among the newly created states, to the improvement or aggravation of the living standards of the people, to the replacement of a bipolar planetary power by more equitable power and a greater solidarity in international relations, or else to a worse world dictatorial order. Nevertheless, the main question is whether there will be a lesser or increased probability of apocalypse. It is not inconceivable that nuclear, chemical, and biological weapons might be used in inter-nationality and inter-state conflicts on the territory of the former USSR and even of their falling into the hands of terrorists. Compared with such dangers, the panicky migration of peoples in that area and from it to the rest of Europe and Asia, would even appear tolerable.

One thing, however, is certain, the positive and negative fascination with Gorbachëv and the debate about him will continue into the next century and perhaps even longer.

The Categories of Social Change

Because they assessed the weaknesses of their social and state system better than the communist reformers, the communist conservatives and reactionaries insisted that attacks on it should be cut short at the very outset. It was as though they had a premonition that the guardians of the system would one day relinquish their readiness and firmness to defend it with all their means.

True, state terror came under attack in the ranks of the ruling class beginning with Khrushchëv's condemnation of Stalin in 1956. And it is practically impossible to repeat a totally discredited past in a brief space of time. In addition, it would not have been at all simple to commit mass killings in the name of "socialism," which could only legitimize itself by insisting it was "real" socialism. It was much easier to do this in the days of the quasi-religious belief and sacrifice for the sake of a communist utopia. But we are here speaking of a ruling class that not only no longer believed in its "*historic mission*" but was moreover permeated with a "mendacious consciousness."

And yet besides all this, who could have supposed that the ruling class would simply wash its hands of its own system? This is exactly what happened in a number of countries bound together in a military, police, economic, and ideological bloc, under the leadership of a superpower. The rulers did indeed in several countries find themselves confronted by the unarmed masses, which, in a way, meant an added difficulty in any eventual use of violence. But they did not even need to resort to violence; it would have been enough for them not to hand over power and leave the initiative of violence to the opposing side. This would have morally eased their defense with all the means at their disposal. It was because of moral scruples that a part of the ruling class was not prepared to use violence. It would be of no less interest to study those rulers who also opposed violence but not for moral reasons. Among them one must differentiate between the orderers and the executors, as well as between the older and younger ones. Why would the communist leaders, innocent of criminal doings, share the responsibility for any mass violence with those who had already been steeped in such crimes?

Practical experience conditioned the wide difference in moral and political conceptions such as between the Chinese and Soviet top leaderships. That is why Deng's leadership reacted to the liberal-democratic movement in a repressive way and Gorbachëv's in a benevolent manner. Before becoming a reformer, Deng was an active fighter and leader in the civil war, the revolution and in totalitarian Maoism; whereas Gorbachëv in Stalin's time was a child or at worst a small functionary in the Party.

The demonstration effect of the peaceful surrender of power from country to country was of unquestionable influence in Eastern Europe and a matter that finally impacted on the actions and reactions in the USSR as well. Fortunately, we saw Ceaucescu's violent reaction only at the end and not at the beginning of the East European anti-system avalanche.

Gorbachëv's signal that the USSR would not save them discouraged any would-be orderers of state violence in Eastern Europe. This of course, could not have a significant effect on the break-up of the central power in the SFR Yugoslavia in 1990, as it was not dependent on the USSR. However, it is true that the rulers in Yugoslavia felt quite isolated after the East European changes and were frightened by Ceaucescu's fate. In addition, they were under great pressure from the West.

The relevant literature has long been using sharp dichotomies such as revolution or evolution and revolution or reform. In order to find their way through experiential variety, theoreticians, researchers, and journalists were compelled to introduce transitional instances of "revolution from above," "peaceful revolution," "radical reform," and the like.

However, insurmountable category difficulties arose only when governments and systems collapsed in Eastern Europe and in the USSR in 1989–1991. These changes were sudden and yet nonviolent; implosive and not explosive; caused both by mass movements and by the self-negation of the ruling class; radical but without revenge-ful "expropriation of the expropriators" nor depriving the erstwhile "expropriators" of their civil rights.

For those reasons, the following conceptual combinations were launched: "consensual revolution," "velvet revolution," "consti-tutional revolution," "revolutionary reform," "reformist revolution," and so on.

However, Th. G. Ash immediately sensed that it was no longer helpful to add adjectives and that there was a need somehow to change substantives. So he began using the coinage "refolution" (more revolution than reform). In 1990 I myself coined two expressions: revorm (more reform than revolution) and (r)evolution (more evolution than revolution). Thus we have the following continuum: *revolution, refolution, (r)evolution, revorm, reform and evolution.*

Due to the sudden and violent change of power and system, we can freely speak of a revolution in Romania. Since in East Germany and in the Czechoslovak Federal Republic, a relatively sudden change took place without violence, these cases can be described as refolutions. Since vital social changes accumulated over a decade or two, and since finally a systemic change was effected more gradually than in the above-mentioned countries, what happened in Poland and Hungary can be called (r)evolutions. The processes in the SFR Yugoslavia, the USSR, Bulgaria, and Albania, were for a while more akin to reforms than to revolutions—and that is why they should be called revorms. However, there, too, they grew into (r)evolutions and into refolutions. Thus Gorbachëv started out with reforms and then opted for more and more revorms and finally did not even offer any resistance to (r)evolution and refolution. Naturally, besides Gorbachëv's *nondoing*, Yeltsin's *doing* was and has remained of vital significance for radicalization in the USSR.

Parallel with the collapse of the communist *social system* in the USSR, in the SFR Yugoslavia, and in the Czechoslovak Federal Re-public, the *states* also fell apart so that among the new states differ-ences have increased as to the speed, the manner, and the radicality of the postcommunist changes. This signifies that we are in need of a new, richer, and more varied conceptual apparatus for social change, not only because of the disintegration of communism but also because of the postcommunist developments.

Eight

Postcommunism

The Contradiction between Democracy and Capitalism

Postcommunist development ensued following the demise of monopolistic structural control on the part of the communist-statist class over the state and, through it, over the economy and the other sectors. Until the nature of the new social orders crystallizes sufficiently, we have to designate as "postcommunism" a "transition period" in which, along with the supposed break, considerable continuity with the previous situation will persist, particularly as regards cadres and the economy.

Postcommunism is *a mix of communism, precommunism, capitalism, nationalism, authoritarianism, and democracy* that differs significantly from country to country and the final result of which depends on what prevails from among these three tendencies. For this reason I argue for a comparative research on postcommunism.

With regard to the extent of the break with communism, we can arrange postcommunist countries along a continuum. In East Germany we encounter the greatest break with communism as it rapidly integrated into West German capitalism. At the opposite pole we find several examples. In Serbia, for instance, communism did not implode; rather it (self)transformed into postcommunism. However,

Serbia is not unique either in that respect or with respect to the violent collapse to which multinational Yugoslavia has succumbed. Serbia represents a *completely* separate case due to the international blockade imposed against it.

One can, as well, classify postcommunist countries according to the continuity with the precommunist juncture of authoritarianism, nationalism, an immensely powerful state, and a weak "civil society." Of all the postcommunist countries, in the Czech Republic, prior to the establishment of communism, those characteristics were least pronounced. At the opposite end of the postcommunist spectrum stands Croatia as one of the leading states in perpetuating precommunist traditions (particularly those nationalistic in nature).

The theory of the disintegration of communist statism is still in its infancy, while the theory of postcommunist development is still in the embryonic stage. The previous chapter dealt with the major structural reasons for the fall of communist statism. We now turn to the structural dimensions of postcommunist development.

I will begin with *the tension and even contradiction between postcommunist democracy and postcommunist capitalism*, all the more because the ideological illusion prevails that democracy and capitalism always go hand in hand.

In truth, until recently (prior to the break up of communist statism) *all* democratic states functioned as market economies. Conversely, a number of market economies still function within undemocratic states. Indeed, there is no strict parallelism between a privately-based market economy and democracy, much less is there a cause and effect relationship between the two. Not only does democracy not necessarily always lead to a market economy, but at times it can even constitute an impediment to it. Such an economy and such a political arrangement represent forms of social organization as well as aspects of culture and mentality that only *in the long run* are mutually supportive and reinforcing.

In capitalism, it was only *partial democracy* that had existed until relatively recently: the right to vote had been limited to taxpayers and literate citizens (exclusively men), i.e. to those who were interested in seeing capitalism succeed. As capitalism spread and increased in strength, the electorate also grew. Only much later and under great social pressure did *the symbiosis between capitalism and general democracy* come into being. Marx envisioned that in some highly developed countries the capitalist system would be eliminated by the universal right to vote, while it is precisely in those countries that a capitalism imbued with democracy blossoms.

In postcommunism as a rule there are no electoral limitations and consequently *general democracy* (in a formal sense) already exists within it. However, between postcommunist democracy and the postcommunist aspirations as to the development of market-based production, entrepreneurship, and distribution, there is a tension and even a contradiction. More specifically, a great part of the electorate does not support the procapitalist parties, particularly those who threaten it with the social-Darwinistic measures of "instant capitalism." Pro-capitalistic elitism is encountering enormous resistance on the part of anticapitalistic populism.

History knows of no mass popular movements in the name of private, profit-oriented market business practices. Instead, such movements have been in the name of justice, equality, freedom, and civil, national, and human rights, and against hunger, unemployment, exploitation. In postcommunism as well one should not expect any mass movements in support of capitalism.

Some anticommunist dissidents fantasized about a *sui generis* "original position" in which they almost at will build a new society. But communist nihilists already attempted "a complete break of the new with the old," and it is well known how their radical social engineering wound up. Both the former and the latter are characterized by the belief in a magic effect of systemic changes in history.

It is as if the pendulum of social illusions has been moving from one extreme to the other: while for the communists private ownership, the market, and profit exemplified a negative utopia, for many anticommunists these institutions have come to represent a kind of positive utopia. The anticommunists hope that the "visible hand" of their government will suddenly ("the great leap forward") make possible the functioning of the "invisible hand" of the market. But that u-topia also suffers from u-chronia: it turns out that capitalism cannot burst forth and abruptly spring into being.

Since there is no capitalist class, the procapitalist political elite has to play the role of "class substitute"! In a certain sense one could say that in postcommunism there is still not even a working class. Stated more clearly: the labor force inherited is in keeping with the system of communist statism, and, with regard to interests, mentality, and expectations, it bears little resemblance to the for-hire market work force that is indispensable for the development of capitalism. The "old working class" still needs to be transformed into the "new working class." That assertion sounds ironic if we recall leftist discussions in the West regarding the "new working class" as being the principal socialist hope in capitalism 30 years ago.

It is from politics as the dominant factor in postcommunism that many are expecting to bring about by intervention from above the sudden transformation of statism in its entirety as a socio-*political* formation into capitalism as a socio-*economic* formation. The postcommunist political elite is principally made up of elements from the noneconomic sphere that attempt to maintain the dominance of politics over the economy despite their noisy declarations in favor of capitalism in which the relationship between politics and the economy is precisely the opposite. The economic *dilettantism* of a good part of the postcommunist governments resembles the economic incompetence of the leading communists at the time of assuming power.

It is estimated that due to enlarged reproduction of the communist-statist "sin" at least one-fourth of the communist super-enterprises are not economically viable. Indeed, the ruling class's industrial grandomania was not in the least accidental: it was easier to run large enterprises by "plan" and, in so doing, garner prestige at home and abroad. Which of today's postcommunist governments possesses the power and mandate required to eliminate that *enterprise-leveling (uravnilovka)* overnight?

Such statist egalitarianism constitutes only one aspect of the "monopolistic-paternalistic syndrome": in order for it to accept or at least tolerate its lack of any control over the ruling class, the citizenry was "corrupted," among other things, by guaranteed jobs in secure nonmarket enterprises. The masses gladly approved the elimination of the dictatorial aspect of communism but, in return, they have not been prepared to renounce the social security obtained under its auspices. After all, economic reforms in statism had failed owing to resistance both on the part of conservative communists and on the part of citizens reluctant to trade those guarantees for the uncertainties of economic liberalization.

Postcommunism will have major difficulties with inherited *prolet-production* (my concept from III–7) in which the manual labor of the "immediate producers" was proclaimed as the main source of newly created economic value. In communism extensive development based on cheap labor was acclaimed, but communism lapsed into a "comparative crisis" as soon as knowledge, information, and innovation became the main "productive forces" in capitalism.

By means of deconstruction it is not difficult to show that "equality," as the supposedly central value of statist communism, concealed class privileges and other types of privileges as well:

The ruling "vanguard" eliminated the labor market ostensibly to prevent exploitation, but, in the process, it came to have at its disposal a labor force considerably below its potential market value. Since the power structure was of a class nature, the distribution of housing under "social ownership" also favored the ruling class and other well-positioned groups, while an *anti-private-property ideology* masked this structure. As a rule, those in power by no means wanted main income discrepancies to be expressed in monetary terms (so that the haves would build apartments at their own expense, while the have-nots would live in socially-provided living quarters), since the extent of social differentiation would then be totally transparent. The absence of private medical practice played a similar role because in any event the more wealthy and powerful already had privileged access to the best physicians in public practice.

Such an atmosphere strongly provoked the resentment of the masses, but it also redirected it away from the statist class toward the private sector—getting rich, entrepreneurial activity, competition, innovation, etc. In good measure this continues to be the case under postcommunism as well. The masses continue to attack "enrichment without work," subsuming under that heading (also) enrichment on the basis of private ownership, as if the market economy could exist without it. People speak out in favor of private ownership, market incentives, and competition, but only as long as it adversely affects someone else. Thus strikes continue to be of a exceedingly political nature: they demand of the government that redistribution satisfy the needs of those employed in the public sector, even at the expense of someone else's money.

One of the most ironic consequences of the fall of communism is the sudden acquisition of private wealth on the part of a number of members of the former ruling class and their descendants, who in their private business dealings make use of previously acquired connections, experience, information, knowledge, and material resources. At one time Trotskyists warned that by usurping the nationalized means of production Stalinists could easily become a class of private owners. Somewhat similarly, but in a different way, a part of the former statist class is currently becoming just that.

However, the working people do not want to see the fruit of many decades of their labor, manifested as social and state ownership, expropriated for a song through privatization. The Proudhonian ideological formulation of "Property is theft" takes on a convincing ring as the masses get the clear impression that private ownership originates with the *sui generis* theft of state-social ownership. Some countries attempt to avoid such forms of *primitive postcommunist accumulation* through the allotment of enterprise shares to employees or even to the entire populace. However, that idyll of share-holding egalitarianism quickly gives way to new class differentiation between those who, for a trifle, purchase shares and those who have to sell them.

With regard to the ideological rationalization of this newly created situation, a very interesting reversal has occurred. In order to discredit capitalism, communist ideologues used Marx's opposition of *formal equality and material inequality*, while the new capitalists from the ranks of the former communists do not even wish to hear of this distinction. For them it is totally unimportant that a material handicap exists for those who have to sell their shares; all that matters is that these transactions take place under formal conditions of equality.

The same type of reversal has occurred with a view to democracy. The communist-statist class had the habit of discounting bourgeois democracy as merely *formal*, while simultaneously proclaiming its own dictatorship as being a *substantially* democratic form of government. With the fall of communism the monopolistic structural control over the state on the part of that class disappeared, but that of course does not mean that no difference exists between social groups as to the real possibilities to influence the state in postcommunism. On the contrary, the new power holders, often former communists and now usually nationalists or liberals, make use of the mass of inherited advantages (as to cadres, organization, finances, information, etc.), while they define democracy as a mere formal procedure (the existence of the universal right to vote and multiparty elections). On the other hand, opposition parties who are in that aspect handicapped, even when they declare themselves anti-Marxist, still (unconsciously) use the Marxist-substantive view of democracy in order to attack the new situation as being undemocratic.

In analyzing the relationship between democracy and capitalism in postcommunism one must take into account international factors as well. International "capitalist encirclement" had significantly influenced the collapse of communism, and its effect on the postcommunist development and denouement will surely not abate. Nevertheless, the West had better guard well against triumphalistic postcommunist social engineering from outside. It is extremely important to know, for example, that the Russian people have experienced the external pressure in favor of "capitalist shock therapy" as an attack not only upon their material interests but also upon their national independence and dignity.

It is essential not to lose sight of the tension and even contradiction between postcommunist democracy and international "capitalist encirclement": the preferences of the domestic electorate do not coincide with the radically capitalist demands on the part of Western governments, business circles, and financial institutions. True, foreign capital can help a great deal, but it is not in a position to supplant completely a (yet nonexistent) capitalist class in the postcommunist countries.

President Clinton's strategy of a "proliferation of market democracies" fails to take sufficiently into account the aforementioned contradiction. To say nothing of the vicious circle into which that strategy falls, in that the US is not prepared to extend more abundant material assistance to the postcapitalist countries (above all, to Russia) prior to their exhibiting clear evidence of having successfully undertaken a capitalist path, though the US knows that these countries are not in a position to do that without generous foreign aid.

How to find a way out of this postcommunist situation in which a great deal of the electorate does not support capitalism? Increasing numbers of its protagonists (for example, H. Kissinger and Z. Brzezinski) are reaching the conclusion that, in order for the capitalist transformation to be speedy and more successful, what will be needed are authoritarian rather than democratic postcommunist governments. That is why, in the final analysis, the West supported Yeltsin's violent crushing of the opposition Parliament in the Fall of 1993.

In that context, however, an analogy with the Bolsheviks immediately comes to mind. They relied on dictatorship, unpreoccupied with any expectation that the masses would give an advantage via free elections to their own "long-term and objective interests" (as viewed by the Bolsheviks) over their own "short-term and subjective" preferences. Nevertheless, we all know to what extent that dictatorship was "temporary." Moreover, where is the guarantee that the authoritarian forces under postcommunism would use the "temporary" suspension of democracy to effect just capitalist changes?

THE FALL OF YUGOSLAVIA

From Multinational Federations to National States

Three multinational communist federations disintegrated into 22 states (as a rule, national) and, most likely, this process of dissolution is still not complete. If the break up of communism was an enormous surprise, it is not clear why it was also a real explosion of nationalism, since it is a significantly older and more studied historical phenomenon than communism. Many former communists in nationalist-separatist confrontations employ violence, which they had otherwise not used to defend their governments and system.

Soviet power holders imagined that they could adequately deal with their nationalities' problems by reducing them to national *cultures* and these in turn to "national *forms*" whose differences were allegedly overcome by a common "socialist *content*." Czeslav Milosz correctly pointed out ("Swing Shift in the Baltics," in *The New York Review of Books*, 4 November 1993) that "Soviet" nations took the official formula "*National* culture as to form, *socialist* culture as to content" and turned it around in practice to read: "Socialist culture as to form, national culture as to content."

Naturally, the former ideological formula would not have been of any use to the Soviet government—save as a self-delusion—had it not by means of dictatorship imposed a single "socialist content" (more often than not, as *kitsch*), i.e., had it not hindered "national forms" from creating and manifesting differences of content. When that dictatorship weakened, and especially when, under Gorbachëv, radical liberalization was introduced, then the differentiating, nationalistic, and even separatist potential of "national forms" put an end to the obligatory "Soviet content," not only in culture but also in politics. Were the new slogan formulated explicitly, it would be expressed as: Politics and culture—national both in form and in content.

One should not be too amazed that in the new politics many former communists again play an important and, at times, crucial role. Above all, since communists already utilized nationalism and separatism for the destruction of the previous regimes and to gain power, it was totally logical that many of them were prepared to use nationalism and separatism in postcommunism as well to remain in the political game. Moreover, the transition from one (communist) type of manicheism to another (nationalist) one was not so difficult. In discovering a (new) enemy in other nations of the former common state, such communists quickly found a common language with the original nationalists whom they had formerly severely persecuted. They even compete with such nationalists in radicalism, to some extent owing to a feeling of guilt and somewhat due to an attempt, via political noise, to divert attention away from their own repressive antinationalist past. That political-psychological mechanism strongly recalls the effort of the communists of bourgeois origin to demonstrate the most extreme anticapitalist position possible in the eyes of their party comrades of proletarian origin.

I have no intention here of going more exhaustively into the doctrinaire-historical background of the Soviet government's underestimation of "form." Suffice to remind that it began with the Bolsheviks' belittling of the liberal and democratic "form" of capitalism and their reducing it to an "illusion" behind which was supposedly hidden, from the point of view of "content," merely the class rule of the bourgeoisie. For that communist nihilism vis-à-vis social "form," Lenin bears full responsibility. In truth, he elaborated that position with a series of simplifications drawn from Marx's analysis of the ontology (architectonics) and ideology of capitalism. But, nonetheless, it should be said that Marx himself in some of his formulations significantly opened up the possibility for such vulgarizations (III–3).

During the first 20 years in power the declared position of the Yugoslav communists toward the nationality question was considerably reminiscent of that of the Soviets. However, in the second half of the 60s the CPY rejected "Yugoslav-ness" and initiated a nationalization (ethnization) of the constituent republics, and somewhat later, of its own (party) make-up.

In the independent national states that separated from the communist federations there is a strong tendency to create *nationality societies*, and not "*civil societies.*" True, the nationalist-separatist forces, for instance in the former Yugoslav republic of

291

Slovenia, abundantly employed the ideal-logy of *"civil society,"* but only as long as they did not break away from the federation, and then, in practice, they have shown that they had their own *nationality* (Slovenian) *society* in mind. There existed at least two reasons for this ideological cover-up: that way it was incomparably easier to mobilize domestic liberal-democratic circles to fight against the central Yugoslav government, and also to obtain legitimacy and support from the West.

We have already established that democracy represents a certain impediment to the capitalist transformation in postcommunism. However, that transformation is incomparably more frustrated by the aspiration of a closed nationality society. I say incomparably more, because in the long run between capitalism and democracy there is a universalistic homology, since the institutions of "buyer-seller" and "citizen-voter" disregard diverse characteristics of people, while nationalism adopts the discriminatory particularity that contradicts capitalist logic both in the short and the long time frame. After all, in postcommunism capitalism has yet to be established while nations have been in existence a long time. Superficial critics of nationalistic tendencies usually point out that a nationality is an "abstract collective," overlooking that it is more concrete and closer to the masses than the totality composed of "buyers and sellers" and "citizens and voters."

In nationalist circles the communist system of the past and its remnants are less and less being blamed for the difficult economic situation. Instead, accusations are increasingly being leveled at other nations, particularly the former "ruling nation." The new ruling parties attempt to establish "nationality sovereignty" over economies in which state-social ownership still predominates. Owing to the symbiosis of nation and state, political interventionism in the economy does not abate. In a nationality economy and a nationality society it is difficult to develop profit-market business dealings because the basic agents would have to be owners, entrepreneurs, capitalists, workers, and not a political-demographic totality like a nation.

Radical nationalist governments are concerned that, through privatization, state-social ownership (especially of the "national soil") will fall into the hands of those who belong to other nations. There-fore, *postcommunist nationality society* is in conflict with the inter-national "capitalist encirclement." The West should not be amazed that the masses offer resistance to the capitalist domination of out-siders. How to convince them to accept the competition of over-bearing international capital if it is known that the far more powerful capitalist economies enjoy state protectionism? If the transfer of "national wealth" into foreign hands cannot be avoided, nationalist power holders would rather relinquish it to foreigners from faraway nations (and not to their former countrymen), and even more to their own compatriots and their descendants abroad ("nationality-business").

The war and other conflicts with the breakaway states, and also with the separatism which, from within, threatens the new inde-pendent states—constitute one of the basic reasons for establishing an *nationality-command economy*. What is at issue is a *war-national-ity postcommunism*. While, in the name of a communist utopia, ear-lier power holders called upon the populace to sacrifice during the "transition period," the new power holders now demand sacrifice from it for the sake of nationality interests, the nationality state, and the nationality future.

How to reconcile all these observations regarding nationality so-ciety with my assertion that general democracy is established in postcommunism? Obviously, I have to introduce one qualification into that assertion: in postcommunist countries with dominant na-tionalist orientations, the right to vote is tacitly limited in the sense that citizenship is automatically granted to the members of the na-tionality group whose name the state bears, while other inhabitants face numerous obstacles. Thus, the former Stalinist "political correct-ness" is substituted by nationality correctness.

Great conceptual and emotional confusion has been generated among internationalist-leaning intellectuals in postcommunist coun-tries, particularly where inter-nationality and inter-faith wars have broken out. Those who have not degenerated into nationalists and chauvinists, but have not either attained a realistic approach to the nation and the national state, compensate their lack of comprehension by a surplus of condemnation.

True, it is difficult to orient oneself in collective "limit situations" that came about with the break up of the states, civil wars of nationality and religious origin, crimes that yesterday's countrymen carry out against each other, mass flight. That return to a "natural state" tragically validates the thesis of "foundational violence" in the history of nations and their states. The newest evidence for that is represented by the case of the Muslims of Bosnia and Herzegovina. Up until the disintegration of Yugoslavia and especially until the outbreak of the war there with the Serbs, and somewhat later with the Croats as well, many Muslims vacillated between a Muslim, Yugoslav, an "undefined," a Serb, or a Croat *nationality* identity (while there was no such hesitation regarding their religious identification). And afterwards it took "only" two years of war to feel and nationally define themselves definitively as Muslims. The analysis of this sudden shift in identification could stimulate us to an elaboration of the notion of "late-comer nations," but we will not go into that at this time.

What practical effect can one's opposing of the nationalist metaphysics via the characterization of a nationality as an "historical construct" exert, when a people in practically no time moves from being a *nationality construct* to being a *nationality given?* After all, the thesis about a historical construct is valid only in a collective-diachronic perspective, while, for the individual, the nationality is, as a rule, a given (ethnicity, language, religion, culture, tradition, custom) in which one is born.

Therefore, in the newly formed postcommunist states in political competition with the nationalist antidemocrats, the national democrats have an incomparably better chance than do the non-national democrats. The latter remain impotent as to, for instance, the question of the former, of why even the democratic Germans wanted to reunify with the Germans, but not to unify with the East European democrats, and why democratic Germany automatically adopts into its citizenry only those foreigners that have German and not some other ancestry. They also cannot convincingly answer the question of why the combined force of Czech and Slovak democrats was so ineffectual that it could not impede the break up of the Czecho-Slovak federation into two national states. It is unclear why the West was so surprised by the success of national and nationalistic parties and by the relative failure of the a-national-democratic parties in the recent Parliamentary elections in Russia. How is it that they expected the Russians to lend electoral support to those parties in which they did not see the best guarantee for their *national* interests?!

Postcommunist nationalism cannot successfully be countered by simply counterpoising a civil state to the national state, and even less by reactions of the type "It is not borders that matter, but rather democracy," because it is widely known that many states in the West are predominantly national and that democracy functions there as well in a state framework in which only its citizens have the right to vote. Therefore, the real dilemma for the 22 states originating with the collapse of three communist federations is: either a *democratic national* state or an *antidemocratic nationalistic* state. The first nurtures equality of all citizens without regard to whether or not they belong to the *majority* nationality group for whom the state is named, while the second is disgraced by nationality discrimination and the implementation of ever greater "nationality purity."

Those intellectuals have led themselves into an embarrassing position who are trying to persuade the nations drawing borders between themselves in blood, that in "the European world"—particularly since it has taken on a postmodern characteristic—time is a far more important factor than is space. Moreover, behind "European-ness" is often concealed an attempt to impose the identity and power of one-half of the continent upon the other half. I have nothing against "European identity" being further defined, say, by humanism and democracy (which in any case constitutes a "Balkan" invention and creation!), but solely on condition that fascism and colonialism are also included in it. Why the effort to define the national, regional, or continental identity as homogeneous, instead of as a structure full of internal tensions and contradictions?!

The Model Societies

The fall of communism in Eastern Europe and the Soviet Union should stimulate a reevaluation of the entire democratic-socialist tradition. Some democratic leftists will surely dismiss this with a wave of the hand since they start from the position that communism had nothing in common with the democratic-socialist legacy and that, consequently, the fall of the former is irrelevant for the future of the latter. It is true that the democratic Left has been long since immune to the political influence of communism, but I doubt that the same can be said for the communist position regarding private ownership, the profit motive, and market competition.

On the other hand, some former communists have gone so far as to proclaim the collapse of their system as the end of any socialist ideal, thereby continuing even in defeat to monopolize socialist tradition. However, let us imagine that the Western social-democrats, while in power, have renamed their countries as "socialist," as the communists arrogantly did with theirs. Would it not then be possible to conclude that it is only the authoritarian communist systems that had failed and that realistic and democratic socialism is alive and well in the West? It goes without saying that I am employing such a thought experiment merely as a polemical devise, without thinking that it represents a way out of the impasse into which the left has fallen.

Now is the real opportunity for the left definitively to get free of the pressure of those who continue to situate utopian "responsibilities" in the non-Western countries (this time postcommunist), although they themselves enjoy the blessings of capitalist hedonism in the West. If their leftist utopias stand no real chance in the rich and democratic West, with what right do they expect that these utopias will be politically embraced under far less favorable conditions in postcommunism?

Today *utopian* constructs of the good society are truly of no use to the left. What is required instead is the project of an *efficacious and feasible good society* for our times, and not for some unforeseeable future. Of course, "feasibility" means here both the material-cultural preconditions and the democratic manner to establish such a society. The tragic experience of the Left validates the notion that imposed social order inevitably becomes bad because it excludes the majority from defining and constituting it.

Now I would like to move to a comparison of the anarchist and social-democratic threads in the socialist legacy. Starting with the ideal of a democracy without parties and the "withering away of the state," one part of the left was opposed to the "dictatorship of the proletariat" from the standpoint of a system of self-governing councils. Such councils came about, as a rule, in times of revolution and war, but they were quickly eliminated, primarily on the part of the communist parties with which they had temporarily shared power. Moreover, even independently of those more powerful competitors, self-governing councils always met with one insurmountable existential obstacle: when the war and revolution had passed, the council members had to return to their usual life and work, thereby renewing the differentiation into producers on the one hand and economic and governmental leaders on the other. A great mistake is made by those thinkers and practitioners who normatively generalize institutions originating under exceptional circumstances.

And that is precisely what Marx did when he set forth the "Paris Commune" as a model for the new social organization. But, even had that form of *self-government in war* not been immediately destroyed with the help of external enemies, would it not have practically expired on its own under peaceful circumstances? Marx was a utopian because for him every state and every law represented a form of human alienation that should be eliminated. In contrast, post-Marxists do not fantasize about a good society without a state (legal, pluralistic, social and democratic).

During the 60s the "New Left" resuscitated the anarchist belief in direct democracy. To counter political parties the theoreticians of the New Left used Michele's "iron law of oligarchy," but they did not see that a nonparty system of self-governing councils would also be exposed to a strong oligarchic tendency and that the majority within them would easily become the victims of manipulation on the part of the informally organized minority. In order to focus attention on that danger, in previous books I formulated the "law" of the *manipulation of the nonorganized majority on the part of the informally organized minority.* It is not possible to overcome that tendency without the mutual balance and control of openly organized political parties.

Naturally, party-representative democracy still does not constitute any maximum democracy. Therefore, its "democratic elitism" is often attacked by new social movements and extra-Parliamentary opposition. In fact, it would be best if a multiparty arrangement were combined with forms of direct democracy. That would add a new component and force to the democratic mechanism of "checks and balances." After all, the information-communications technology already exists to enable the instant, direct participation of the entire citizenry in social decision making, and through the political struggles in our century the normative concept of the *"citizen"* has been broadened and deepened, so there is no compelling reason to limit citizenship to politics and totally exclude it from work and production.

Yugoslavia experimented incomparably more than others with self-management. In order to avoid repeating what I have already written about Tito's pretensions regarding a third, "self-management" path between communist statism and capitalism, I will limit myself to the issue of the compatibility of self-management with ownership and production efficiency. That relationship is of vital importance for the future of the humanization and democratization of labor and management.

Since in Yugoslavia self-management was inherently linked to the utopia of the "withering away of the state," it is not surprising that it was basically an ideal-logical myth, and not a reality. Contrary to the myth, some participation of employees in management, which really existed, should have been interpreted much more realistically and modestly as a component of a reemerging "civil society."

In Yugoslavia workers were told that they had the right to self-management, though they had no ownership-market responsibility. Nevertheless, experience has shown that this does not work, for anyone who disposes of and manages the abstract and anonymous "social ownership" will relate to it like unclaimed property—particularly when the state, through general redistribution, sustains many unprofitable enterprises and superfluous institutions and when employees enjoy a life-long monopoly on their jobs. It goes without saying that if employees become co-owners, they should then manage and dispose of those enterprises and institutions, and, until that is the case, they should merely co-participate in management. The right to self-management originates from ownership, while the right to co-participation in management should be drawn from the idea of citizenship construed in a radically democratic fashion. Naturally, this latter right has no real future if the state safeguards it against market competition from the other forms of ownership and management.

The Yugoslav experience, among others, also demonstrates that it is wisest to divide mandate and responsibility between the employees participating in management on the one hand, and the professional managers on the other—similarly to the relationship between democratic Parliament and the executive. In the absence of professional managerial autonomy, decisions become extremely dilettante-like and populistic, and individual responsibility gets lost in the collective decision making in which incompetent managers easily exonerate themselves.

We have had enough of those who derive their notion of the good society from some definition of socialism. It is time for normative ideas to be founded much more on historical practice. To that end we must base ourselves on an amalgam of capitalism, democracy, and socialism. If democratic-socialist theoreticians search the map for the economically most successful and, at the same time, most humane states on Earth, they will find out that, in them, as a rule *capitalism with a social-democratic or social-Christian face* predominates.

Social-democratic parties are largely to be credited for the social face of capitalism in Europe. They have made an enormous contribution to transforming partial into general democracy. Social democrats have also greatly helped the working class in the struggle to eliminate despotism in the organization of production, to establish free unions, to introduce collective bargaining between labor and management, etc.

Today also the weaknesses of social-democracy are widely known. Their common denominator is an exaggerated dependence on party politics, and an insufficient emphasis on the democratic self-organization of citizens. Thence the social-democratic accent is on the "welfare state," and significantly less stress on *welfare society.*

After the fall of communism, social-democracy has been the only real winner on the left. It is as if history wanted to offer it the opportunity to avenge itself against the Bolsheviks for having been persecuted. To save whatever they could, some communist groups and parties immediately changed their name to social-democrats.

In the conceptualization of a feasible and efficacious good society, the left should, in my opinion, lean most on the social-democratic legacy. However, since the ecological disposition is also of crucial importance, concern for the biosphere must by all means find expression in the definition of that political orientation—thence I derive my syntagma: *social-eco-democracy.*

Of course, there is a close tie between a well conceived ecologism and feminism. It will be difficult for the human race to survive if it perpetuates its "male" (instrumental) relationship with nature. Without the contribution of contemporary feminism it generally is not possible to sketch the contours of a better society. I only mention this in passing, since I am not in a position to add anything original to the rational ideas and literature of the feminist movement.

The philosophical weave of my newer normative approach, aside from other things, constitutes a departure from the Hegelian-Marxist dialectic of *overcoming* the basic oppositions in societal organization (III–1) and a proposal for maintaining these oppositions, such as those between: "civil society" and the state, private and state ownership, market and social regulation, representative and participatory democracy, institutionalized democracy and social movements, competition and solidarity, freedom and equality. Such oppositions should be built into the social organization—while attempting, of course, to see that they should not turn into destructive contradictions.

It should be honestly acknowledged that both the best socialist and the most advanced capitalist traditions are relevant for the conceptualization of a humane and democratic society. Many leftists now tend to include in their project a market of all productive factors—competition, the profit motive, and private ownership—but they continue, unjustifiably, to shun "capitalism" as the common designation for those institutions.

It is well known that social-democracy has provided very few economic innovations, particularly on the level of the enterprises and their mutual market relationships. Most probably, this is because until several decades ago, it essentially adopted the market merely as a necessary evil. Social democracy did not sufficiently value the fact that the market stimulates, for example, initiative, independence, creativity, innovation, rationality . . . . The logic of profit or losses at the market teaches us to set only those goals for which we have the means at our disposal.

For the sake of an optimum functionality, any democratic and humane society and state today should organize its production and primary distribution along competitive, market-profit lines. By means of its "creative destruction" (J. Schumpeter), capitalism daily eliminates the unprofitable enterprises and creates new ones. That system has shown itself to be superior because in it firms have the task of producing a profit, rather than being a vehicle of the social policy of the state, as in communist statism.

Nevertheless, the best existing societies do not typify capitalist principles only. On national levels they function according to non-capitalist principles: of democratic direction and planning, solidarity, ecology . . . . Primary distribution is based on ownership or work results, while redistribution guarantees a living minimum. Social differences stimulate the growth of productivity, whereas solidarity should make possible the satisfaction of basic needs, independent of property and work results. Such a society is, naturally, constantly threatened by opposing dangers: on the one hand, the exacerbation of class conflicts, and, on the other, a drop in production and creativity due to an exaggerated redistribution.

The basic value of such societies is freedom, which institutionally means democracy. Freedom always exists in a certain tension with equality, but it is not true that their tension inevitably grows into an irreconcilable contradiction, as conservative and reactionary thinkers affirm. "Escape from freedom" as a rule even leads to inequality, but *escape from equality* also almost always results in a lack of freedom for the majority.

But still the societies that we are using here as an example are without a doubt class societies. As soon as appropriation based on capital and information exists—classes are also present. One task, among others, of social-eco-democracy consists of keeping the richest and most informed classes from using democratic procedure for perpetuating and even strengthening their structural domination over the rest of the populace.

The option I favor obviously has all the features of pragmatism and minimalism. That is undoubtedly the most radical step toward accommodating leftist aspirations to a real life and history. The height of these aspirations was represented by the "international proletarian revolution," which allegedly should have established the basis for a society without a market, classes, a state, and laws, and since that revolution did not happen, so-called permanent revolution was invented; later on in contrast to it, "socialism in one country" was proclaimed; the critical reaction to it was called "market socialism," "socialism with a human face," etc.

Evidently the sharp division on the left and the right must undergo radical change, primarily due to the totally altered attitude of the left toward a market economy, private ownership, and political-party pluralism. Up until a few years ago, leftists categorized the supporters of such institutions as right-wing, while now the dividing line between left-wing and right-wing on the political spectrum has shifted to such an extent that one could, in my opinion, speak of a *democratic left with a capitalist face*. That means that the left favors a regulated market and supports a socially and ecologically responsible private ownership, while the right upholds the laissez-faire

market and laissez-faire private ownership. Further, the right reduces democracy to its representative-procedural form, while the
left adopts this form as a necessary condition for democracy, insisting also on the need for its more direct and more substantial
dimensions.

The leftist opposition in communist countries often ran up
against the incomprehension and opposition of the left in capitalist
countries. When I myself came out to some extent in support of the
market, the profit motive, private ownership, a multiparty system,
civil rights, and "civil society," my leftist friends in the West criticized
me from the standpoint of a planned economy, distribution according to work, social ownership, direct democracy, socio-economic
rights, and overcoming "civil society."

With the idea of a convergence of capitalism and communism, it
was suggested several decades ago that the future belonged to a
mixed society that would adopt the market, private ownership, and
democracy from capitalism, while assimilating planning, state ownership, and economic and social regulations from communism. Although the two systems did not come to resemble each other, but
instead, one of them collapsed, I have long since considered the
idea itself of a mixed society a fruitful one. After all, the most humane capitalist countries are already characterized in great measure
by opposing organizational principles: the capitalist mode of production, political democracy, and social regulation and redistribution. The basic difference between those two systems is that capitalism was structurally in a position to weather a transformation from
partial to general democracy, and from laissez-faire "regulation" and
distribution to social regulation and redistribution, while the communist-statist structure could not incorporate private ownership, the
market, and democracy, and, consequently, it fell apart.

Understandably, the genesis and environment in which it oper-
ates, the center of activity, and the perspectives of social-eco-
democracy in postcommunism are quite different from its situation
in the West. In any event, it is the task of social-eco-democracy to
see that the postcommunist transition exhibits the most humane face
possible and that the tension and contradiction between democracy

and capitalism (which I analyzed in the first section of this chapter) is diminished as much as possible.

In the former communist part of Europe new social-democracy has most often ensued with the demise of communist parties, precisely the opposite of the manner in which at one time communist parties were begun (with the separation from social-democracy). In the social-democracy in postcommunist countries a struggle will long be waged between crypto-communist and true social-democratic tendencies. The latter are squeezed between the social bloc inherited from the communist-statist economy and the emerging bourgeoisie that exerts pressure in the direction of a privatization of nearly the entire public sector of the economy and the elimination of almost any government intervention in it. But even Western capitalism does not function in such a way, to say nothing of the economically most successful Asian countries. It would be useful for the postcommunist elites to study the experiences of these countries exercising state interventionism, instead of repeating the history of laissez-faire capitalism.

It would be best to allow, free from ideological prejudice, market competition in postcommunist countries to show which forms of ownership and to what extent have a future. On the basis of world experience we know for certain only that public ownership must be drastically reduced and transformed into state ownership with a clearly defined owners.

As we have seen, social-eco-democracy is only one component of my viewpoint, while the second is capitalism. My position is both postsocialist and postcapitalist.

Those who still define their viewpoint as socialist, albeit democratic, encounter a veritable resistance in all the former communist countries. In fact, most people react that way verbally, while at the same time being in favor of free medical care and education, a guaranteed minimum wage for those employed and social assistance for the unemployed, social housing for the poorest segments of the population, meaningful participation of the employees in the management of enterprises and institutions, etc.—as if these were not socialist measures (best realized in Western democratic countries with a capitalist mode of production).

For me democracy is the most important feature of the social-eco-democratic point of view, because people ought to choose freely (in this I find the primary meaning of an "open society") their social system, and advocates of that viewpoint should only try to win others over to it.

If the failure of communism indicates the triumph of one social conception, it is *postliberalism* rather than liberalism that has triumphed. The socialization of liberalism has taken on such an extent and depth that that term is much more adequate.

There is no justification in generalizing a very specific case of USA in which unsocialized capitalist liberalism still prevails. Such capitalism now finds itself under great pressure to socialize itself, both for domestic reasons and due to the challenge of capitalism with a social-democratic and a social-Christianized face in Europe and Canada.

The American thinker J. Rawls, for instance, has introduced into his conception so much social-democratic content that we could in no event classify him simply as capitalist liberal, but rather as postliberal. And if, for example, we take the American thinker M. Walzer as his counterpart on the left, then we will encounter in his work so many elements of capitalist liberalism that we will have to dub him postsocialist.

Nine

From Marxism and Post-Marxism to Anti-Apocalyptism

Humanist Marxism versus Communist Statism

Marxist humanist criticism of communist statism and of its Stalinist-Leninist foundation passed through at least two phases: *"authentic Marxism"* and *"revisionist Marxism."*

Initially, the humanist Marxists called for a "return to the authentic Marx," since for them communist statism represented a radical deformation of his thought. Starting from a naïve hermeneutics, however, some of them expected to reach an essentially homogeneous construct.

But the most talented and best informed among them knew that that construct was full of tensions and contradictions and that, consequently, a "return to the authentic Marx" had to be selective, fragmentary, and critical. That, indeed, logically led to an increasingly profound revision of Marxism, which would eventually call into question even the very basis of Marx's social vision.

Nonetheless, how could one do that and still remain a Marxist? In fact, sooner or later, consciously or unconsciously, revisionist Marxism had to grow into *post-Marxism*. My first two books on communism, socialism, and Marxism were consciously revisionist, while the third was to a significant degree post-Marxist, or even non-Marxist, though I was as yet not completely aware of it.

One of the basic dividing lines between revisionist Marxism and post-Marxism is the idea that it is necessary to maintain, and not to "overcome," the opposition between "civil society" and the state. From the struggle of Solidarity with the communist state in Poland, the radically revisionist Marxists drew the conclusion that it was necessary to restore and build "civil society" that should be as independent of the state as possible.

Nevertheless, only a few years had passed since the birth of Solidarity when Marxists had to come to yet another conclusion: that "civil society" must have obvious capitalist components, such as the market for all factors of production, private ownership, and the profit motive. In truth, some of the Marxists persisted in their self-delusion, characterizing even that answer to statist practice and the crisis of Marxism as Marxist revisionism. But that was no longer even post-Marxism but rather the abandonment of Marxism.

Critiquing communist statism from a humanist Marxist point of view undoubtedly played a *progressive* role in that: (1) it denied the Marxist legitimation of that system and its ideology; (2) it brought into question the monopoly of the ruling class over public discourse; (3) it prompted the communist reformers to liberalize the system and to develop an adherence to humanist principles; (4) it provided an example of critical courage and perseverance, which in any case undermined the self-assuredness of the ruling class and (5) it contributed to establishing a free space for non-Marxist intellectuals as well.

Since much is known regarding the other four functions of humanist Marxism, I shall only touch here on its influence on humanist inspiration and humanist scrupulousness of the communist reformers (3). I have already pointed to this theme when speaking, with regard to Gorbachëv, about not resorting to violence for the sake of defending the system in Eastern Europe and in his own country. Gorbachëv's "new thinking" lent an explicit *priority* to universal human interests over those of class. This could not have been Marxist but rather post-Marxist humanism, since for Marx, there existed an *identity* between proletarian interests (at first only "objective," and, with the development of the class consciousness of the proletariat, its "subjective" interests as well) and the interests of humanity. What is at issue here is a radical turn which had to influence both Gorbachëv's critical "nondoings" we spoke of before. There is no doubt that both he and his political-intellectual collaborators and supporters were subjected to the influence of revisionist Marxist and post-Marxist critiques of communist statism. The supposition would be unfounded that other conceptions (specifically liberalism) exerted a greater effect than revisionist Marxism and post-Marxism on the ultimate and crucial decisions of that group. That was even less true for earlier communist reformers in Eastern Europe.

However, with the question of the extent and depth of the contribution of *humanist Marxism* to liberalization and, ultimately, to the fall of communist statism, we are already in the realm of a new research program. A great deal of Marxology, with its anti-Marxist bent, has taken the opposite path, even affirming that the genesis and development of Leninism and Stalinism were already predetermined in Marx. Therefore, the farthest thing from the minds of such Marxologists was the possibility of a humanist Marxism that could seriously stimulate radical reforms in communism, let alone its collapse. Knowing that communism could not be overturned by foreign intervention on the part of the West, and underestimating the humanist Marxist undermining from within, an approach to Marxism and communism thus construed could have no presentiment as to the self-negation of communist statism. However, with regard to the undermining from within, even those histories of Marxism and communism written from the humanist Marxist standpoint have to undergo significant revision, not just addition. In truth, they have already dealt with the first part of the job affirming those humanist dimensions of *Marx's thought* that facilitated the genesis and development of humanist Marxism and its critical account of Stalinism, Leninism, and of communist statism in general.

But let me get back to my basic train of thought. Through the exasperation of officials and the persecution of critics it became clear that the indication of the gap between communist statism and the humanist interpretation of Marx truly hit a sore point. Essentially touching on the ideological legitimation of the ruling class, that seemingly dogmatic argument over who was right to and who unjustifiably called Marx to witness, adopted an increasingly political rather than academic character and significance.

Nonetheless, as soon as the real prospects for the liberalization of communist statism opened up, the danger arose that humanist Marxists could become sociopolitically irrelevant. Here though, we need to make a distinction between *realistic* and *utopian* humanists.

The former resolutely supported political liberalization and decentralization of government, the partial rehabilitation of private ownership and market competition, along with the reaffirmation of some other elements of "civil society" and the rule of law, but, in so doing, they exceeded the framework of Marxism. To "real socialism" they countered with "socialism with a human face," "democratic socialism," "self-government (self-management) socialism," "market socialism" . . . . For such Marxists, the transformation into social democrats has been the most natural and the easiest.

On the other hand, utopian Marxists *continued* their attacks on "real socialism" from the standpoint of a Marxist classless communism without a state, private ownership, laws, or markets. Understandably, they lost their attractiveness and influence because the people were interested in ever-greater economic development and political emancipation, and not in a polemic regarding whether or not communist statism had the right to invoke Marx's communism.

For utopian-humanist Marxists who failed to change themselves at that turning point there arose the danger that they would evolve into conservatives or even reactionaries wielding a Marxist criticism of the bourgeois political economy and liberalism to attack progressive social change. For Marx, for instance, even distribution according to work done in the "lower phase of communism" possessed a bourgeois nature, and it is easy to guess what he would have said about a reaffirmation of distribution according to market results. After all, Marxist criticism from the point of view of a society without classes, a state, laws, private ownership, and markets had, from its inception, a *conservative potential* as well, since the ruling class could use it to preserve the status quo by diverting attention from the real problems and their prospective resolutions.

As opposed to the utopian, realistic criticism concentrated on diminishing and limiting the structural control of the ruling class over the state and the law, and not on its "withering away."

And that, in my estimation, should have been sufficient reason for a radical revision of Marx's standpoint by means of separation of the principles of *radical humanism* from the vision of *communist social organization*, although he would certainly have protested against it.

Here are some of the fundamental principles of Marxist humanism: collective conscious control over the historical process, praxis, de-alienation, the elimination of reification, de-ideologization, the satisfaction of authentic human needs, the freedom of every individual as the precondition for the freedom of all. Marx believed that those principles would be definitively realized in the communist classless and stateless society in which there would be neither private ownership nor a market economy, and distribution would be carried out in proportion to human needs. Nevertheless, life has convincingly shown that that vision of communism is utopian. That perhaps would be a flawless society, but an unattainable one.

From that, of course, it does not have to follow that Marx's radical humanism has also been rendered irrelevant; only on the condition that we separate it from Marx's project of a communist society and we construe it as a sum of ultimate *regulative-critical ideas*, and not as *constitutive-operative principles*. Subjected to further revision and mediation, those ideals can still prove useful for an evaluation of the degree of humanization in existing societies (including postcommunist ones), as well as for an evaluation of the projects of a *better society*.

Marx based his own vision of communism on the anticipation of an end to scarcity and the coming about of abundance. However, we know that projects for a better society can count on wealth, but not on unlimited plenty. To make things even worse, Marx's non-market and noncompetitive "association of producers" would not have been the most optimal framework even for creating material wealth, to say nothing of abundance.

Instead of drawing radical consequences from the inexorable historic experience, some Marxists amazingly even now seek solution in a neocommunist utopia. They argue roughly like this: as a political program, communism really has failed because the Bolsheviks and other communists "skipped" the long and necessary stage of capitalist development, and now we must take *a big step back to capitalism* in order to build the necessary material basis for a future communism of a truly Marxist character.

The social democrats, on the other hand, proceeded opposite to the Bolsheviks. But not even that most developed capitalism in which they have significant or even predominant influence has indicated a need for or the plausibility of Marxist communism. Is it now necessary to proclaim that capitalism is insufficiently developed? And how far should we continue like that in order to salvage Marx's utopia? After all, he insisted that developed capitalism constitutes a necessary precondition for communism, and simultaneously, nonetheless, he expected the outbreak of proletarian revolutions in the Western capitalist countries, which were at the time rather undeveloped, not merely by our contemporary standards, but also by those *theoretical* standards Marx himself set.

With that, in my opinion, there is no way to avoid recognizing that Marx succeeded only in his critical and not in his constructivistic approach, and that radical conclusions ought to be drawn from that.

As criticism, Marxism today has yet to exhaust all its possibilities as relates to capitalism, and it has not yet been tested in the critique of postcommunist societies. Naturally, the humanist impetus of Marx's regulative-critical ideas is not sufficient for a Marxist subterranean river to break through to the postcommunist surface, but concrete criticism of the new relations of power and of the new class-economic differentiation and alienation is indispensable, as is criticism of the ideology that conceals and justifies these relations. The experience with statist communism has demonstrated that state and social ownership can be a powerful source of alienation and that it does not abate without extensive reprivatization. In its stead, however, private ownership again prompts alienation and the disproportionately big influence of the rich on the democratic political process, thereby renewing the need for a Marxist-inspired criticism.

In the previous book (III–5), I analyzed Marx's paradigm for a critique of the bourgeois ideology of "freedom" and "equality" as "forms" and "appearances" behind which is hidden the "content," "essence," and "reality" of the capitalist domination. I also pointed out why that paradigm is not applicable to the communist statist ideology of the "objective interests" of the working class. Now I would like to add the notion that that Marxist paradigm, revised of course in a post-Marxist spirit, could prove useful for the criticism of the privatistic-liberalistic *ideology* that, along with the nationalistic one, is increasingly permeating postcommunism.

The Yugoslav Praxis Group

Much has been written, at home and abroad, about the Yugoslav group of Praxists, to which I belonged. What I said in general about humanist Marxism more or less holds true for this group, but it would not be amiss for me to add something of its particularities.

Usually the question is posed why our group functioned longer on the public scene than did other humanist Marxist currents in communist countries. Was it because Tito's dictatorship at the time was the most enlightened and the most manipulative? That, though, only explains why the Praxists were neutralized later than other groups of critical Marxists and why they did not emigrate to the West, but not why humanist Marxism was socially and politically relevant for a longer time in Yugoslavia.

It is well known that the Yugoslav ruling communists were the first to attack Stalinism and that they experimented the longest with "self-management socialism." Consequently, it was harder for the

Praxists to attack the system in their own country than in the other communist statist countries. In that, they were also fettered by moral and patriotic considerations: since Titoism established independence from Moscow, no one among them wanted, by criticism, to help a still worse foreign power.

The inception of the *organized* group of Praxists falls in the time of the end of Khrushchëv's reforms and the beginning of Brezhnev's counter-reformation in the Soviet Union and in international communism. The Soviet leadership constantly attacked Praxis as a "center of international revisionism" and exerted pressure on Tito to stifle it.

Tito also publicly criticized Praxis, but up until 1974 he put off overt and direct repressive government action against our journal, against our international meetings in Korčula and against the eight of us Praxists at the University of Belgrade. Why? Because, for him, we served a purpose as critics of the policy and of the ideology that Moscow imposed, but also because we represented an argument vis-à-vis the West that Tito's communism was different.

When communism collapsed in Yugoslavia, some intellectuals began to ridicule the Praxists, affirming that their conflict with Tito and his regime was just a "disagreement within the family." Even a well-meaning group of these critics was misled by the similarities in the lexicon of official Marxism and the opposition-Praxis Marxism in Yugoslavia, but also by the fact that, as a rule, the Praxists had been members of the League of Communists of Yugoslavia (LCY). It is accurate that Titoists at times employed a similar terminology to that of the Praxis group, but they were still fully aware of the enormous differences in the meanings. It is astonishing when even the *intellectual* critics of Praxis underscore the linguistic similarities while ignoring the basic conceptual differences.

But, regardless of that, any talk of a "family squabble" is altogether misplaced because the Praxists had denounced the ruling class, had identified new forms of alienation, had shown that worker and social self-management in Yugoslavia was an ideological myth, had criticized the privileges and immorality of communist officials, had affirmed that the structural monopoly of the League of Commu-

313

nists of Yugoslavia over the state constituted the main hurdle to de-mocratization, had upheld the right of workers to strike, to organize in free trade unions, and to demonstrate peacefully. In addition, some Praxists had criticized Tito personally.

And as to membership in the LCY, it is important to realize that almost all the Praxists had been expelled from the party or quit it of their own volition by 1968 at the latest (ultimately convinced that its leadership had no intention of permitting significant democratic re-forms in the Yugoslav society), thereby setting a dangerous example in this manner as well.

Praxis was very open toward non-Marxist viewpoints and groups, not only abroad but also in Yugoslavia. Who but the Praxists helped the phenomenologues, the positivists, the structuralists, the analytical philosophers, the existentialists, the system-theoreticians, etc., to teach, research, and publish in Yugoslavia? And precisely some of those people today talk arrogantly of a "family squabble," although they kept quiet about political conditions under commu-nism in order not to jeopardize their careers. It was their political passivity and cowardice that suited the "communist family" and Tito much more than did the Praxists' public and vocal opposition.

As an influential current of humanist Marxism, Praxis deserves a much more serious critique. After all, what is this book other than the critical self-analysis of a Praxist? Such an analysis is to be ex-pected from the other Praxists as well, because the individual differ-ences among us were great. Our consensus was of a primarily nega-tive character: anti-Stalinism, antistatism, antidogmatism . . . . There-fore, it should be no surprise that the Praxists set off in very different political directions as soon as political parties began to be formed in Yugoslavia.

Many of the weaknesses in the criticism of communist statism on the part of several of the Praxists arose from utopian standpoints. That can be most clearly seen from their position toward private ownership, the market, multiparty democracy, and the nationalities' question.

With the exception of the treatment of the nationality phenome-non, I was not a typical Praxist. Those who have followed my intellectual and political development know that from early on I began to favor a certain rehabilitation of private ownership and market for goods and services. True, it was only much later that I accepted the inevitability and desirability of markets for capital and labor as well, along with a fundamental privatization. I did not succeed in resisting the pressure of *the antiprivatist, antimarket and antiparty-political* disposition of the democratic leftist student movement of 1968 in Belgrade, which we Praxists supported wholeheartedly. Fortunately, that did not hold me for long; perhaps because as a child in an enterprising and politicized capitalist home prior to World War II, I witnessed many positive aspects of private ownership, market competition, and opposition *party* activity.

The Praxists had little knowledge of contemporary capitalist economics. The mastery of Marx's *Capital* did more to hinder than to help in that regard. Therefore, the market-oriented economists in Yugoslavia sympathized (more privately than publicly) with the Praxists' critique of official policy and ideology, but not with the Praxists' views on economics.

Until the end of the 80s the Praxists generally supported a *partyless* social and worker self-government and self-management. Already in my first politically committed book (*Between Ideals and Reality*) I differed to some extent from them in that I pointed out that developed democracy is truly impossible not only without self-government but without complete freedom of political organization as well. However, from concerns that such organization in the second Yugoslavia, as was the case in the first, would take on an excessively nationalistic-religious character, and for fear of foreign interference, I supported a gradual, organized, and cautious introduction of political pluralism in place of a one-party structure.

And, once I have touched on the nationality question, I must recognize that it constitutes the most far-reaching *cognitive* weakness of the whole of Praxis. As its bloody collapse will definitively reveal, Yugoslavia was a country in which social science and philosophy needed to concentrate significantly on an analysis of nationalities' relations and conflicts. Nonetheless, all the Praxists started from the standpoint of a noble, while simultaneously considerably utopian, Yugo-internationalism, and criticized nationalistic manifestations incomparably more than they truly comprehended them. Because of that, the explosion of nationalisms and separatisms that hit Yugoslavia generally caught us Praxists totally unprepared intellectually, emotionally, and politically. That is one of the most important reasons why in our individual trajectories we have ultimately grown so far apart.

Up until this point at issue has been the political-theoretical utopianism of Praxis. Now it is necessary to add a few words regarding its purely theoretical utopianism. It reached its peak in the case of those Praxists for whom even morality constituted a form of alienation which in a future communist society would supposedly "wither away" together with the state and the law. According to them, Marx's interpretation of "revolutionary praxis" transcended every ethical (=bourgeois!) point of view with the establishment of total unity of "being" and "ought." For them a moral "ought" (like any other) represented an expression of "abstract" and "mediated" sociality as well as of an "illusory" humanity.

And I criticized them, reasoning, to the contrary, that the opposition of "being" and "ought" was inherent to the "generic being" or to the "essence" of humanity, and that, in that regard, no society could function without a moral-normative minimum. I maintained that humans are alienated solely in an heteronymous morality, while in the autonomous one they manifest sociability and humanity in the most concrete and direct way. I constantly expressed the complaint that Praxis wasted a great deal of time and energy in a doctrinary dispute about whether a *normative ethic* and a *moral* critique of society was compatible with Marx's viewpoint, while at the same time philosophers of other orientations in the world were working as hard as they could on a normative ethic and its application in social criticism. It is indicative that the communist leadership and ideologues were not very concerned about theoretical discussions on Marxism and ethics, but instead axiomatically claimed the alleged moral superiority of their "revolutionary praxis."

A review of the results of the realistic-humanist Praxists in normative ethics and moral criticism transcends my immediate intentions, but I still feel the obligation to say a few things about them before the end of this book. We realists, by immanent criticism of the utopian position as well, tried to show that a normative ethic and moral criticism of "the proletarian revolution," "the transition period toward communism" and "the lower phase of communism" are—from a Marxist standpoint—not only possible but also indispensable, even if the fantastic premise of the future unity of "being" and "ought" in a "higher phase of communism" were to be adopted.

In keeping with this, I was much involved in the critique of the *communist ideal-logical suspension of humanist morality*. Under that I included the misuse of humanist ends for the sake of justifying immoral means, such as dictatorship, terror, the sacrifice of the current generation in the name of the well-being of future generations, the destruction of human dignity, etc. I was motivated by the firm conviction that, in the long run, means (save in the instance of a few heroes and saints) are, ontologically speaking, more powerful than ends, and, owing to that, easily degenerate into self-purpose. Accordingly, the relationship of revolutionary ends and means was at the core of the critical clash of a Kautsky with Lenin and Trotsky, and later also of the American philosopher Dewey's critique of Trotsky, as well as at the center of interest for Sartre and Merleau-Ponty. A study of these discussions and analyses helped me to see that the obligation of moral justification falls upon those who—citing the "new man" and the "future"—in practice break completely with the humanist tradition and its scruples.

True, we are no longer in a communist, or a Marxist, but rather a postcommunist and post-Marxist situation. With the fall of communism there opened up a whole series of moral problems. In the first place, one needs to examine the *moral implosion of communism*. How could it be that communism was not ready to employ decisive means in its self-defense when its previous history is characterized otherwise by the use of all disposable means?

As a Praxist I wrote critically about the communist characterology, and now it is necessary to elaborate an excommunist characterology. In fact, the least complicated subject would be the conversion of communist to anticommunist careerists, while the most diffi-

317

cult would be the transformation of communist into postcommunist idealists.

Here we have yet another important subject. Now that we have come full circle with the return to the "old man," to "civil society," to private ownership, market economy, the multiparty system, and the rule of law, there is posed the dramatic question: In what were so many human lives, suffering, and energy invested? Was it worth it to sacrifice so many communists and their fellow travelers and to destroy or make suffer many other people as well, particularly in the USSR, in order finally to see the rehabilitation of a social system of which there should not have remained one stone on top of another, and experience even the collapse of inherited multinational states? Self-delusion here does not help: enormous human sacrifices cannot be justified by pointing to results in economic development, urbanization, the number of the literate and educated, broad social and health care, even if these results had been incomparably greater and more lasting.

And those former communist internationalists who have included themselves in nationalistic-chauvinist "vanguards"—even leading them—will have on their conscience as well the *nationalistic ideal-logical suspension of humanist morality.*

Human Nature and History

We are approaching the boundary between two centuries and two millennia. As none other before it, our century has accumulated a large amount of diametrically opposed experiences.

(A) The conflict between *totalitarianism* and *democracy* has essentially characterized our century. Totalitarianism represents a new historical phenomenon, but not because earlier power holders had not wanted all-encompassing and terrorist control over society, but rather because only in the 20th century were the appropriate means created. The totalitarian potential of these means, unfortunately, can never again be eliminated. It would benefit democracies to bear these lessons in mind as well:

318

Nazism originated, grew in strength, and came to power in the democratic Weimar Republic, which means that democracy and totalitarianism are not necessarily *external* oppositions.

In the world war from 1939 to 1945 the democratic powers had to make an alliance with Stalinist totalitarianism in order to defend themselves against Nazi totalitarianism and to impose by force upon defeated Germany (though only in the western half) a democratic order, while Stalinism was extended in its eastern part.

Let us imagine that, at the last moment, Hitler had called off his scheduled attack on the USSR realizing that it was virtually impossible to seize and occupy so much territory and populace, and since he already controlled practically all of Europe, the risk was not worth the potential cost. Instead of undertaking a war adventure with the Soviet Union, Hitler could have offered peace to Great Britain. And, even under the assumption that it would not have accepted it, he could have unilaterally stopped the war. Most importantly, the United States was not yet in the war. How would European and world history look in light of this alternative "past"? The time gained would have allowed Hitler even to acquire nuclear weapons. It is frightening to imagine that he could have blackmailed us with "mutually assured destruction."

It is amazing that the literature has neglected that genre possibility (let us call it *history fiction*) based on a "documentary" treatment of the "past" which was not, but easily could have been. More frequent visits to that "cemetery of possibilities" (W. Benjamin) could help us to resist repeating the triumphalistic-deterministic mistakes in the explanation of history.

The capacity for self-delusion of the two greatest totalitarian tyrants of our century was almost limitless. Hitler was convinced that he was laying the foundation for a 1,000-year German Reich, and it lasted a mere 12 years.

But, not even Stalin's totalitarianism was more resistant to the ravages of time, though it spread the belief that it was building the basis for the communist culmination of history. That it was of longer duration than the Nazi intervention in the name of one people and one race, Stalinism owed also to having taken refuge behind a universalistic ideal.

(B) Stalinist totalitarianism had developed from the Bolshevik dictatorship at the end of the 20s in the USSR; it was militarily imposed on Eastern Europe after the Second World War; 10 years later it began to be transformed into communist authoritarianism; finally, the entire system in Eastern Europe and Soviet Eurasia ultimately collapsed. That is how our century became acquainted with *communist dictatorships*, and their totally unexpected *peaceful implosion*.

(C) Among the characteristic phenomena of the 20th century belongs *colonialism* (some of the most highly developed democracies were also the most powerful colonizers), and all-inclusive *decolonization*.

(D) *The collapse of imperial and other multinational states*, and, more recently, strong *regional and even continental integration* also constitute a feature of our century.

(E) This is the century both of *world wars* and the renewal of *hope for a lasting peace*.

(F) The human experiences in the 20th century span from horrifying *genocides* to numerous examples of *planetary solidarity*.

(G) While for all contradictions mentioned thus far there exist similarities in earlier historical experiences, our century provides at least one complete novelty. That is, only approximately 10,000 years have gone by since the birth of agricultural civilization, and the incipient industrial civilization had already begun *to create the means that could destroy all of humanity*.

All in all, our century is characterized both by an unlimited faith in *progress* and nearly *apocalyptic* shocks.

What are the consequences of the above-mentioned contradictions for the Marxist philosophy of humanity? In order to answer we must recall that on the theoretical level Marx never completely exceeded the philosophical-anthropological bounds assumed from Feuerbach, not even when he took labor as his point of departure. Only, how can we explain so much evil in history, especially totalitarian evil, if we use labor as the starting point?

Power creates many fewer difficulties for us in that regard—for example in Hegel's model of *the master and the servant* (which, indeed, includes labor as well), particularly their mutual "struggle for recognition." Nevertheless, even that approach is unsatisfactory when we apply it to a Hitler or a Stalin, as well as to the organizations and systems which they personify. To me, Auschwitz and the Gulag symbolize a relationship between *criminal rulers and literally reified people*. Here we are not dealing with any "struggle for recognition," but simply with the annihilation of millions of people as if they were refuse. H. Arendt's formula of the "banality of evil" falls short of reaching this scope and depth of evil.

In the spirit of philosophy as the problematization of the limits of literature I would pose the question of why there are no impressive literary representations, say, of a Stalin or a Hitler. I offer a sketch as an answer:

Before becoming the criminal of criminals (the meta-criminal), Iosif Vissarionovich was, of course, born into a family, educated as a child and a young man by parents, school, and the social community; here he acquired his own particular complexes; he was later expelled from theological school . . . . The best literature cannot content itself with the more or less ready-made character of Stalin the tyrant (as we find, for example, in A. Rybakow's novel *The Children of Arbat*), it must describe its genesis and development. But, as a convincing portrait of Stalin's development from childhood to systemic criminal, literature could easily fall into an ethical trap in which the explanation of his personality development spontaneously slides into human understanding for him. How to reconcile the biological, psychological, and social determinism—the fact that, prior to becoming Stalin, Iosif Vissarionovich was formed by circumstances and influences—with his responsibility for almost absolute evil? The writer who convincingly explains Stalin's evil as the result of biological, psychopathological, and social factors, therefore calls into question his personal responsibility. On the other hand, a literary work would unavoidably lose persuasiveness to the extent that Stalin's evil were portrayed as some type of *causa sui*. As a result: writers instinctively are disinclined to attempt developmental portrayals of colossal historical criminals. Enough has been written about how evil in the case of Stalin or Hitler exceeded the imagination, and in that regard the question was posed as to whether or not literature is even possible any further. But I have something else in mind: the impossibility of literature to humanize (by a developmental portrayal of) the characters of grandiose criminals (this is some kind of unconscious taboo).

To add yet another question: since evil has long reigned in history, why is it a greater enigma than good? Why are we more astonished by the criminals than by the heroes and the saints? Perhaps it is that Christianity optimistically misleads us with its image of humans "created in the likeness of God." Perhaps that is the reason why so many educators start from naïve premises regarding the nature of humanity and overemphasize good, heroic and saintly examples. But, precisely to the contrary, after the experiences with boundless evil in our century we should systematically point out the range of our potential from almost absolute evil to nearly perfect good. Daydreaming constantly reminds us of that. And what of dreams?! Why then, of all knowledge, is humanity's knowledge of itself as individuals and as a species the most difficult?

Unprepared for the above-mentioned evils, often done by the people who cite it, the Marxist philosophy of humanity inevitably fell into a difficult crisis. This does not mean that Marx did not know that humans were inclined not only to freedom, sociability and creativity . . . but also to nonfreedom, egotism, destructiveness . . . . The trouble is, however, that his optimistic-essentialistic philosophical conceptual apparatus did not enable him to lend the latter series of human potentials the same importance it granted the former. Accordingly, for Marx only freedom, sociability, creativity . . . belong to the *essence* of humans, to their generic being, while lack of freedom, egotism, destructiveness . . . represent the nonessential, nongeneric potentials of humans. By the way, Marx periodically treats "sociability" as an essential, generic characteristic in too universalistic a manner, and, therefore, generally he fails to grasp the power of group membership as in the case of, for example, nationality.

Such a depiction of human nature could not withstand the pressure of historical experience and scientific knowledge in our century. Long ago I perceived that Marx's assumption about the "essence" or the "generic being" of humanity was too axiologically restrictive and ascertained that people are, in their very essence and generic being, inclined both toward freedom and to an escape from freedom, both to sociability and to egotism, both to creativity and to destructiveness . . . . To the basic, generic human characteristics, of course, should be added the awareness of mortality, as well as the inclination toward its suppression—which Marxists tellingly neglect to do.

The Bolsheviks treated human nature in a completely contradictory manner: exceedingly optimistically when referring to themselves and pessimistically when others were in question. They saw themselves as "people of a special mold" and "engineers of the human soul" who were creating "the new human," and, at the same time, they saw the working class merely as "a class in itself," which they alone could elevate to the level of a "class for itself." But, as if that class pessimism were not sufficient, *in practice* they divided their "vanguard" into a "party for itself" (the leadership) and the "party in itself" (the membership).

To Acton's dictum, "Power tends to corrupt; absolute power tends to corrupt absolutely," utopian Marxism had nothing better to counter than the superstition: Proletarian power tends to fight against the corruption, absolute proletarian power tends to fight against it absolutely.

In contrast to the utopian Marxist, the realistic Marxist, and even more so the post-Marxist, exercises systematic caution against the human substance of *any* power. They have learned this from experience but also from the liberalism that, in the spirit of anthropological pessimism, supports the division and control of power and the opposition of one will to another for power so that neither can gain too much impetus.

The above-mentioned changes in viewing human nature led me early on to corresponding changes in the notion of "alienation" as well, though I came to see only much later on that they already possessed a post-Marxist and even non-Marxist character. Other Praxists limited themselves as a rule to an identification of new forms of alienation, particularly in communist-statist countries, without calling into question the meaning of "alienation" itself. According to Marx, humans become alienated when they cannot realize their own essence, their generic potential, and when, therefore, they are destructive, selfish, unfree . . . . Thus, for the Praxists and other typical humanist Marxists, Stalinism represented merely the alienation of people from their essential, generic potentials (freedom, sociability, creativity . . .), while for me it was also the realization of the opposite, but no less essential, generic human potentials (lack of freedom, egotism, destructiveness . . .).

It goes without saying that as soon as we, in addition to freedom, sociability, creativity . . . , also add the inclination to nonfreedom, egotism, destructiveness . . . , as I did, to the essential, generic potentials of humanity, then we must exclude from our definition of "alienation" all reference to the essential, generic potentials of humanity. Long ago I did that, defining "alienation" in the following manner:

> The term "alienation" ought to apply to a particular kind of relationship between humans, on the one hand, and their activity and creations, on the other. We can locate this relationship on a continuum which begins with the state in which humans lose control over their activity and creations. Further, their activity and creations can assume a position of domination over them—they become dependent upon them and even begin to serve them. Finally, they can enslave, terrorize, threaten, and even destroy them.
>
> "Activity" here refers to all types of human mental and physical activity. And "creations" is used in the broadest sense of the word, corresponding to the connotation which we have given to "activity"; thus, for instance, it can embrace things, organizations, institutions, ideas, scientific and artistic works, linguistic creations, and myths. The terms "activity" and "creations" enable us to embrace a good deal more than is embraced by the concept of al-

ienation of labor and of the products of labor: the alienation of the state and other political institutions, ideological alienation, and so on.

Activity can become alienated from humans in two ways. First, if the activity is not freely chosen by people but rather compelled, both the goal of the activity and the conditions under which people perform it are imposed upon them—in Marx's terms, this is not "self-activity." Second, the entire personality becomes a slave to one of its activities, as for instance in the attempt to secure one's material existence; instead of leading to self-affirmation, such activity comes to dominate the person. In both cases people are more mere creatures than real creators (I, p. 30f).

In the post-Marxist and even non-Marxist spirit, already then I rejected Marx's "great story" about the definitive de-alienation of humanity in a communist future: "The possibility for human activity and creations to become alienated will always exist" (Ibid.).

Indeed, just when people imagine that they have attained some quasi control over the historical process, changes resembling a natural elemental force emerge. As if some force wishes to put the pretentious power-holders back in their puny place in the world by alienating the consequences of their actions. Some such "avalanche" occurred at the end of the ninth and the beginning of the last decade of our century. Thus Gorbachëv in the fall of 1989 attempted to encourage communist reformism in Eastern Europe, and, in fact, initiated the implosion of communism. He also tried to democratize communism in his own state and truly to federalize it, and of that system and state little remains. The participants in the coup against Gorbachëv in August 1991 tried to save the social and state system by force, and they only accelerated its implosion. Thus the democratic-capitalist West triumphed over communism and its superpower, but finds itself increasingly on the brink of apocalyptic chaos in its stead. Therefore the West exerts pressure on the breakaway nations to renounce nuclear arms for the benefit of Russia whom the latter fear and against whom they seek guarantees from the West.

That situation offers the newest proof for a ranking of alienation such as I did long ago:

> Students of alienation still feel a compulsion to devote their primary attention, as did Marx, to the production of material goods and its influence on the totality of aliena- tion in society. Even in the most advanced countries so- cial and individual life has not ceased to revolve about the procurement of material existence.
>
> But today the greatest and most important form of al- ienation is encountered not in the production of means to life, but rather of means to death. We are all witness to su- per-alienation: human creations are now revolving around the earth, threatening not only individuals or classes, but humanity as a whole. The apocalyptic "revolt of things" against their creator—the anthropological form of the Last Judgment—is in sight. A cynic might say that the defini- tive disappearance of alienation may coincide with its irre- versible triumph (Ibid., p. 34).

The persistence of philosophers in drawing a sharp demarcation between the nature of humans and the nature of the highest animals has not been, as a rule, successful because the distinctions have ul- timately turned out to be gradual. However, about the middle of this century humans began to develop the capabilities that separate them by an unbridgeable chasm from other animals. Since then we have been quickly becoming *a species capable of self-destruction as well as genetic self-transformation and the creation of completely new living beings.*

Between Triumph and Apocalypse

Although the "remainder" of history characterized by potentially apocalyptic alienation has begun, a false sense of security has spread through the world following the fall of the USSR because the probability of war between the superpowers and the respective blocs is drastically reduced. The question to be pondered is: what if on the territory of the former Soviet Union conflicts break out in-

326

volving the use of nuclear and other apocalyptic weapons? There are obsolete nuclear reactors in operation there, and there is no small probability that in the ensuing chaos some kind of a "Super Chernobyl" could occur. It is asserted that the Chernobyl disaster involved fifteen cubic meters of such radioactive substances that would take the waters of all the rivers on the planet the next fifty years to dissipate and render harmless (see the German weekly *Der Spiegel*, 27 January 1992). A possibility also remains that the unemployed or poorly paid scientists and engineers from the military-industrial complex of the former Soviet Union may place themselves at the service of states or groups given to blackmail by means of nuclear, chemical, or biological weapons.

But, even apart from the situation in the former USSR, we are menaced by the catastrophic danger of the proliferation of apocalyptic means, especially should they fall into the hands of terrorists. The "satanic" combination of apocalyptic technology, the gaps between the developed and the poor parts of the world, the demographic explosion, and the ecological degradation seriously threaten the survival of humanity.

Even under the fantastic assumption of universal and total disarmament, humankind will never forget how to create apocalyptic means. People will continue to be in a position temporarily to move back the hands from twelve midnight on the symbolic apocalyptic clock, but they will never again be able to turn them completely back. It is as if we have been truly visited by divine punishment because the first people dared to taste the forbidden fruit from the tree of knowledge! And in the context of the ancient Greek myth that would be the consequence of the unbridled hubris of our kind: as if it were not enough that we have at times transgressed the limits established by gods, we have now directly taken some divine power and prerogatives into our own hands!

The possibility and probability of self-destruction has become *the overdetermination of all overdeterminations* in history. All future social formations, no matter how creative otherwise, will remain potentially apocalyptic. The most developed part of the world already transits into an information-apocalyptic formation.

The self-apocalypse of humankind represents an almost un-bridgeable linguistic limitation. We have no quite adequate words to describe an earth from which human race has eliminated itself. Even *science fiction* seeks a humanlike being.

Once intellectuals warned about the danger of "The Decay of the West," and now many are captivated by its "definitive triumph." Focusing on that, I have no wish to underestimate the victory of the West over communism, in the name of which the "New World Or-der" is being established, but rather simply to caution that that order will either become an order of concern for the survival of human-ity—or humankind will be no more.

The basic conceptions and institutions, even in the most devel-oped and most advanced countries, point to all the indices of a fatal self-delusion. Humankind is threatened by an even greater danger of carelessness than it is by that of intentional evil. The *carefree hu-man* is, in my opinion, the most dangerous manifestation of "mankind's obsolescence" (G. Anders). How absurd: in the shadow of the apocalypse the "end of history" has been triumphantly proclaimed!

Our concept of power continues to base itself on competition and struggle, and not on the capabilities of associated humanity to resolve potentially apocalyptic problems. What indeed is the mean-ing of the sovereignty and the security of individual states, even of the strongest among them, when the mutual security and sover-eignty of humankind over its own survival does not exist? It is evi-dent that *realpolitik* based on a zero-sum game is, in that situation, transformed into *unrealpolitik*, even into the politics of the absurd. As the victor of the Cold War, the United States is at most prepared for a combination of rivalry and cooperation with Russia, although the position in which humanity finds itself imperatively demands their total partnership to resolve global problems and neutralize apocalyptic dangers. These countries feel that they will quickly lose their monopoly because small nations, and even some groups, will fairly soon acquire the apocalyptic capability.

It is recognized that, owing to enormous scientific and techno-logical progress, humanity is rapidly bringing about long-term, all-

encompassing consequences, while its moral, institutional, and political arrangements are, at the same time, adapted to less rapid,
short-term, and limited scope.

There is no doubt that democracy is the best social order. However, the more foresight-prone thinkers and states(wo)men have already noticed one weakness in it, the final result of which could
prove fatal. Specifically, due to the short term of office of the elected
officials, and the narrow nation-state framework in which democracies operate, they are not in a position to concentrate even on their
own long-term problems, much less on the universal ones affecting
humankind. The periodic democratic elections favor political candidates motivated by the interest and sovereignty of their own states,
and not political visionaries who would show a primary interest in
worldwide solidarity and the sovereignty of humanity as a whole.
The mass media suffer from the same weakness, even those with a
global range, because they express the interests of their own states
or multinational corporations. There are no planetary media who
would function on behalf of humanity as a whole or at least the
United Nations.

The market, private ownership, the profit motive, capitalism,
"civil society," social democracy, the nation-state, regional integration—none of the above address the lurking question posed by the
state of possible apocalypse.

Only now, after the collapse of communism as its main rival, the
capitalist world and others along with it are indeed faced with the
question of whether or not the planetary universalization of a profit-
market economy and the social organization based on it is possible
and desirable, even in its most humane and advanced forms, such as
social-democratic and social-Christian capitalism. Distinguished intellectuals have long warned that an *unlimited* capitalism-ization of
the planet would bring about a rapid depletion of economic resources, a deepening of the explosive North-South gap, and an
ecological catastrophe. And that is to say nothing of the incompatibility of free enterprise and free trade *per se* with the attempt to ar-
rest the spread of apocalyptic technology and arms. All these problems are now additionally exacerbated by the increasing gap in de-

velopment and living standard between the West on the one hand and Eastern Europe and the former Soviet Eurasia on the other. A further plummeting of the living standards on the territory of the former Soviet Union to a poverty level like that of the Third World could really spell apocalyptic consequences.

I doubt that humanity can survive if it does not become a community based *more* on principles of solidarity than on capitalist ones, and if it remains a conglomerate of nation-states and fails to become a global federation. Judging by everything, the left must now seek its real prospects on that level. I call it *social, democratic, (con)federal, and ecological mondialism.*

Can the United Nations be the embryo for such a world order? It is doubtful since they cannot even credit themselves with democratic equality. Thus, for example, the five permanent members of the Security Council, without whose agreement no crucial UN decision regarding peace is possible, participate in 80 percent of the global export of arms. And what if the United Nations actually represent the most efficient form of humankind's self-delusion? Indeed, numbers grow of those who see the chance for its salvation in some type of worldwide dictatorship rather than in a democratic federation. I anticipate that in the next century the forces interested in establishing their world domination will more and more use as their *ideological* justification the survival of humankind rather than human rights and democracy.

In my previous book I pointed out that not one philosophical or spiritual tradition is in a position conceptually to deal adequately with this absolute novelty in history (apocalyptic danger). And I would like to strengthen my thesis further: there is not one tradition remaining that should not evolve in a kind of *post-post* direction. That will be illustrated by post-post-Marxism, post-postmodernism, post-post-Christianity, and post-post-humanism.

Since we have already spoken enough about Marxism and post-Marxism, I will simply add two comments here. Marx envisioned that humankind would quickly end up its "prehistory" unfolding "behind its back" and would initiate a "real history" characterized by conscious control over social processes. However, development has gone in exactly the opposite direction: if, up until now, people exercised some control over at least local social processes, they themselves are now seriously threatened as a species. In this manner we have gone from history into a *new prehistory*. Fifty years have passed since its beginning indicating the possibility and probability of the self-destruction of humanity.

Marx's conceptualization regarding the role of leadership in history is also entirely untenable. According to Marx, there is a "general course of development" subject to anonymous and collective factors, and the leadership can only contribute to the acceleration or delay of that course (see, for example, his letter to Kugelmann of 17 April 1871).

However, Marx was refuted to the greatest extent by precisely those who incessantly cited him. Leadership played a decisive role in the communists' coming to power, the totalitarization of their power, and, ultimately, in their fall from power. It is recognized that without pressure from Lenin the Bolsheviks would not have carried out the October Revolution. And if we fail to take into account the crucial role of Stalin, how can we explain the terrorist liquidation of the NEP and, generally, the totalitarization of the Bolshevik dictatorship in the Soviet Union and the Comintern? Finally, how would that alleged "general course of development" look in recent years, had there not been a Gorbachëv?

At the time of the August coup of 1991 in the USSR the world held its breath: to whose hands would the nuclear trigger pass? That means that the old theme about the role of "great men" in history has taken on a radically new significance. Following Isaiah Berlin, under the notion of "great men" one should value-neutrally subsume all those who produce unforeseeable key turns in history. But a leader with a finger on the apocalyptic trigger is no longer even in the position of a "great man," but rather is, in a manner of speaking, "god-like." Unfortunately, apocalyptic power and the number of people wielding it will increase exponentially. Thus the difference between the *human condition* and the *divine condition* is further reduced.

As a consequence, the question is posed: how can Marxists continue believing in the "general course of development" independent from leaders—when even the survival of humanity itself increasingly depends on them. And if it is possible to foresee anything with certainty, then it is an even greater dependency of the "general course of development" on this type of contingency. When one adds to it other contingencies of human origin, then it becomes clear why humankind is increasingly incapable even precisely to *situate* the power for its own destruction or survival, let alone to *control* this power.

Interpreted from this perspective, postmodernist assumptions regarding, for example, the "fragmentation," "decentering," and "diffusion" of power touch directly on the contemporary collective *human condition*. Moreover, among the ideas of postmodernists about "deconstruction," "small stories," "relative truth" (as opposed to insisting on one Truth), and "ambivalence," there are useful insights for the critique of enlightenment, liberalism, Marxism. Contrary to the assertion of the modernists, history has no progressive or any other kind of meaningful direction indeed. I would venture to say that for history, "direction" and "meaning" are increasingly the possibility and probability of self-annihilation and avoiding it. But, even if we believed in the postmodernist "great story" of the "definitive end of all great stories," the indispensable need for a *sui generis* "great story" about the *being-toward-self-apocalypse and the action to avoid it* would not cease to exist. But, with that we have already gone beyond postmodernism, into post-postmodernism. Were we seriously to apply the thesis of the relativity of all values to the survival of humankind, then we would merely, willy-nilly, increase the chances for self-destruction. What use could there possibly be for value skepticism and nihilism at a time of the necessity of a universal human perspective and of gathering all forces for the sake of preserving humanity?

I also fail to see how Christianity, even a radically revised Christianity (post-Christianity), would be in a position logically to reconcile God's love and mercy and the forgiveness of the *original sin* with the possibility and probability that humankind, through suicide, may commit the *definitive sin*. I have written on this in my previous book (III–1) as well as elsewhere, and I here develop it further.

On the occasion of the first atomic test to which he himself contributed substantially, J. R. Oppenheimer lamented: "We have known the sin!" The thought that humankind can, by self-destruction, commit the *absolute sin*, in my opinion, cannot be integrated into any type of post-Christianity, to say nothing of Christianity itself. I do not believe that humanity has much chance to survive as long as Christianity, otherwise a key religion in the dominant part of the world, is preoccupied with the repentance of *original sin* and not with the *avoidance of the irrevocable sin of self-apocalypse*. In its own radicalness, for instance, liberation theology could not at all stand up to an eventual *theology of the survival of humanity*. Of course, the introduction of this negative-regulative idea into Christianity and even into post-Christianity would result in a genuine conceptual and emotional chaos. It already belongs in post-post-Christianity.

The chasm between the "secular" and the "sacred" has provided us with the blessings of the scientific-technological revolution, but it has also brought us to the brink of extinction. I doubt that humanity stands any serious chance of surviving if it continues to relate in a hyper-secular manner to the issue of its own survival. How can the human species survive if it treats its own existence merely as a tacit precondition for other values, and not as its highest value and concern?

A. Malraux announced that the next century would be the century of religion or it would not be at all. I take that as an affirmation that humankind should (quasi) sanctify its existence if it wants to survive. To that end, in my opinion, it would be good to reinterpret Feuerbach's support for a "religion of humanity," especially because we can conceive of religion in a minimalist sense as a "preoccupation with the ultimate." From a Marxist and post-Marxist perspective in this sense one could learn a lot from E. Bloch.

The *post-post-humanism with an anti-apocalyptic face* that I propose here implies a convergence of postsecularism and postreligiosity. But if we are unprepared for that, are we at least capable of poeticizing our existence in the cosmos? Admiration, thrill, amazement, awe . . . —that is how the astronauts describe the spectacle of Earth when they are temporarily separated from it. Perhaps pedagogy, which needs to concentrate on nurturing an active concern for the survival of the human species, should seek support in that experience.

The history of philosophy knows of many turns: epistemological, ontological, linguistic, pragmatic, postmodernist, just to name a few in no particular order. But the thesis that is being put forth here represents the most radical change in thinking, sensitivity, and action. The definition of human beings as a species capable of its own destruction and even prone to it constitutes the anthropological basis for such an *(anti)apocalyptic turn.*

Many philosophical and theological problems appear quite different if we use an (anti)apocalyptic key to them. As an illustration, let us take the conflict of principledness (de-ontologism) and consequentialism (utilitarianism) that runs throughout the history of moral philosophy.

The principle-ists claim that there are moral principles which we must respect (even) without regard for the consequences. They are opposed by the consequentialists who maintain that morally right actions are *by definition* those which produce some nonmoral good (positive consequences).

At one time I was also more inclined toward principledness than to consequentialism. Here is one observation on that:

> Opposed to that type of interpretation, a number of recent and contemporary philosophers find in Marx a de-ontological or a mixed de-ontological moral theory. Also many Marxist humanists of the Yugoslav Praxis group, like Mihailo Marković and Svetozar Stojanović, emphasize Marx's support for the concept of human dignity and freedom (like self-determination) and self-realization, and conclude that Marx was not a utilitarian but rather a de-ontologist (R. G. Peffer, *Marxism, Morality and Social Justice*, Princeton University Press, 1990, p. 83).

However, at the time I was discussing the interpretation of Marx's thought and political issues, and not the survival of humankind. Some years ago I reached the following conclusion: the more long-term the consequences of human actions are and the more people that are affected by them, the more relevant are the consequentialists for a moral community than are the principle-ists—and their dispute is in my view definitively decided in favor of the consequentialists if we ponder the *absolute limit situation* in which the survival of humanity as a whole is threatened.

It seems that theological language is the least inappropriate for an exposition of such a situation. Therefore, let us imagine that humankind is afflicted, for instance, by catastrophic radiation, infectious disease, or genetic mutation; that the only exception is a tiny group of men, women, and children on some isolated island; that God is in a position to bring about the continuation of the human species by saving this little group from the aforementioned plagues (a new version of Noah's ark), but that the price of achieving that end is the annihilation of the rest of humanity. How would God proceed in such a dilemma. Would He be a principle-ist or a consequentialist? To reiterate: the assumption is that we are dealing with a good, but not omnipotent, God. In a word, if He wants the continuation of the human race, God *must* destroy nearly all existing humankind. In so doing He would certainly suffer from a "most unhappy consciousness" because He would be forced to choose between absolute evil (the permanent disappearance of humankind) and nearly absolute evil (the destruction of practically all of existing humanity).

The distinguished Jewish thinker Hans Jonas, after a long, unsuccessful effort to reconcile the goodness of an omnipotent God with his allowing the Holocaust, decided that God is limitlessly good and, therefore, only limitedly powerful (in the essay on "The Concept of God after Auschwitz," 1984). In my imagined absolute limit situation Jonas would surely have been even more obliged to effect such a choice.

Caring exclusively about individual survival and the perpetuation of one's closest descendants, but not about humanity as a whole, is *biologically* inherent to human beings. Concern about humanity as a whole can be only a *moral and political* task. Humankind will not survive if it does not build a *global morality of a super-categorical imperative* that has as its highest duty caring for its own survival.

And now I ask the reader to go back to the very beginning of this book. It began with a motto which greatly radicalizes the myth of Sisyphus, and I want to conclude it with a total radicalization: *the stone that human beings incessantly and repeatedly push unsuccessfully toward the summit—ultimately falls upon them!* But this picture should by no means be construed as bowing to an apocalyptic fate, but rather as a warning and a stimulus to action. Though in a certain sense the most minimal program possible, the survival of humanity today represents as well the most radical utopia, even the utopia of all utopias (the meta-utopia). *Philosophers have only interpreted the world in various ways; the point, however, is to change it in order to save it.*

Index

Index

Index